MY JOURNEY OF GRACE

Lessons from My Ninety-One Years

REV. DANIEL A. KOLKE

WESTBOW
PRESS®
A DIVISION OF THOMAS NELSON
& ZONDERVAN

WestBow Press books may be ordered through booksellers or by contacting:

WestBow Press
A Division of Thomas Nelson & Zondervan
1663 Liberty Drive
Bloomington, IN 47403
www.westbowpress.com
844-714-3454

Because of the dynamic nature of the Internet, any web addresses or links contained in
this book may have changed since publication and may no longer be valid. The views
expressed in this work are solely those of the author and do not necessarily reflect the
views of the publisher, and the publisher hereby disclaims any responsibility for them.

Any people depicted in stock imagery provided by Getty Images are models,
and such images are being used for illustrative purposes only.
Certain stock imagery © Getty Images.

ISBN: 979-8-3850-2632-6 (sc)
ISBN: 979-8-3850-2633-3 (hc)
ISBN: 979-8-3850-2634-0 (e)

Library of Congress Control Number: 2024910929

Print information available on the last page.

WestBow Press rev. date: 06/25/2024

CONTENTS

Foreword.. vii

Chapter 1   My Journey of Grace... 1
Chapter 2   How Did It All Begin?... 7
Chapter 3   Humankind Is God's Handiwork, and So Am I 15
Chapter 4   My Call into the Ministry 22
Chapter 5   My Family Is Grace Manifested................................ 28
Chapter 6   What Is God Like to Me?...................................... 33
Chapter 7   Christians Are Not Alone 40
Chapter 8   Life: What Have I Learned about Living? 46
Chapter 9   The Source of Life Is God's Spirit............................ 52
Chapter 10 How Does God Feed Us?... 59
Chapter 11 Grace Comes in Small Portions 65
Chapter 12 Grace Offers Endless Hope..................................... 72
Chapter 13 Is Grace a Gift, or Is Grace Earned?.......................... 79
Chapter 14 Grace Has a Huge, Merciful Heart.............................. 86
Chapter 15 Quenching the Spirit in Us.................................... 92
Chapter 16 Taking Grace for Granted...................................... 98
Chapter 17 Afraid to Fail 106
Chapter 18 Beware of Self-Incrimination 114
Chapter 19 Can Grace Bend the Law?....................................... 123
Chapter 20 How Is Grace Back to God?..................................... 130
Chapter 21 Practice Made Grace Real...................................... 137
Chapter 22 Has Grace Freed Me from Sinning?.............................. 143

Chapter 23 How Do I Stay Saved? 149

Chapter 24 Why Am I in This World? 156

Chapter 25 My Loss of Self-Confidence 165

Chapter 26 What Has Self-Confidence Done for Me?.........173

Chapter 27 Losing Confidence in Faith............................182

Chapter 28 Elementary Faith Is Basic............................... 190

Chapter 29 How Did I Keep Believing? 199

Chapter 30 The Apostles' Manual 207

Chapter 31 The Apostles' Manual, Part II 215

Chapter 32 The Apostles' Manual, Part III....................... 222

Chapter 33 What Is a Christian Doing in This World? 230

Chapter 34 Why Does God Not Stop Evil?....................... 238

Chapter 35 How to Face Deception and Temptation 246

Chapter 36 Who Causes Deception and Temptation? 254

Chapter 37 Chosen in Christ before the World Began........ 264

Chapter 38 Walking in the Shoes of Grace........................274

Chapter 39 Each of Us Has Our Turn............................... 283

Chapter 40 Remembering Rev. Daniel A. Kolke 286

FOREWORD

My Journey of Grace is a series of works that my father wrote and published on his blog from July 2020 through April 2021. Each chapter of this book is a blog post, published in chronological order, and the final chapter is a eulogy written by my mother as an announcement for Dad's blog. Since it is the last blog entry on his blog, it seemed appropriate to include it as a conclusion and final chapter.

My dad was very passionate about sharing the lessons he had learned during his ninety-one years of living. We spoke often during the last year of his life about the topics in this book. He was very excited about the grace he had experienced in his life and what it meant. He wanted to share that passion with everyone.

Dad loved life, and he felt truly blessed by all that life gave him. This final work of his certainly shows that. I hope you will take from these pages a bit of his passion for life and share it with the people in your life.

Please enjoy *My Journey of Grace* by my father, the Reverend Sir Dr. Daniel A. Kolke.

—Danny Kolke Jr.

CHAPTER 1

MY JOURNEY OF GRACE

JULY 11, 2020

At the time of this writing, I have been granted ninety years of grace, and it has yet to run out. I was a gift, a package of grace, given to my parents to be shared with my fellow people, and that, too, has yet to end. I invite you on my journey. It has been both smooth and rocky, and a few times, our Lord sent angels to keep me alive. He sent a ship of grace that still keeps me sailing. Come and sail with me, for it is the best ship on earth.

WHAT DOES GRACE MEAN TO ME?

The word *grace* is music to my ears, as it is to every human being who is shown grace. Christians and God-fearing people have played and continue to play grace's tune to the outer limits of heaven. To them, it is a kind of special music—the kind that only God in Christ can play. No one has ever made us aware of grace as much as Jesus Christ did himself, and he commanded us to live and practice grace every day.

Many think that it is ludicrous to suggest grace is limited, but this is precisely what I have experienced and endeavor to share. I believe that grace not only has limits, but grace also has conditions. Grace has both a divine and a human side that do not always see eye to eye. While you may argue that God's grace does not have limits, humankind's grace certainly does. Just look at what humanity has done with the grace God has given to them.

WHERE DOES OUR VIEW OF GRACE COME FROM?

Let us begin by exploring where today's prevailing view of grace comes from. Grace has been subjected to different interpretations that do not always represent it adequately. I confess that I had great difficulties in finding an adequate definition of grace. I feel like the soldier who told his chaplain about a sermon he heard on the grace of God. The soldier recalled almost every detail in the message: that the grace of God was plentiful, sufficient for all our needs, and near at hand. "But," the soldier added, "the minister never told us what the 'grace of God' was. Perhaps you will be good enough to do that?"

THE HEBREW *HESED*

The Hebrew word origin is vague. *Hes* is used to describe human behavior, like attractiveness or pleasantness, in seeking God's favor and love. *Hes* did not depict all that the writers understood God was doing, so they made it *hesed* to give it a broader and more personal meaning.

THE GREEK *CHARIS* OR *ELEOS*

The Greek equivalent became *charis*, meaning goodwill, loving kindness, and favor. The Greek also uses *eleos*, meaning the personification of pity, mercy, clemency, and compassion.

THE ENGLISH *MERCY*

In English, we would use the word *mercy*. Mercy gives the concept of grace a more workable application. All that changed when Paul, the apostle of grace, added his interpretation.

Paul learned about grace from his own experience, from his Hebrew religious background, and from his spiritual encounter with Christ. Paul gave grace a redemptive meaning that only Christ could fill. He claimed that he had a direct revelation from Christ, whom he had once persecuted. He and he alone lifted grace to the very throne of God, and that is where grace should be. Out of 152 references to grace in the New Testament, 101 are Paul's; his associates wrote forty-eight, and only six directly belong to Jesus. All the other references are about Jesus and his Father.

SIX REFERENCES TO GRACE

How can it be that only six references actually belong to the sayings of Jesus?

There is a profound reason for this. The evangelist of the fourth Gospel holds the key. The prologue of John laid down a foundation for grace. Grace came into the world through Jesus Christ. He was the source of "grace in person" (John 1:15–18). It was from Jesus that his followers have drawn "grace upon grace." Through Jesus, God supplied an endless resource of God's favor, love, mercy, and forgiveness to redeem humankind from sin.

Grace was incarnate in Jesus of Nazareth on earth. Apart from within Jesus, true grace was not and is not available. Jesus not only defined grace in his teaching, but he also lived grace. He was grace himself. Jesus's birth was an act of grace, and so was his childhood and his adulthood. In Luke, the account states that the child Jesus grew strong and became filled with wisdom and the grace of God (Luke 2:40). At twelve, Jesus was continuing to grow in "wisdom, stature, and grace before God and man" (Luke 2:52). When Jesus finally began his ministry, people marveled at the gracious words that proceeded from his mouth (Luke 4:22). No one ever said, "What credit [grace] do you show if you love only those that love you back or reciprocate for the good you did for them" (Luke 6:32–34). Jesus himself appreciated the gracious act when a woman anointed him with costly ointment and kissed his feet (Luke 7:47). No one thinks of thanking his servant for doing his duty (Luke 17:9), but Jesus did by taking on the role of a servant himself. These six references of the word *grace*, in connection with Jesus, are more than sufficient to show what kind of person he was and what grace meant to him.

Now, how did Jesus intend to spread grace or himself to all men and women in the world? Jesus told his disciples that God and his Spirit would fill them with grace, and they would live it and disperse grace among their fellow men who also would become bearers of grace (Acts 1:23; Matthew 28:19–20). When the Son of God was on earth, he was a vessel of grace, and men and women could draw from him (John 1:16). When Jesus had to return to where he had come from, his followers became disciples of grace, and their fellow men drew grace from them. With the permanent arrival of the Holy Spirit, every believer became a vessel of grace to be shared in the world. Thus, grace became the content of God's heavenly kingdom on earth. The vessels, or dispensers, of grace became the evidence that God's Spirit was at work in the world. The Holy Spirit revealed grace in action to Jesus's disciples and followers. All of this was set in motion by the Father, the Son, and the Holy Spirit before the world was created.

> Jesus said, "I have yet many things to say to you, but you cannot bear them now. When the Spirit of truth comes, he will guide you into all the truth; for he will not speak on his own authority, but whatever he hears, he will speak, and he will declare the things that are to come. He will glorify me, for he will take what is mine and declare it to you. All that the Father has is mine; therefore, I said that he will take what is mine and declare it to you." (John 16:12–15)

What if God, desiring to show his power, held back his wrath (in Greek, *orgen*), and instead, he endured with patience those vessels deserving of destruction? God has done this in order to make known the riches of his glory. In doing so, he has transformed these very vessels into vessels of grace and mercy—vessels that he has called not only from the Jews but also from the Gentiles.

> "Those who were not my people I will call 'my people' and her who was not beloved I will call 'my beloved.'" (Romans 9:25)

> "And in the very place where it was said to them, 'You are not my people,' they will be called 'sons of the Living God.'" (Romans 9:26)

> Blessed be the God and Father of our Lord Jesus Christ, who has blessed us in Christ with every spiritual blessing

in the heavenly places, even as he chose us in him before the foundation of the world, that we should be holy and blameless before him. He destined us in love to be his sons through Jesus Christ, according to the purpose of his will, to the praise of his glorious grace which he has freely given to us in the Beloved. In him we have redemption through his blood, the forgiveness of our trespasses, according to the riches of his grace which he lavished upon us. For he has made known to us in all wisdom and insight the mystery of his will, according to his purpose which he set forth in Christ as a plan for the fullness of time, to unite all things in heaven and things in heaven and things on earth. (Ephesians 1:3–10)

The Jews took up stones again to stone him. Jesus answered them, "I have shown you many good works from the Father; for which of these do you stone me?" The Jews answered him, "We stone you for no good work but for blasphemy; because you, being a man, make yourself God." Jesus answered them, "Is it not written in your law, 'I said, you are gods'? If he called them gods to whom the word of God came (and scripture cannot be broken), do you say of him whom the Father consecrated and sent into the world, 'You are blaspheming,' because I said, 'I am the Son of God'? If I am not doing the works of my Father, then do not believe me; but if I do them, even though you do not believe me, believe the works, that you may know and understand that the Father is in me and I am in the Father." Again, they tried to arrest him, but he escaped from their hands. (John 10:31–39)

JESUS CAME TO DISPENSE GRACE

Jesus came to dispense grace, and he sent his Spirit to partner with us so that we each would become a vessel of grace in the world. Paul's life was an example of grace, and so are our lives.

> But how are men to call upon him in whom they have not believed? And how are they to believe in him of whom we have never heard? And how are they to hear without a preacher? And how can men preach unless they are sent? (Romans 10:14–15a)

> How beautiful upon the mountains are the feet of him who brings good tidings. (Isaiah 52:7a)

> Who has believed what we have heard? (Isaiah 53:1a)

> So faith comes from what is heard, and what is heard comes from the preaching of Christ. (Romans 10:17)

But they have not all heeded the gospel.

SUMMARY

- Grace has limits as well as conditions, divine and human.
- Jesus was grace incarnate. He handed it down to the disciples, who in turn handed it to the followers of Jesus then and to us today.
- Jesus challenged the leaders to show grace to all Jews and Gentiles.

CHAPTER 2

HOW DID IT ALL BEGIN?

JULY 18, 2020

God did everything he intended to do in six of his days. He then put his creation in motion, and his creation will continue to progress until the time he chooses. It then will complete its course.

Everyone was in the mind of God before the world began (Ephesians 1:4; Colossians 1:15–16). *Everyone* includes you and me. Learning this blew me away. Somewhere down the corridor of history and time, the very Son of God would want me to be one of his "vessels of grace" in the world (Ephesians 1:4). What is there about us—me and you—that God loved so much and that the Son of God himself would lay down his life for us (Psalm 8:3–6; John 3:16; John 10:14–18)? And what would you, I, or anyone else have to do to be a friend of Jesus the Christ (John 15:12–17)? Let's pursue this together.

WHERE DID WE COME FROM?

I learned that I was created long before I was born, and so were you. I came to this conclusion with the help of the two accounts of Genesis, which put the creation story into script. Yes, there are two accounts of the origin of humankind, and there is a distinct difference between the two writers, especially with regard to "man."

THE FIRST GENESIS ACCOUNT

Genesis 1 introduces God in the plural, as "Gods" (Elohim and not El) and as an "Us." The plural *Gods* have only one Spirit that unites them. The *Us* creates the universe, our planet with all plants and animals, before the six days are up (Genesis 1:1–25). Toward the end of the sixth day, the Us decided to make humankind, both male and female, in the plural, and give them instructions. And then the Us retired permanently. And the Us (Gods) leave the management of the earth in the hands of the human beings. Our English text uses the singular for God, but the Hebrew text has the plural *Gods*.

Then God(s) said, "Let us make man in our image, after our likeness; and let them have dominion over the fish of the sea, and over the birds of the air, and over the cattle, and over all the earth, and over every creeping thing that creeps upon the earth." So God created man in his own image, in the image of God he created them; male and female he created them. And God blessed them, and God said to them, "Be fruitful and multiply, and fill the earth and subdue it; and have dominion over the fish of the sea and over the birds of the air and over every living thing that moves upon the earth."

And God said, "Behold, I have given you every plant yielding seed which is upon the face of all the earth, and every tree with seed in its fruit; you shall have them for food. And to every beast of the earth, and to every bird of the air, and to everything that creeps on the earth, everything that has the breath of life, I have given every green plant for food." And it was so. And God saw everything that he had made, and behold, it was very good. And there was evening and there was morning, a sixth day.

Thus the heavens and the earth were finished, and all the host of them. And on the seventh day God finished his work which he had done, and he rested on the seventh day from all his work which he had done. So God blessed the seventh day and hallowed it, because on it God rested from all his work which he had done in creation. (Genesis 1:26–2:1–3)

THE SECOND GENESIS ACCOUNT (GENESIS 2:7–9, 18–25)

Genesis 2 begins at verse 6 and not with verse 1. The plural Elohim (Gods) has become one Lord (Yahweh), and it is this one Lord that undertakes the task of creating a man and then a woman. This man received something extra! The Lord blew his own breath and his own Spirit into man. This man has the knowledge to distinguish between good and evil. This man is allowed to choose what he wants to be and even what he wants to eat (Genesis 3).

> Then the LORD God formed man from the dust from the ground, and breathed into his nostrils the breath of life; and man became a living being. And the LORD God planted a garden in Eden, in the east; and there he put the man whom he had formed. And out of the ground the LORD God made to grow every tree that is pleasant to the sight and good for food, the tree of life also in the midst of the garden, and the tree of the knowledge of good and evil. (Genesis 2:7–9)

> The LORD God took the man and put him in the garden of Eden to till it and keep it. And the LORD God commanded the man, say, "You may freely eat of every tree of the garden; but of the tree of the knowledge of good and evil you shall not eat, for in the day that you eat of it you shall die." Then the LORD God said, "It is not good that the man should be alone; I will make him a helper fit for him." So out of the ground the LORD God formed every beast of the field and every bird of the air, and brought them to the man to see what he would call them; and whatever the man called every living creature, that was its name. The

man gave names to all cattle, and to the birds of the air, and to every beast of the field; but for the man there was not found a helper fit for him. So the LORD God caused a deep sleep to fall upon the man, and while he slept took one of his ribs and closed up its place with flesh; and the rib which the LORD God had taken from the man he made into a woman and brought her to the man. Then the man said, "This at last is bone of my bones and flesh of my flesh; she shall be called Woman, because she was taken out of Man."

Therefore a man leaves his father and his mother and cleaves to his wife, and they become one flesh. And the man and his wife were both naked, and were not ashamed. (Genesis 2:15–25)

Then the LORD God said, "Behold, the man has become like one of us, knowing good and evil; and now, lest he put forth his hand and take also of the tree of life, and eat, and live forever"—therefore the LORD God sent him forth from the garden of Eden, to till the ground from which he was taken. He drove out the man; and at the east of the garden of Eden he placed the cherubim, and a flaming sword which turned every way, to guard the way to the tree of life. (Genesis 3:22–24)

WHAT DO THESE SCRIPTURES TEACH US?

To begin with, they shed light on many things that I have misunderstood and have been misled to believe. The popular belief that God is in control of the world is incorrect—as if God were pulling levers to control everything? Controlling every act, every deed? Rather, God—"Gods"—made a self-sustaining good world and then handed it over to humankind to manage. God abstains from interfering in human affairs, letting humankind manage the world until Judgment Day, the end of time (2 Corinthians 5:10). (Unfortunately for humankind, this is why atrocities are "allowed" to happen. Humankind is managing this world.)

God, however, will not withdraw his Spirit from humankind because they are like, and they resemble their Creator with a similar behavior and mentality of independence. It is the humankind's spirit, which is part of the eternal Spirit of God. And it is the eternal Spirit of God who is the ultimate Spirit and source of life on earth. Life in humankind is on a time clock and in a period of grace in which humanity can choose to be either good or evil. It is also the only time when all persons can open their spirits to the Spirit of God and allow God to supply them with assistance to make the right choices. And it is the time when the serpent Satan will try to endear himself to humankind and mislead them. Humankind, like the Gods ("Us"), have a free will and can choose whom they want to serve. Humankind's choices will decide their destiny (Genesis 3).

> Jesus issued this warning: "Either make the tree good, and its fruit good; or make the tree bad, and its fruit bad; for the tree is known by its fruit. You brood of vipers! how can you speak good, when you are evil? For out of the abundance of the heart the mouth speaks. The good man out of his good treasure brings forth good, and the evil man out of his evil treasure brings forth evil. I tell you, on the day of judgment men will render account for every careless word they utter; for by your words you will be justified, and by your words you will be condemned." (Matthew 12:33–37)

All good gifts come from God, and they are dispersed through God's "vessels of grace" (James 1:16–18). Satan, too, is busy handing out gifts, which rob humans of their relationships with God and their fellow individuals. Satan is very generous with the material blessings that the human body desires, but Satan perverts them into harm and evil.

VESSELS OF GRACE

My role and your role are to be "vessels of grace" that distribute what is good and healthy for everyone. For instance, my spirit and soul existed with God before the world was created. Thousands of years into history, my parents brought me into the world to become a vessel of grace for my Lord Jesus Christ. My arrival brought great joy and hope to my parents, family, and friends. God gave me over ninety years to practice his grace. And God sent many angels to keep me alive and prepare me to share the insights, which his Spirit granted me.

The first thing the Lord wants me to share with you is that he is as close to you as he is to me, but you must be willing to open your spirit and let his words in, and he will tell you what you must do. God's Spirit has provided all you need to know—how to please and how to serve the Lord.

God's grace was given to us that we may serve him. It may not be an easy path, and we may suffer. *Grace* does not mean our lives will be easy. Those who regard this as ludicrous should ask themselves why the innocent suffer. Why does God not stop atrocities? Why does he allow them to happen? Also, what happens when we neglect guarding the good things God gives us? Do we play no part at all?

If we let sin and evil tear up our lives, it will be very difficult to put our lives back together.

SLAIN FOR THE WORD OF GOD

When he opened the fifth seal, I saw under the altar the souls of those who had been slain for the word of God and for the witness they had borne; they cried out with a loud voice, "O Sovereign Lord, holy and true, how long before you will judge and avenge our blood on those who dwell on the earth?" Then they were given a white robe and told to rest a little longer, until the number of their fellow servants and their brethren should be complete, who were to be killed as they themselves had been. (Revelation 6:9–11)

AN ENEMY HAS DONE THIS

In another parable Jesus put before his disciples, he said, "The kingdom of heaven may be compared to a man who sowed good seed in his field; but while men were sleeping, his enemy came and sowed weeds among the wheat, and went away. So when the plants came up and bore grain, then the weeds appeared also. And the servants of the householder came and said to him, 'Sir, did you not sow good seed in your field? How then does it have weeds?' He said to them, 'An enemy has done this.' The servants said to him, 'Then do you want us to go and gather them?' But he said, 'No; lest in gathering the weeds you root up the wheat along with them. Let both grow together until the harvest; and at harvest time I will tell the reapers, Gather the weeds first and bind them in bundles to be burned, but gather the wheat into my barn." (Matthew 13:24b–30)

There is more we can read in scripture about this:

- Who is messing up the world? (Revelation 12:7–12).
- Who has all the power and wealth that man has handed over? (Matthew 4:8–9; Luke 4:5–7).
- Who were the enemies of Jesus, if not the children of the devil? (John 8:39–47).
- Who angered and defied the Spirit of God? (1 Thessalonians 5:19–21).
- What did Jesus find when he went to the temple? (Matthew 21:12–17).
- Who disregarded the Law of Moses? (Matthew 5:20–45).

And they came to Jerusalem. And he (Jesus) entered the temple and began to drive out those who sold and those who bought in the temple, and he overturned the tables of the moneychangers and the seats of those who sold pigeons; and he would not allow anyone to carry anything through the temple. And he taught, and said to them, "Is it not written, 'My house shall be called a house of prayer for all the nations'? But you have made it a den of robbers." And the chief priests and the scribes heard it and sought a way to destroy him; for they feared him, because all the multitude was astonished at his teaching. And when evening came they went out of the city. (Mark 11:15–19)

Who allows dulling the humans' consciences so they end up as slaves to sin? (See Romans 6:16–19.)

SUMMARY

- God had all of us in mind before the world was created.
- There are two creation accounts in Genesis.
- Genesis 1 introduces God in the plural—*Gods* and as *Us*.
- God (Gods) made a self-sustaining good world, and he then handed the world over to humankind to manage until Judgment Day (the end-time).
- God will not withdraw his Spirit from humankind because he is part of the eternal Spirit of God.
- Humankind, like the Gods, have free will and therefore their choices will decide their destinies.
- God has brought grace through Jesus Christ to everyone, and we can become dispersers—vessels of grace.
- Satan perverts the blessings of God into harm and evil.
- God's grace was given to us to serve humankind through him.

CHAPTER 3

HUMANKIND IS GOD'S HANDIWORK, AND SO AM I

JULY 25, 2020

Humankind was and still is foremost in the mind of God (Ephesians 1:4). Humankind is God's special project. He made us in the "likeness and image of God," filled us with his Spirit, and enabled us to be children of God, capable of managing the whole world. How and when did humanity lose its worth? And when did humankind become in need of total reconstruction?

It was to the fallen Adam that God entrusted the world. Adam's mistake in disobeying God cost him the relationship with God but not his leadership of the world. Evil came into the world when Adam and Eve did what the devil serpent suggested. Did the evil spirit prove more powerful than the good spirit in man? No, but this was and still is Satan's most profound lie. The will and the spirit that God put in humans is more than powerful enough to reject and resist evil. And that spirit, inside us, is also strong enough to choose the good and to do what is right. This has been my experience as a vessel of grace.

WHAT AM I TO THINK OF MYSELF?

I have learned that I am not a weak earthling. I have been given a strong body and mind to endure abuse—the most excruciating pain and suffering created by humans and even Satan, the evil spirit. I am not a grasshopper who is too weak to cope with the difficulties in life (Numbers 13:33). I am not a mysterious being with superpowers, as king David believed (Psalm 8:4–6). I am not merely a disposable refuse of sin, as Paul describes in Philippians 3:8. Are my deeds so worthless that they embarrass God and my fellow humans (Ephesians 2:8–9; John 10:34–35)?

WHY HAVE I BEEN SAVED?

I marvel at why God granted me my life. Why would God allow me to be a vessel of grace for all these years? Why have I been shown grace? Why am I still on this journey? The answer to all my questions is that God sent his Son to save me—not only my soul but also my life—so I could serve him (John 3:16).

MY STORY IS A MIRACLE OF GRACE

Before I was twenty-two, I nearly died many times. I should have died from poison as a baby; I should have drowned at age twelve. Before I turned fifteen, I was almost run over by Russian tanks.

At twenty-one, I was the victim of a terrible fire accident while working in a lumber camp. I should not have survived. I was severely burned on 75 percent of my body. My body turned into a living torch from my knees to my head. While I was between life and death, God placed two "angels" there, a German and an Italian, who knew how to stop the fire and who took me to the hospital.

Can you imagine how many human angels God used to keep me alive? My first blood transfusion, which was through my legs, took the blood of eleven men. Two ministers came to give me last rites. In fear of death, I swayed back and forth, in and out of consciousness. I was unprepared to face my Maker. I had been a believer from the cradle, but I was not living as a vessel of grace. Nevertheless, my soul was worth more than the whole world to my Lord (Matthew 16:24–28).

HUMAN ANGELS

During those days, God's human angels were doing their very best to keep me alive so that I could be transferred to the burn center in Toronto, Canada. There, I spent eighteen months with expert human angels. For six months, three nurses were with me around the clock, feeding me like a baby and soaking me in tubs of water to loosen the scabs, which the oil had formed when it was applied to my wounds to kill the pain. This procedure was more painful than the fire itself, but my body was strong enough to endure and recover.

At this time, I required a lot of extra attention. I still needed to be dressed and fed, and my visitors were instructed how to behave. I had not yet been allowed to see myself in a mirror. Some people who knew me before the accident showed up, but when I saw their faces, it made me wish they had not come.

I looked forward to seeing two particular ministers and some of their parishioners. They helped me over the hardest time in my life. These ministers also helped me to map out a future and showed me how I could become a vessel of grace.

Eventually, I had to meet the public, which I dreaded. Between the skin graft procedures, I was taken to a rehabilitation center in Malton, near Toronto. It was located where the Toronto International Airport is today. This was long after the nurses were dismissed, and I could again walk on my own, and I even played shuffleboard with my feet.

Malton's military barracks became the housing for people like me, with injuries requiring long-term rehabilitation. I befriended two German lads with minor injuries. Just for fun, they put me in a wheelbarrow and wheeled me around on the outside lawn.

During this time, I still needed help with dressing, feeding, and turning the pages in my German Bible, which I began reading constantly and extensively. Across from my bed was a chair that I used as a table. My Bible was on it, opened flat so I could read, and an attendant frequently came by to turn a page.

GOOD FOR NOTHING

I remember an older Ukrainian man, who sat in a chair talking to some of his friends in his native language. After he had assessed my condition, he sympathetically said to them, "That German is good for nothing." He didn't know that I understood him. Unfortunately, I also felt that way. Although I was very hurt by his statement, we became friends and checkers companions.

When the bandages were taken off my hands, a specialist set my fingers in a fixed position so that I could start to help myself. I could now become independent. Both of us marveled how God had used a physician to restore me to be a useful human being again. The marvelous burn specialist was Dr. Farmer, whose skin grafting saved many soldiers during World War II, as it did me. At the end of eighteen months, I was sent back into the world for a year of healing and exploring, after which I would return to finish my physical reconstruction at Toronto General Hospital.

I BECAME A NEW MAN IN AN OLD WORLD

Physically, I was reconstructed, and I managed to get by with just 25 percent use of my hands. My mind assisted me at times, helping me improvise ways to make my life more feasible and useful. My mind, however, also required reconstruction, and that would take years. I was plagued by teachings that I was made to suffer as an atonement for my sins. My sins were very similar to the sins of the young ruler in Mark 10:17–22, except I already had become poor.

My grandmother and parents taught me how to distinguish right from wrong at an early age. If I should neglect or forget to obey them, they promised me that God would punish me. I spent many nights sweating, fearing that God would punish me. When I went swimming with friends on a Sunday, which was forbidden, and I nearly drowned, I heard my conscience accuse me of violating the Sabbath. I was twelve at the time.

It was nine years later when another man and I accidentally fell at the lumber camp and started the fire. My mind again reminded me that I had failed to commit my life to the Lord God of my parents. I was atoning for my mistakes, like the apostle Paul (Acts 9:15–16). Two ministers, like

Ananias, came to assure me that God loved me, but my conscience could not let go of my feelings of guilt.

My parents were common, ordinary people who believed and trusted their preachers and teachers, who themselves followed their leaders. These leaders turned the Hebrew God into a supernatural being who was involved with everything that happened in the world. This God chose certain people as his own and blessed them with prosperity when they obeyed him and punished them when they disobeyed his laws. This is not uncommon. Many have been led to believe that it was because the Jewish people were disobedient that they were replaced with Gentiles (Romans 9–11). Also, the ones who teach this dogma believe that they were led by the Spirit of God to arrive at their conclusions, while most of their decisions favored humankind and pleased them (Matthew 15:1–20). As a result—and for nearly forty years—I, too, hid behind this teaching. I was full of guilty feelings, rejecting the inconsistency of God as a benevolent being, in charge of a world that is falling apart, just as my life was falling apart. I was looking for an answer. *Where was the answer that would appease my guilt?*

During furlough from surgery, I enrolled in the high school department at the Christian Institute in Edmonton, Alberta, to gain qualification for college entrance.

EDMONTON BECAME MY SPIRITUAL TESTING TIME

On my arrival in Edmonton, a young Christian man looked at me a bit bewildered and said to my face, "If you put on horns, you would look like the devil."

I tucked this lesson away quietly.

We all met for chapel daily, and the Bible students appeared to be full of spirits on predictions. One day, I stood up and opened my mouth, but my conscience cried out, *Sit down! I did not tell you to talk!* This experience I also tucked away quietly, in embarrassment and humiliation.

I belonged to the people in World War II who were stripped of their countries, homes, properties, businesses, and loved ones. I lost a brother and a sister. I had come to Canada to find my fortune, but I found misery—and a handicapped life. At the time, the churches in Edmonton were filled with immigrants from my part of the world. They brought with them their hard losses from the war, and this had turned them into ardently religious people. They regarded their thoughts and emotional stirrings as the movement of God's Spirit.

When a fiery evangelist came to Edmonton to hold meetings, at least a thousand experienced emotional awakenings. I, however, was left in limbo, as my conscience rejected the idea that all the converts had to do was believe, and Christ would take care of all their wrongdoings. It was with that unsettled conscience that I returned to Winnipeg for the summer, where my parents and siblings had made their home.

REVIVAL IN WINNIPEG

Winnipeg was alive with revivalists. My mother had taken in a boarder, and he took me in his little Volkswagen to a big tent meeting. There, I consulted with a famous evangelist about my unsettled conscience. All he told me was, "Pray."

Prayer did not wash away my guilt.

The next Sunday, the same gentleman took me to his church, and he introduced me to a friend of his, who sensed something about me and insisted that we join him for lunch at his home. While we were eating, he shared his story and what he had done to find peace in his conscience and soul. He had to apologize, ask for forgiveness, compensate, and try to make up for the wrong he had done. He did what Jesus said we must do (Luke 12:57–59).

His testimony was what I needed to hear. I followed his advice, and peace came over me that even made me forget that I was injured and handicapped. This was the kind of person Jesus was looking for me to be.

SUMMARY

- Humankind is God's special project.
- Adam and Eve's disobedience cost them their relationship with God but not their leadership to the world.
- Satan's most profound lie is that the evil spirit is more powerful than the good spirit in humans.

- The will and the spirit that God has put in humans are more than powerful enough to reject and resist evil and are strong enough to choose good and what is right.
- I am not a grasshopper who is too weak to cope with the difficulties in life.
- In order to find peace, this is what Jesus said we must do (Luke 12:57–59). Prayer alone does not wash our sins away. We need to apologize, ask for forgiveness, compensate, and try to make up for the wrong we have done. This is the kind of person Jesus wants us to be.

CHAPTER 4

MY CALL INTO THE MINISTRY

AUGUST 1, 2020

I was called into ministry no differently from the way Jesus called some of his disciples. In the Gospel of John, John Zebedee and Andrew followed Jesus on their own. John stayed with Jesus, but Andrew went to find his brother Simon and introduced him to Jesus. Jesus went after the other disciples in person (John 1:35–51).

In the Gospels of Matthew 4:18–23 and Mark 1:16–20, Jesus himself called Simon (who became Peter), his brother Andrew, and the Zebedee brothers James and John. In the Gospel of Luke 5:1–11, Simon and his brother Andrew partnered with the Zebedees; for some reason, they had not left their boats and followed Jesus. Even after Jesus showed them a miracle, Simon felt unworthy to follow Jesus. This was how I felt when it was suggested to me that I become a minister of the gospel.

THIS IS HOW IT TOOK PLACE IN MY LIFE

God does not always work in mysterious ways—at least not in my life. God is Spirit (John 4:24), and to communicate with me, he had people who willingly partnered with him to lead me in the direction of becoming a vessel of grace. I myself had to open my spirit to God's Spirit and the Holy Spirit to listen to those who had come to direct me. I had to have the will to be considered for the task. I chose to follow Jesus, my Lord, and not the world, which would have paid for any other profession

I could have chosen. Without these godly volunteers, I doubt very much that I would have become a minister of Christ. What does it mean to be a minister of Christ? The word *minister* means being a servant, not one who wants to be served.

RUBY WAS GOD'S PARTNER

There was one person who rendered unmatched service for me. Her name was Ruby Leal, a wonderful Lutheran Christian who had a heart of endless love. Her husband was a mining engineer; they had no children. She volunteered at the hospital in Larder Lake, Ontario, where I was taken and kept until I could be moved to Toronto. Ruby took me on like a mother. She joined a nurse on my five-hundred-mile train trip to Toronto. Once there, she made arrangements for people to look after me. Ruby was in my life for many years to come. She saw me recover, reeducate myself, and become a minister, and she met my lovely wife and two sons before she passed away.

When I was in the hospital, Ruby brought three people into my life who proved to be invaluable help to me at that crucial time—the Reverends Lukas, Price, and Stinner. These men knew what I needed most.

Ruby had that special sense of recognizing my mental and spiritual dilemma, which required instant moral guidance. When I regained consciousness, I saw Ruby, Reverend Lukas, and a visiting pastor from Holland, who spoke German. No doubt they prayed and did what preachers do to rescue a sinner from hell, only I was fading and swaying between life and death, jabbering in a language they could not have understood. I was not crying out for being lost but for failing to do what I knew I should have done—commit my life to Christ.

WHAT MADE THESE MINISTERS SO IMPORTANT?

Reverend Lukas, in addition to keeping me in his prayers, passed on my name to the Reverend Alfred Price in Toronto, who took special interest in me and my future. Faithful and gracious Ruby stayed close by me until I was properly placed in medical care and was introduced to her brother and caring friends. Only then did she go home to be with her husband. Reverend Lukas and family also moved to Toronto, and we were reacquainted.

The Reverend Alfred Price appeared tall and handsome at my bed. His smile was backed by a gentle voice and very few words of encouragement, like, "Dan, you are coming along," or "You are fine." Not once did he try to open my Pandora's box. From the start, he helped me see a new future. He stopped by every week, and so did another couple from his church, Des Eagle and Gwen Wilcke. Des became my first English Bible teacher, and we became lifelong friends.

LET THE LORD DO IT

Reverend Price sensed my need for someone to whom I could fully explain myself, so he brought into my life Reverend Skinner of the Hungarian-German Church. Reverend Price noticed my uneasiness regarding what I would do when I had to leave my sheltered environment. Without any discussion, he smiled while he said, "Dan, you belong in the ministry." He stunned me, and I objected, saying, "How is that possible, with no English and only six years of foreign elementary schooling?"

With the same smile and tone of voice, he said, "Let the Lord do it," and then he left. That was my call. Reverend Price had me testify in his church, introduced me to his family at dinner, and saw me become a minister before he unexpectedly passed away.

NOW, HOW WAS I TO GET THE LORD INVOLVED IN ME?

Well, God's Spirit inspires all who are willing and ready to assist those who seek to do his will (Psalm 40:8; 143:10; Matthew 6:10; 7:21). I had to will myself to attempt the impossible; I had no idea how hard it would be and how long it would take for me to become a minister of Christ. I shared my decision with my compensation board counselor, and he did not deem it feasible, but he promised to obtain pay for college—that is, if I could get in. Ontario, where I'd been hurt, had no institute where a person could make up eight years to qualify for college.

That was when Reverend Stinner came to my aid.

Reverend Stinner had come to see me in the hospital and brought some of his people with him. When I was discharged from the hospital, I was baptized at his church, and for the first time in my life, I confided in him as if he were my father. When I told him of my dilemma, Reverend Stinner said that he knew of the Christian Institute, under Dr. Wahl, in Edmonton, which had such a high school department for dropouts and adults like me. After Edmonton, I qualified and was accepted to attend the United College in Winnipeg. And in three years, I received a bachelor of arts degree from the University of Manitoba.

THE "IMPOSSIBLE" HAD HAPPENED (MARK 9:27)

I became a graduate of a Canadian university that was modeled after England, and I even was knighted by the chancellor. I took it for granted that I would go to the German Baptist Seminary in Sioux Falls, South Dakota, and I earned my bachelor of divinity (pastor's) degree in two and one-half years. I finished seminary half a year faster than expected because after the first two semesters, I went to Princeton for the summer to take biblical Hebrew and received nine credits. Going to Princeton proved to be the most important thing I ever did in my life. The Lord made something happen, for which I have been overwhelmingly grateful for more than sixty-one years.

IS IT HARD TO GUESS WHAT IT WAS?

While I attended Princeton, my uncle and aunt insisted that I spend my weekends with them in Union City, New Jersey. I was twenty-nine years old, handicapped, and scared. Looking for a mate who could please the eyes of a spoiled youth was an unlikely task.

One Saturday morning, my uncle had us board his huge Plymouth station wagon with his wife, his ten-year-old son, and some friends of theirs, a widow and her two daughters. Off to the lake we went to spend the day. We did this all summer long. On Sundays, I joined them at their German Church of God, which was meeting in a house. The older daughter's name was Selma. She played the organ and sang with her mother and sister. She very much pleased my eyes, but I would not have dared to approach her without some motivation.

After several Sundays, my uncle remarked that Selma's mother would like to see me take out Selma. So, I asked her to go on a boat ride around Manhattan. She consented and came with Elvira, her friend who stayed between us all the time. On the way home, Elvira had to go another way, and we were finally alone. We went through the park, and it began to rain. I extended my hand and Selma hesitatingly took it, and we ran to avoid getting wet. This was on a Sunday in July 1959.

A week later, after church, Selma remained shy and distant. I took her behavior as a sign that I should return to Princeton, and I began to walk away. But Selma's sister, Teofila, stopped me and pushed me into her car, next to her sister, as they were getting in. Soon, I was riding around with three girls in the car, and Selma began warming up to me. Over the next few weeks, we also went for walks and talks and for ice cream.

It was the first week in August, and we strolled in the woods at the beach. I casually asked whether everything was all right between us. She nodded and said yes. When we went back to our group of friends, who regularly met there, Selma announced, "We are getting engaged." With joy and surprise, I welcomed the announcement, and so did everyone else. Who expected this to happen? I, of course, was the happiest person in the world.

On August 15, 1959, we officially became engaged. I spent the rest of the year in seminary, while Selma continued at her job in New York City. We wrote to each other every day, saw each other on Christmas, and were married on May 28, 1960, in Union City, New Jersey—sixty years ago as of this writing.

OUR MARRIAGE WAS VITAL TO MY CALL

What was and still is our secret? I was not happy alone, and I needed help being a vessel of the Lord Jesus Christ. Selma and I came from the same part of the world, with similar backgrounds and beliefs. We believe marriage was and is instituted by God, and we are commanded to be as one until death dissolves that bond. We decided to treat our marriage like a storehouse. We tried to put more into our relationship than we took out. We built up our understanding of love, tolerance, loyalty, patience, forgiveness, and many other things. Each one of these attributes has a reserve that we use when one of us faces doubts, fears, and many other problems on our long journey of grace. And we do make it a journey of grace by being affectionately gracious with each other.

> We still bear one another's burdens, and so fulfill the law
> of Christ. (Galatians 6:2)

SUMMARY

- We are not unworthy to be followers of Christ.
- God brings people into our lives to lead us to him to become vessels of grace.
- God's Spirit inspires all who are willing and ready to do his will (Matthew 6:10).
- With God's help, we even can do that which seems impossible.
- Our journey of grace is being affectionate with each other, bearing one another's burdens, and fulfilling the law of Christ (Galatians 6:2).

CHAPTER 5

MY FAMILY IS GRACE MANIFESTED

AUGUST 8, 2020

My family was a very essential part of my journey of grace. How can I possibly talk about grace and love when I do not love those who are closest to me? (1 John 3:11; 18; Mark 12:28–31). In my life, my wife, Selma, came first above my relationships. When we became parents, our children came first; we had to care for them above all else. I learned this from my parents, who, in hard times during the war, fed us children before they would eat.

It was Jesus who set up that rule himself.

> "What father among you, if your son asks you for a fish, will instead of a fish give him a serpent; or if he asks for an egg, will give him a scorpion? If you then, who are evil, know how to give good gifts to your children, how much more will the heavenly Father give the Holy Spirit to those who ask him?" (Luke 11:11–13)

MARRIAGE IS THE REASON FOR PARENTING

To manage the earth, humankind must procreate. Procreation was and still is a command of Elohim (Gods) (Genesis 1:26). God made the world and put it in space. And then God made humans to multiply so they could keep up with a re-creating world.

God made a special person for Adam (and all men) to manage himself and give himself some offspring. Without the reproduction of humans, the world would become a useless jungle. Thus, the family of a man and a woman is the key foundation of civilization. And that foundation is key to preserving the maintenance to sustain the world. A people or a nation that stops having children or becomes promiscuous will soon cause its own demise. Adam and Eve let Satan, the devil, in, and their lives became a shambles. They lost their affinity to God, their unity between themselves, and their godly environment (Genesis 3).

In the Bible, every leading family was disrupted and broken up. Noah blamed his grandson for his exposure. Abraham had to throw out his son Ishmael. Jacob cheated and ran from his brother Esau. Jacob's sons sold their brother Joseph. David's lusting for Bathsheba nearly cost him his life, and his grandson Rehoboam lost the kingdom of Israel. The people, who were led by their priests and prophets, insisted that this was approved by God. And there was Jesus himself, who his friends regarded "as being beside Himself" (Mark 3:21, 31–35).

What role could God have played in their lives—or in mine or in ours?

THE IMAGE OF GOD

From the beginning of human beings' appearance on earth, they have tried to picture who and what the Creator was and what he was doing. The first writer imagined God was like "a spirit and the wind," moving over water and saying (*amar*), "Let there be: 'light, land, waters separate from the land, day and night, waters fill with life, earth bring for vegetation, animal and birds appear, and men and women appeared.'" In Genesis 1, the writer says that God does not create or make, but God "commanded" that the world and everything in it appear alive as it is. This mystery, Jesus promised his disciples, would be resolved when the Holy Spirit and the Spirit of God returned to the world (John 14:23–26).

God had withheld his Spirit from humankind before the flood of Noah (Genesis 6:3). God's Spirit returned in Jesus Christ, the Son of God, who was begotten of the Holy Spirit and not of man (Matthew 1:18–25; Luke 1:26–35). The Holy Spirit shed light on how and what God had done and still continues doing in every human life, saint or sinner. The writer of the Gospel of John received this insight:

> In the beginning was the Word, and the Word was with God, and the Word was God. He was in the beginning with God; all things were made through him, and without him was not anything made that was made. In him was life, and the Life was the light of men. The light shines in darkness, and the darkness has not overcome it. (John 1:1–5)

SIMILAR INSIGHT THE HOLY SPIRIT CONVEYED TO THE APOSTLE PAUL

> The God who has made the world and everything in it, being Lord of heaven and earth, does not live in shrines made by man, nor is he served by human hands, as though he needed anything, since he himself gives to all men life and breath and everything. And he made from one every nation of men to live on all the face of the earth, having determined allotted periods (grace) and the boundaries of their habitation, that they should seek God, in hope that they might feel after him and find him. Yet he is not far from each one of us, for 'In him we live and move and have our being'; as even some of your poets have said, 'For we are indeed his offspring.' (Acts 17:24–28)

MAN IS FEEDING ON GOD'S GRACE, AND HE DOES NOT EVEN KNOW IT

I sponged off grace during the first twenty-one years of my life. I was not cognizant of what *grace* stood for. Grace is not some gift, but grace was and is the period of life granted to me, during which time I can render valuable service on earth, which builds up credits in heaven. In my first twenty-one years, I was not useful, and neither shall I be when I am dead, for it was Jesus who restored grace among men and declared,

He is not God of the dead, but of the living. (Mark 12:27a)

And the Word became flesh and dwelt among us, full of grace and truth; we have beheld his glory, glory as of the only Son from the Father. (John bore witness to him, and cried, "This was he of whom I said, 'He who comes after me ranks before me, for he was before me.'") And from his fullness have we all received, grace upon grace. For the law was given through Moses; grace and truth came through Jesus Christ. No one has ever seen God; the only Son, who is in the bosom of the Father, he has made him known. (John 1:14–18)

PAUL HAD A VISION OF THE RESTORER OF GRACE

He [Jesus] is the image of the invisible God, the first-born of all creation; for in him all things were created, in heaven and on earth, visible and invisible, whether thrones or dominions or principalities or authorities—all things were created through him and for him. He is before all things, and in him all things hold together. He is the head of the body, the church; he is the beginning, the first-born from the dead, that in everything he might be preeminent. For in him all the fullness of God was pleased to dwell, and through him to reconcile to himself all things whether on earth or in heaven, making peace by the blood of his cross. (Colossians 1:15–20)

SIMON PETER KNEW FIRSTHAND HOW CLOSE HE CAME TO BEING TRAPPED BY THE DEVIL

The Lord is not slow about his promise as some count slowness, but is forbearing toward you, not wishing that any should perish, but that all should reach repentance. (2 Peter 3:9)

Humble yourselves therefore under the mighty hand of God, that in due time he may exalt you. Cast all your anxieties on him, for he cares about you. Be sober, be watchful. Your adversary the devil prowls around like a roaring lion, seeking someone to devour. Resist him, firm in your faith, knowing that the same experience of suffering is required of your brotherhood throughout the world. And after you have suffered a little while, the God of all grace, who has called you to his eternal glory in Christ, will himself restore, establish, and strengthen you. To him be the dominion for ever and ever. Amen. (1 Peter 5:6–11)

God's Institution

The family is God's institution, not humankind's. The family was and still is "in the family," where I learned to practice grace—first in my parents' life and now in my own family. It called me to be humble and willing to suffer for my loved ones. I learned more about God and his Son Jesus by practicing grace. I will share more in the next chapter on human perceptions of God and grace.

Summary

- Jesus set up the family structure (Luke 11:11–13).
- Marriage is the reason for parenting (procreation). It is the key foundation of civilization.
- God withheld his Spirit from humankind before the flood of Noah (Genesis 6:3).
- God's Spirit did return in Jesus Christ, the Son of God, who was begotten of the Holy Spirit and not of man (Matthew 1:28–25; Luke 1:26–35) and still continues doing so in every human life, saint or sinner.
- God gives life, breath, and everything to all people.
- Humankind is feeding on God's grace and does not even know it.
- The family is God's institution, not humankind's.

CHAPTER 6

WHAT IS GOD LIKE TO ME?

AUGUST 15, 2020

My perceptions of God began in very early childhood. They were childish and silly then, and in some ways, they have continued to be that way. Upon reflection, this has been for my own satisfaction, but my perceptions are not unique to me.

God did not give humankind a description of himself; instead, God allows us to form our own perceptions. Some have developed very strong opinions, and they force their perceptions on us as being God's truth. I was born into such a theologically set world. There, I learned that everything began with fearing God more than anyone else.

> The fear of the Lord is the beginning of wisdom; a good understanding have all those who practice it. His praise endures for ever! (Psalm 111:10)

WHEN DID I FIRST BECOME AWARE OF GOD?

I was brought into the world by my father's mother, my grandmother. When I was one year old, we moved to another town where my father had bought land, and with the help of my mother's father, they built a new home. Mother's parents moved in with us, but after a year, my grandfather died. My grandmother stayed with us for nine years after that. It was during this time that she and my mother planted in me their perceptions of God. They taught me that he was an awesome being who had angels everywhere and who heard and saw everything I said and did. It was simple. God was good to those who obeyed his laws, and he punished those who did wrong. God would hold whatever I'd done wrong against me when I faced him in the afterlife.

By the age of six or seven, I had made enough mistakes to fall asleep in fear almost every night. And when bad things happened to me, I felt that God was punishing me. When, at the age of twelve, I went swimming on a Sunday with some friends and almost drowned, I was intensely afraid to face God. At the age of twenty-one, I was in a terrible accident when I fell with a kerosene lamp in my hands. My life would be forever changed. My fear of facing God was unbearable.

This fear of God that my parents and grandparents instilled in me has been with me for ninety years. Fear is legitimate and even necessary at times. Fear curbed my appetite, endless times, for doing wrong. It also kept me from inflicting harm on others, and I avoided enduring embarrassment and humiliation.

GROWING UP WITHOUT A HOME

I was born in what is now Ukraine, but in 1930, it was Poland, and not long before that, it was Russia. My family was German, living in Poland, so we were in the minority where we lived.

The year was 1939, and war with Germany was imminent. At the time, I was nine years old and toward the end of second grade in a Polish school. The class was made up mostly of Ukrainians, very few Poles, and three Germans students (two sisters and one boy), and, of course, an ardent Polish lady teacher. The Polish children began to call me Hitler and even threw stones at me. The teacher even outdid the children. Unintentionally, she made me look silly and even embarrassed my parents in front of all the students over the rumors of war with Germany. Imagine what an attitude of fear I was developing.

WAR DID COME

The war with Germany commenced on September 1, 1939. My father had served in the Polish military and was still in the reserves, so he was immediately called to active duty. The Russian army invaded Poland on September 17, 1939, as part of the Molotov–Ribbentrop Pact with Nazi Germany. The Polish army was quickly defeated, and my father was among a few who were taken prisoner and then released by the Russians and sent immediately home. We were now in a part of Poland occupied by Russian forces. Months later, we were gathered up like animals, sorted, and shipped in boxcars to the German military.

We were sent to an indoctrination camp, where we lived for several months. This was a difficult and fearful time for us. We didn't know what would happen. Eventually, they placed our family in northern Poland to work on a local farm, raising food for the German army. The locals didn't like us because we were put there by force. They considered us to be German. Even though my father was a Polish soldier, and I was born in Poland, we were Germans.

This is where I grew up during World War II.

THE END OF THE WAR

In 1945, the Russian army was advancing, and one day there was a knock at the door. My father was ordered to grab me and join the militia to defend the town. He told them I was working in the fields, but he would get me and report immediately. Well, that's not what we did. My father told us to gather what we could, and we fled on a horse-drawn wagon out of town, following the German troops as they retreated. We traveled for many weeks until we settled after the war in what was US territory.

AFTER THE WAR

After the war, we decided not to go back to Russian-occupied territories. My father was very afraid of what might happen. I lived in Germany after the war for six years. There, the locals didn't welcome us as Germans either.

I became known as the Polack. Once again, I was teased for my awkward background. In 1951, I decided to immigrate to Canada.

A German-Speaking Immigrant in Canada after World War II

I felt very out of place in Canada too. It was not shaping up to be the promised land I was looking for. I had taken a job working in a lumber camp to earn money to return to my family in Germany. It was then, after being in Canada for only six months, that I had a very serious accident. I was forced to start my life all over again. I had to develop new skills, which led me to a Bible school in Edmonton, Alberta. Even in Bible school, I was mistreated. I remember overhearing a group of young Christian men, wondering what could possibly become of the "worthless immigrants" in their school.

But I Persisted

Well, this immigrant did make it through their high school, college, and seminary, then past seminary, and then I qualified for doctoral studies in Toronto, Ontario.

What and Who Do I Fear the Most, Here on Earth?

I do fear God. I try to please him by following and practicing his laws. In doing so, I stumble from time to time, and I need the help of Jesus, my Lord, to make it past my mistakes. But there is another problem that I constantly face, and that is maintaining a relationship with those who have no sense of fear. I live in a time—and so do you—that is no different from the days of David, when there also was no longer a fear of God. We, as a people, ought to take to heart the warning that Samuel gave to King Saul and Israel. The hand of God is the law, and we ourselves have turned it against our nation.

Hear my voice O God, in my complaint; preserve my life from the dread of the enemy, hide me from the secret plots of the wicked, from the scheming of evildoers, who whet their tongues like swords, who aim bitter words like arrows, shooting from ambush at the blameless, shooting at him suddenly and without fear. They hold fast to their evil purpose, they talk of laying snares secretly, thinking, "Who can see us? Who can search out our crimes? We have thought out a cunningly conceived plot." For the inward mind and heart of a man are deep! But God will shoot his arrow at them; they will be wounded suddenly. Because of their tongue he will bring them to ruin; all who see them will wag their heads. Then all men will fear; they will tell what God has wrought, and ponder what he has done. Let the righteous rejoice in the LORD and take refuge in him! Let all the upright in heart glory! (Psalm 64:1–10)

If you fear the Lord and serve him and harken to his voice and not rebel against the commandment of the LORD and if both you and the king who reigns over you will follow the LORD you God, it will be well; but if you will not hearken to the voice of the LORD, but rebel against the commandment of the LORD, then the hand of the LORD will be against you and your king. (1 Samuel 12:14–15)

FEAR IS THE WAY—HOW TO PLEASE GOD

It is only in this life that I am able to honor and serve God. God does not need anything, but his children do. They are in the clutches of God's enemy, Satan. To set these victims free, the Lord Jesus Christ wants us to stay on earth as long as we can serve him for his follower's sake. I am (and so are you) included in Jesus's prayer. Like the apostle Paul, I, too, long from time to time to be set free from my earthly housing.

"Father, I desire that they also, whom thou hast given me, may be with me where I am, to behold my glory which thou hast given me in thy love for me before the foundation of the world. O righteous Father, the world has not known thee, but I have known thee; and these know that thou hast sent me. I made known to them thy name, and I will make it known, that the love with which thou hast loved me may be in them, and I in them." (John 17:24–26)

For me to live is Christ, and to die is gain. If it is to be life in the flesh, that means fruitful labor for me. Yet which I shall choose I cannot tell. I am hard pressed between the two. My desire is to depart and be with Christ, for that is far better. But to remain in the flesh is more necessary on your account. Convinced of this, I know that I shall remain and continues with you all, for your progress and joy in the faith, so that in me you may have ample cause to glory in Christ Jesus, because of my coming [staying] to [with] you again. (Philippians 1:21–26)

I retired from the pastorate twenty-seven years ago. Soon after, I was diagnosed with prostate cancer. My doctors were not optimistic, and I was not given much of a chance of beating it. I was at a loss. What should I be doing while I wait for my departure from this world? I even had a lovely vision of paradise. Then, a Muslim friend, who worked with our sons, suggested that I share my thoughts and views on a blog. Our youngest son set me up and showed me how to do it. To date, I have been able to share 1,213 entries that can assist my fellow pilgrims on their journeys. This "journey of grace" is my prime.

To close this chapter, I commend to whoever reads my testimony this message of the apostle Paul:

So we are always of good courage; we know that while we are at home in the body we are away from the Lord, for we walk by faith, not by sight. We are of good courage, and we would rather be away from the body and at home with the Lord. So whether we are at home or away, we make it our aim to please him. For we must all appear before the judgment seat of Christ, so that each one may receive good or evil, according to what he has done in the body.

Therefore, knowing the fear of the Lord, we persuade men; but what we are is known to God, and I hope it is known also to your conscience. We are not commending ourselves to you again but giving you cause to be proud of us, so that you may be able to answer those who pride themselves on a man's position and not on his heart. For if we are beside ourselves, it is for God; if we are our right mind, it is for you. For the love of Christ controls us, because we are convinced that one has died for all; therefore all died. And he died for all, that those who live might live no longer for themselves but for him who for their sake died and was raised. (2 Corinthians 5:6–15)

SUMMARY

- God did not give humankind a description of himself. Instead, he allows us to form our own perceptions.
- At times, fear is legitimate and even necessary.
- Fear curbs our appetites for doing wrong. It keeps us from inflicting harm on others.
- Persisting helps us to finish our goals.
- The fear of the Lord helps us practice God's law toward our fellow humans and therefore please God.

CHAPTER 7

CHRISTIANS ARE NOT ALONE

AUGUST 22, 2020

Our Lord Jesus, before he left this earthly life, promised that you and I will have a companion on our journeys of grace. The Spirit of God and of the Son of God will always be with us (Matthew 28:20). How do I know that the Lord was and is with me? I rely on scripture.

HE WILL NOT LEAVE US; WE MUST KEEP HIS COMMANDMENTS

"I will not leave you desolate; I will come to you. Yet a little while, and the world will see me no more, but you will see me; because I live, you will live also. In that day you will know that I am in my Father, and you in me, and I in you. He who has my commandments and keeps them, is he who loves me; and he who loves me will be loved by my Father, and I will love him and manifest myself to him." Judas (not Iscariot) said to him, "Lord, how is it that you will manifest yourself to us, and not to the world?" Jesus answered him, "If a man loves me, he will keep my word, and my Father will love him, and we will come to him and make our home with him. He who does not love me does not keep my words; and the word which you hear is not mine but the Father's who sent me." (John 14:18–24)

BE AWARE, BE WISE

"Behold, I send you out as sheep in the midst of wolves; so be wise as serpents and innocent as doves. Beware of men; for they will deliver you up to councils, and flog you in their synagogues, and you will be dragged before governors and kings for my sake, to bear testimony before them and the Gentiles. When they deliver you up, do not be anxious how you are to speak or what you are to say; for what you are to say will be given to you in that hour; for it is not you who speak, but the Spirit of your Father speaking through you." (Matthew 10:16–20)

HAVE NO FEAR

"So have no fear of them; for nothing is covered that will not be revealed, or hidden that will not be known. What I tell you in the dark, utter in the light; and what you hear whispered, proclaim upon the housetops. And do not fear those who kill the body but cannot kill the soul; rather fear him who can destroy both soul and body in hell. Are not two sparrows sold for a penny? And not one of them will fall to the ground without your Father's will. But even the hairs of your head are all numbered. Fear not, therefore; you are of more value than many sparrows. So everyone who acknowledges me before men, I also will acknowledge before my Father who is in heaven; but whoever denies me before men, I also will deny before my Father who is in heaven." (Matthew 10:26–33)

"Fear not, little flock, for it is your Father's good pleasure to give you the kingdom. Sell your possessions, and give alms; provide yourselves with purses that do not grow old, with a treasure in the heavens that does not fail, where no thief approaches and no moth destroys. For where your treasure is there will your heart be also. Let your loins be girded and your lamps burning, and be like men who are waiting for their master to come home from the marriage feast, so that they may open to him at once when he comes and knocks. Blessed are those servants whom the master finds awake when he comes; truly, I say to you, he will gird himself and have them sit at table, and he will come and serve them. If he comes in the second watch, or in the third, and finds them so, blessed are those servants! But know this, that if the householder had known at what hour the thief was coming, he would not have left his house to be broken into. You also must be ready; for the Son of man is coming at an unexpected hour." (Luke 12:32–40)

I HAVE BEEN SPARED

I have been spared from death, from evil tongues, and from the wages of war in this world. The fear of the Lord kept us from reciprocating for things that were done to me and my family. The lessons from Jesus have taught me how to cool my temper. Furthermore, they have taught me the impact of my actions—how important it is to be childlike and not to cause anyone to sin.

HUMBLE YOURSELF

At that time the disciples came to Jesus, saying, "Who is the greatest in the kingdom of heaven?" And calling him a child, he put him in the midst of them, and said, "Truly, I say to you, unless you turn and become like children, you will never enter the kingdom of heaven. Whoever humbles himself like this child, he is the greatest in the kingdom of heaven." (Matthew 18:1–4)

WARNING TO SIN

"Whoever receives one such child in my name receives me; but whoever causes one of these little ones who believe in me to sin, it would be better for him to have a great millstone fastened round his neck and to be drowned in the depth of the sea. Woe to the world for temptations to sin! For it is necessary that temptations come, but woe to the man by whom the temptation comes! And if a hand or your foot causes you to sin, cut it off and throw it away; it is better for you to enter life maimed or lame than with two hands or two feet to be thrown into the eternal fire. And if your eye causes you to sin, pluck it out and throw it away; it is better for you to enter life with one eye than with two eyes to be thrown into the hell of fire. See that you do not despise one of these little ones; for I tell you that in heaven their angels always behold the face of my Father who is in heaven. What do you think? If a man has a hundred sheep, and one of them has gone astray, does he not leave the ninety-nine on the mountains and go in search of the one that went astray? So it is not the will of my Father who is in heaven that one of these little ones should perish." (Matthew 18:5–14)

THE LORD HATES SIN

There are six things the Lord hates, seven which are an abomination to him: haughty eyes, a lying tongue, and hands that shed innocent blood, a heart that devises wicked plans, feet that make haste to run to evil, a false witness who breathes out lies, and a man who sows discord among brothers. (Proverbs 6:16–19)

CHILDREN NEED GUIDANCE

God has provided excellent rules, but God needs parents and teachers to teach the rules to the children (Deuteronomy 11:19). That is how I learned to fear God. Even though I was twenty-one years old when I left Germany and immigrated to Canada, my mother still kept feeding me

God's Word. These words continue with me to this day. Let me add two more verses from David and some from Solomon.

> How can a young man keep his way pure? By guarding it according to thy word. With my whole heart I seek thee; let me not wander from thy commandments! (Psalm 119:9–10)

> Thy Word is a lamp to my feet and a light to my path. (Psalm 119:105)

> The mouth of the righteous utters wisdom, and his tongue speaks justice. The law of his God is in his heart; his steps do not slip. (Psalm 37:30–31)

> My son, keep your father's commandment, and forsake not your mother's teaching. Bind them upon your heart always; tie them about your neck. When you walk, they will lead you; when you lie down, they will watch over you; and when you wake, they will walk with you. For the commandment is a lamp and the teaching a light, and the reproofs of discipline are the way of life, to preserve you from the evil woman, from the smooth tongue of the adventuress. (Proverbs 6:20–24)

GROWING UP IN CHRIST

One of Paul's brightest students had a glimpse of his teacher's hope— what the vessel of grace had to accomplish among people with a fixed mentality. It took me half my life to open my mind to this.

> And his [Christ's] gifts were that some should be apostles [missionaries], some prophets [interpreters of languages], some evangelists [preachers], some pastors [counselor] and teachers [show how to live], to the equipment of the saints, for the work of ministry, for building up the body of

Christ, until we all attain to the unity of the faith and of the knowledge of the Son of God, to mature manhood, to the measure of the stature of the fullness of Christ; so that we may no longer be children, tossed to and fro and carried about with every wind of doctrine, by the cunning of men, by their craftiness in deceitful wiles. Rather, speaking the truth in love, we are to grow up in every way into him who is the head, into Christ, from whom the whole body, joined and knit together by every joint with which it is supplied, when each part is working properly, makes bodily growth and upbuild itself in love. (Ephesians 4:11–16)

The wise Solomon gave me these helpful words to end this chapter:

My son, if you have become surety for your neighbor, have given your pledge for a stranger, if you are snared in the utterance of your lips, caught in the words of your mouth; then do this, my son, and save yourself, for you have come into your neighbor's power; go, hasten, and importune your neighbor. Give your eyes no sleep and your eyelids no slumber; save yourself like a gazelle from the hunter, like a bird from the hand of the fowler. (Proverbs 6:1–5)

SUMMARY

- We are not alone! Jesus promised that we will have a companion on our journey of grace.
- The Spirit of God and Jesus, God's Son, will always be with us (Matthew 28:20).
- The Lord hates sin (Proverbs 6:16–19).
- We are to keep God's Word active in our hearts and minds!

CHAPTER 8

LIFE: WHAT HAVE I LEARNED ABOUT LIVING?

AUGUST 29, 2020

What is life, and how can it be defined? Having had a stretch of it myself, I would like to pass on what I have learned. I admit that I am not certain I have made the best use of my time, but at least I have tried. I do feel that life has served me adequately.

OUR TIME IS A PERIOD OF GRACE THAT EVERY PERSON IS GRANTED

I learned early that if I did not look out for myself and do what it takes to stay alive, I would not leave much to show for my life. I had a life full of unforgettable hurdles to overcome. I came into the world before World War II began. My father was a Polish soldier who was shipped off to fight the war, but as Germans in Poland, our family faced persecution. My mother hid with us every night in the woods to avoid being molested and jailed. We prayed for the war to end quickly, and it did. That, however, was only the beginning of our woes.

On a very cold day in January 1940, the Russians disowned us and shipped us to the Germans. In the German indoctrination camp, my sister was born, and there she died. Eventually, we were placed on a Polish farm to raise food for the German army, which turned us into mortal enemies of the Polish locals. In January 1945, the Russians rolled into our town with tanks, this time as enemies. We again escaped with horses and wagons, and we briefly settled in the middle of Germany, where my youngest brother was born. Shortly after the war ended, the Americans withdrew, and the Russian troops moved in. Again, we fled. And this time, it took us the remainder of 1945 to find a place where we could stay, where we felt safe. This was Wrexen, Germany. On the corner outside our home, my second brother was killed. We moved a few miles away to Laubach, where we lived on a farm for six years after the war. I then immigrated to Canada, hoping to start a new life.

Life in Canada did not work out as I expected, and a very serious accident made me aware of the value of time and my life. I, too, began to mark my calendar, as did Paul and his associates from prison. This experience taught me to make the most of the time I have been given.

Look carefully then how you walk (live), not as unwise men but as wise, making the most of the time, the days are evil. Therefore do not be foolish, but understand what the will of the Lord is. And do not get drunk with wine, for that is debauchery; but be filled with the Spirit, addressing one another psalms and hymns and spiritual songs, singing and making melody to the Lord with all your heart, always and for everything giving thanks in the name of our Lord Jesus Christ to God the Father. (Ephesians 5:15–20)

Conduct yourselves wisely toward outsiders, making most of the time. Let your speech always be gracious, seasoned with salt, so that you may know how to answer every one. (Colossians 4:5–6)

"You are the salt of the earth; but if salt has lost its taste, how can its saltiness be restored? It is no longer good for anything except to be thrown out and trodden under foot by men.

You are the light of the world. A city set on a hill cannot be hid. Nor do men light a lamp and put it under a bushel, but on a stand, and it gives light to all in the house.

Let your light so shine before men, that they may see your good works and give glory to your Father who is in heaven." (Matthew 5:13–16)

Do not give dogs what is holy; and do not throw your pearls (lives) before swine, lest they trample them under foot and turn to attack you. (Matthew 7:6)

I BEGAN TO VALUE MY LIFE AND LOVED WHAT WAS LEFT OF ME

I was severely disfigured in the fire. I realized that life is a very small stretch in time. Whatever little time I used could not be replaced. In normal circumstances, every human being should have enough time to live a full life, but circumstances are not normal. Therefore, we should always seek to make good use of the time we have been given.

William James believed that a great use of life is to spend it on something that will outlast it. George Herbert held that a handful of a good life is worth a bushel of learning. And Goethe wrote that a useless life is only an early death. Hence, it is significant to follow the suggestion of J. M. Pace: "What is put into the first of life is put into all of life." Only who is doing the filling and with what? Is there a universal law by which all human beings can be born, brought up, and let loose in the world? Unfortunately, there are drastic differences among people and among individuals as to how life is structured. Is there a biblical perspective on life that we can follow? I found that there was and still is.

LIFE IS A GIFT

All of life is a gift from God. Life is not something that happened by accident (Genesis 1:30). Life is defined as the "breath of life." In particular, man was a special act of creation. God formed man out of the dust of the ground. God breathed into man's nostrils the "breath of life" and man became a "living being" (Genesis 2:7). The physical part or body of man, along with all the other creatures, consists of dust and water. What makes man live is the breath of life, and that comes from God. Without that breath and spirit (*ruach, pneuma*), the body cannot live. This life resides in the blood (Genesis 9:4; Deuteronomy 12:23).

Blood became a synonym for life (Leviticus 17:11, 14). To take a life meant to shed blood. Without blood, man cannot live. Only blood could atone for man's sin (Leviticus 17:11). Moses was ordered to smear blood on and over the doorway for death to pass over. The blood became the covenant between Israel and God (Exodus 24:8). The Israelites were not permitted to drink or eat blood. Christ Jesus renewed his covenant with the shedding of his blood (Mark 14:24). Jesus spoke of his life as being blood, which is shared (John 6:53–56). Without the shedding of blood, there can be no remission of sin (Hebrews 9:22). In other words, without giving a life, there can be no forgiveness. Above all things, the blood has to be pure and undefiled. Once blood is polluted, life is shortened and ultimately terminated. That is why the human body is a temple of the "Spirit and the Breath of life" (God) (1 Corinthians 6:19). And it is the blood that keeps the body healthy and alive.

ELEVEN MEN

I remember as if it were yesterday, although it was almost seventy years ago, when I was given blood through my legs. I felt life coming back into my dying body. Twelve men had come to give blood, and the donated blood of eleven of them matched. I owe my life to those eleven men who donated their blood. Without their blood, in a remote community up north in Canada, I would not have survived. And to maintain clean and lifesaving blood, we must lead clean lives. Since I am plagued with cancer, I am no longer able to save others with my blood.

WHAT DO I NEED TO KNOW ABOUT LIFE?

Fifty years ago, the question did not disturb me. At that time, I had presumed and took for granted that all those who taught and preached really were trustworthy and reliable guides for my salvation. I did notice that many differed in their use of the scriptures, but these differences appeared harmless.

When I enrolled in doctoral studies at Victoria University in Toronto, where seven schools had joined to produce a program that I wanted to be part of, I had difficulties finding my specialty in which I could excel. My tests in theology indicated that I was "too biblical" in the Old Testament. I already had completed two degrees and felt uncomfortable with continuing in it, so I decided that my major would be studying the life of Jesus Christ.

Back to theology, I was not thinking like a theologian or like a philosopher who uses sources to prove ideas and opinions. My goal was to have the Bible tell me what it meant. That, in theological terms, made me an exegete, or an interpreter of words and terms and history. With my background of languages and three years of New Testament Greek, the task looked easy.

That was very presumptuous of me. I set out to prove that the Evangelical fundamental position was the most tangible. My doctoral thesis was titled, "A Setting for the Son of Man." I consulted over 150 Evangelical experts, and I used over four hundred pages to impress the committee that would be reviewing my work. Thinking back, it is highly unlikely that the committee even read my thesis. My adviser was from Oxford, and I was in his classes for two years. The monk from the Pontificia's Institute of Rome had no questions. The two experts passed me, but the man from Harvard was irritated with me and humiliated me. He asked me, "Why did you dare to bring such a work before the committee?" He insisted that I go back and produce my own input, based on the texts and not on anyone's expertise.

Well, my ego was bruised, and my wife cried with me. We composed ourselves and began to use the skills I learned to write my own interpretation of "A Setting for the Son of Man." And this time, it was accepted with praise and recommended that I publish the work. After the review was complete, he dismissed me with these words: "We shall hear from you."

THIS IS WHAT THE BIBLE SAYS TO ME ABOUT LIFE

The living being, in the Hebrew text, is called a living soul, or *Nephesh Chajah*. The Greek has *Psychen Zosan*. According to the creation story, the soul was created, and the soul is synonymous with the being. The soul also appears to be related to breath. And the breath is related to a ghost or a spirit. In simple terms, humankind has the living principle of God within them. This explains the following thought: "Yet thou hast made him little less than God, and dost crown him with glory and honor" (Psalms 8:5). Jesus was accused of making himself equal to God. Jesus countered that the sons of God were called gods and that he, too, was a Son of God (John 10:33–36). This is consistent with the image and the spirit or the breath of God in humankind and that the sons of God intermarried with the daughters of men (Genesis 6:4). This godly presence (the spirit) was to live within every human being for as long as God (the giver) intended.

Adam, however, changed that plan by stepping outside of the godly circle. Adam allowed his passion to dethrone him for his feelings and reason. Hereafter, humankind began to live by their feelings. Man's taste buds became his guide. Man's emotions controlled his decisions. It was as if man had returned to an animalistic state. Man began to kill his own brother. Man no longer was satisfied with what he had, and so man forced others to submit to him. Ultimately, man set himself up as a lord and competed with God for sovereignty. In the process, man seduced the spirit (pneuma) within him. Man allowed the soul, or the psyche, to govern him. Man located the psyche in the heart and subjected his mind to it. Now, for a person to be conscious of God, he had to feel it in the heart and not in the mind. The mind was too rational, too critical, too scientific, and too philosophical to grasp the spirit, which can move the feelings within the human heart. The heart completed the picture of the perfect religious being.

SUMMARY

- Every person has been granted a period of grace.
- All life is a gift from God, so life must be valued.
- God takes special interest in humans because God's breath indwells all of us.
- The human body is the temple of the living God.
- Man has the living principle of God living within him.

CHAPTER 9

THE SOURCE OF LIFE
IS GOD'S SPIRIT

SEPTEMBER 5, 2020

There is an interesting statement preceding creation. It reads,

> The Spirit of God was hovering over the waters. (Genesis 1:2)

Two things are evident, which are essential to life; these are spirit and water. The spirit is similar to oxygen. Without oxygen, life in any form cannot exist. Even blood cannot live without water. Oxygen permeates everything, especially in a human being. If we take away the spirit, the breath, or the air, life ceases to exist. When we stop breathing, we stop living, whether we are saints or sinners.

WHAT MUST I DO TO KEEP THE SPIRIT
IN ME AND IN THE WORLD?

God made us and the world, but to stay alive, we must keep his Spirit in us and in the world. We must keep our bodies healthy and functional, and we must keep the world suitable to live in. As long as we feed ourselves and our environment with the good things God has created, the cycle of life renews itself. Even those who are estranged from God have part of

God in them, and they can be revived and restored into God's family and God's kingdom. The spirit or breath in humankind does not die because they sin or die physically. The Bible gives us vital examples.

Job believed that when his spirit was broken, his days were extinct (Job 17:1). The psalmist begged God not to take his Holy Spirit from him (Psalms 51:11). Jesus held that the spirit gave life (John 6:63). The preservation of the spirit or oxygen is also the preservation of life. The other ingredient is water. Water is just as essential as oxygen. Water and oxygen are closely linked together. For instance, when Samson drank water, he was revived, and his spirit returned (Judges 15:19). An Egyptian ate and drank, and the spirit returned. Nicodemus had to be born of water and of the spirit (John 3:5). When Jesus's side was pierced on the cross, out of his side came blood and water (John 19:34). Death on the cross happened after Jesus had released his Spirit, and Jesus allowed his Spirit to return to God (Luke 23:46).

Death does not end the spirit's existence. The spirit returns to God (Job 34:4; Ecclesiastes 12:7). The point in all of this is that even the secular and the unbelieving human being still depends on oxygen, on the spirit, and on the breath of God. There is an underlying religious basis, whether we acknowledge it or not. God is faithful, and God cannot deny himself (2 Timothy 2:15). God lets his sunshine on the good and on the bad. His rain falls on the just and unjust. God allows both to grow until harvest time, when God will gather the wheat into his barn, and then the weeds will be burned (Matthew 13:30).

Religious and scientific fabrication cannot explain the mystery of creation. Humankind deals in tangible reality, and the Creator is not tangible; neither is the mysterious energy and breath (Spirit) that puts life into matter. Everything moves in the universe. What kind of energy is it that never runs out? For instance, I drive a vehicle only as long as the fuel lasts. God's creation never stops to refill. Only God knows how a human life can function together with all the components. Humankind cannot build a human from scratch, even with all the components. The spirit, the mind, and the soul cannot be scientifically tested, nor can the spirit, the mind, and the soul be theologically diagnosed. The interaction of the Spirit of God with the spirit within man is a mystery. Why the interaction with some human beings is greater than with other human beings is an even greater mystery.

53

The mystery increases when the Spirit of God moves individuals to do what is right, even when these individuals have broken most of God's laws and God's commandments in the process. How could Moses, who altered God's law on marriage, be regarded as one who saw his Maker face-to-face? There was David, a man after God's heart, but David committed adultery and even killed for his passion. Even more puzzling is that these accreditations were made to come from the mouth of God and not from man. Jesus's own statement that the tax collectors and the harlots shall make it into the kingdom ahead of the religious leaders is mind-boggling. How can God, who is a good Spirit, overlook such atrocities? How can God be partial to some who think they get away by simply saying that they are sorry, especially, those who have taken it upon themselves to alter the course of life? They have much to answer for in what they are doing.

No good feeling in the heart can absolve them of the blood of the innocent beings that cry out to God. Life is sacred, and only God has the right to call his Spirit home. Life enters a human body at conception, and life leaves the body at death. Jesus was the perfect example. Jesus was conceived of the Spirit of God. Jesus gave up his Spirit on the cross to the Father (Matthew 1:18; 27:5). That is why the soul and the life principle within a human being can be saved, or it can be lost (Matthew 6:25). There is a dimension to life that is beyond the grave. To get there, life has to cross a few hurdles.

WHAT ROLE DO I PLAY IN SUSTAINING LIFE ON EARTH?

Life depends on the lives of others to exist and to survive. Life does not exist on bread alone, but life exists in relationship to other human beings. There has to be interaction, cooperation, and mutual dependency on each other. One life by itself cannot become a family, a community, a state, or a nation. One life cannot dictate policies or set up rules to govern others. Mutual consent is basic to good leadership and good organization. Life does best in harmony with others.

Life endures longest in a peaceful environment. Human life has been endowed with the potential of creating a mini utopia on earth. Life can be pleasant and satisfying. Life itself is not overly demanding. Life's basic needs can be easily met for most. It is when life seeks after pleasure that life becomes greedy, and when life covets more than it needs, then life gets out of hand. Then, life disrupts the harmony within the system. Life then sets up classes and castes, which separate and divide life into fragments. Fragmentation makes life weak and useless.

To overcome such disruptions, the situations and the conditions require alteration. In most cases, the disrupted life has to be changed, and life has to adapt to the system. It is similar to a religious conversion experience. Life must be changed from within before it can reform the community. More often than not, that reformed life must seek other lives with the same mentality and environment. A classic example was Adam.

The reformed Adam had to leave the comfortable garden and relocate to an unprotected world, where he had to fend for himself. It so happens that the new nations were formed by the same principle. England, for instance, shipped their undesirables to Australia and America. Holland shipped the Mennonites to Russia. And in the United States, persecution forced the Mormons to move to Utah. Every creed, culture, and country has some dark spots in its life that makes it unwilling to provide a place for a life that is different or even reformed.

IN ADDITION TO KEEPING UP PHYSICALLY, AM I ALSO A MORAL AGENT OF CHRIST?

The instructions Jesus gave to his disciples were also intended for you and me. We glory in the cross of Christ and bear with dignity our crosses that resemble our Lord's cross. We are the vessels of grace that serve Christ's redemption in the world. We may not be what the world expects, but we are the ones Christ chose to show the way back to God and to a decent mortal life on earth. The Holy Spirit engages us in spreading grace in the world.

THE WORLD HATED JESUS BEFORE IT HATED YOU

"If the world hates you, know that it hated me before it hated you. If you were of the world, the world would love its own; but because you are not of the world, but I chose you out of the world, therefore the world hates you. Remember the word that I said to you, 'A servant is not greater than his master.' If they persecuted me, they will persecute you; if they kept my word, they will keep yours also. But all this they will do to you on my account, because they do not know him who sent me. If I had not come and spoken to them, they would not have sin; but now they have no excuse for their sin. He who hates me hates my Father also. If I had not done among them the works which no one else did, they would not have sin; but now they have seen and hated both me and my Father. It is to fulfil the word that is written in the law, 'They hated me without a cause.' But when the Counselor comes, whom I shall send to you from the Father, even the Spirit of truth, who proceeds from the Father, he will bear witness to me; and you also are witnesses, because you have been with me from the beginning." (John 15:18–27)

For the word of the cross is folly to those who are perishing, but to us who are being saved it is the power of God. For it is written, "I will destroy the wisdom of the wise, and the cleverness of the clever I will thwart."

Where is the wise man? Where is the scribe? Where is the debater of this age? Has not God made foolish the wisdom of the world? For since, in the wisdom of God, the world did not know God through wisdom, it pleased God through the folly of what we preach to save those who believe. For the Jews demand signs and Greeks seek wisdom, but we preach Christ crucified, a stumbling block to Jews and folly to Gentiles, but to those who are called, both Jews and Greeks, Christ the power of God and the wisdom of God. For the foolishness of God is wiser than men, and the weakness of God is stronger than men.

For consider your call, brethren; not many of you were wise according to worldly standards, not many were powerful, not many where of noble birth; but God chose what is foolish in the world to shame the wise, God chose what is weak in the world to shame the strong, God chose what was low and despised in the world, even things that are not, to bring to nothing things that are, so that no human being might boast in the presence of God. He is the source of your life in Christ Jesus, whom God made our wisdom, righteousness, sanctification, and redemption; therefore, as it is written, "Let him who boasts, boast of the Lord." (1 Corinthians 1:18–31)

Then Jesus told his disciples, "If any man would come after me, let him deny himself and take up his cross and follow me. For whoever would save his life will lose it, and whoever loses his life for my sake will find it. For what will it profit a man, if he gains the whole world and forfeits his life? Or what shall a man give in return for his life? For the Son of man is to come with his angels in the glory of his Father, and then he will repay every man for what he has done. Truly, I say to you, there are some standing here who will not taste death before they see the Son of man coming in his kingdom." (Matthew 16:24–28)

"Whoever does not bear his own cross and come after me, cannot be my disciple. For which of you, desiring to build a tower, does not first sit down and count the cost, whether he has enough to complete it? Otherwise, when he has laid a foundation, and is not able to finish, all who see it begin to mock him, saying, 'This man began to build, and was not able to finish.' Or what king, going to encounter another king in war, will not sit down first and take counsel whether he is able with ten thousand to meet him who comes against him with twenty thousand? And if not, while the other is yet a great way off, he sends an embassy and asks for terms of peace. So therefore, whoever of you does not renounce all that he has cannot be my disciple." (Luke 14:27–33)

SUMMARY

- Two things that are essential to life are spirit and water.
- The spirit, the mind, and the soul cannot be scientifically tested, nor can they be theologically diagnosed. The interaction of the Spirit of God with the spirit within man is a mystery.
- Life, the soul, enters a human body at conception; therefore, life is sacred, and only God has the right to call his Spirit home.

CHAPTER 10

HOW DOES GOD FEED US?

SEPTEMBER 12, 2020

World War II made us destitute, homeless, landless, and nationless and left us starving. My father stood in lines for hours for a single loaf of bread, and it often wasn't enough. He had to come up with other means to feed us. When I lost the use of my hands, I had to learn to make a living a different way. Both my father and I learned that God had put more skills in us to earn bread than we thought we had. The Lord made everything available that we needed, and we were able to prepare our own meals. We survived. Like the miracle of the manna from heaven, which the Israelites had to collect and prepare for it to be edible, so is the fullness of the earth God gave humankind to manage and use (Genesis 1:26–31; Exodus 16; Psalm 24:1).

WE MUST RAISE OUR OWN BREAD AND FEED OURSELVES

Following the presumption that God will supply our needs is the question of how he will do this. The Lord used the Philippians to help Paul (Philippians 4:14–19). God's command to Adam, which is in force today, was,

> "Because you have listened to the voice of your wife, and have eaten of the tree of which I commanded, 'You shall not eat of it,' cursed is the ground because of you; in toil you shall eat of it all the days of your life; thorns and

thistles it shall bring forth to you; and you shall eat the plants of the field. In the sweat of your face you shall eat bread till you return to the ground, for out of it you were taken; you are dust, and to dust you shall return." (Genesis 3:17b–19)

KEEP AWAY FROM IDLENESS

Paul made this sobering charge:

Now we command you, brethren, in the name of our Lord Jesus Christ, that you keep away from any brother who is living in idleness and not in accord with the tradition that you received from us. For you yourselves know how you ought to imitate us; we were not idle when we were with you, we did not eat any one's bread without paying, but with toil and labor we worked night and day, that we might not burden any of you. It was not because we have not that right, but to give you in our conduct an example to imitate. For even when we were with you, we gave you this command: If any one will not work, let him not eat. For we heard that some of you are living in idleness, mere busybodies, not doing any work. Now such persons we command and exhort in the Lord Jesus Christ to do their work in quietness and to earn their own living. Brethren, do not be weary in well-doing. If any one refuses to obey what we say in this letter, note that man, and have nothing to do with him, that he may be ashamed. Do not look on him as an enemy, but warn him as a brother. (2 Thessalonians 3:6–15)

MORE THAN BREAD ALONE

Jesus, the Lord, laid down this law, but can he live without it? Jesus was led by the Spirit into the wilderness to be tempted by the devil. There, he fasted forty days and forty nights, and afterward, he was hungry. And the tempter came and said to him, "If you are the Son of God, command these stones to become loaves of bread." But Jesus answered, "It is written, 'Man shall not live by bread alone, but by every word that proceeds from the mouth of God'" (Matthew 4:1–4; Deuteronomy 8:3).

There is another reason why our lives cannot exist on bread alone. Life depends on and exists because of the Creator's Word (Deuteronomy 8:3). In the Bible, a number of individuals were chosen to be the Creator's mouthpiece. According to Jesus, these individuals were Moses and the prophets (Luke 16:29–31). Moses received the Law, and the prophets preached the Law. Some, like the psalmists, had inspirations (Matthew 22:43). But the highest representation of the Word of the Creator was in life itself. The Word was embodied in the life of Jesus, the Christ (John 1:14).

CHRIST'S MISSION WAS TO FULFILL
THE LAW AND THE PROPHETS

"Think not that I have come to abolish the law and the prophets; I have come not to abolish them but to fulfill them. For truly, I say to you, till heaven and earth will pass away, not an iota, a dot, will pass from the law until all is accomplished. Whoever then relaxes one of the least of these commandments and teaches men so, shall be called least in the kingdom of heaven; but he who does them and teaches them shall be called great in the kingdom of heaven. For I tell you, unless your righteousness exceeds that of the scribes and the Pharisees, you will never enter the kingdom of heaven." (Matthew 5:17–20)

Christ lived by the Word and the law, and Jesus Christ set an example for us. Jesus also separated the law of God from the Jewish tradition, which had replaced the Law that Moses had received.

And he said to them, "You have a fine way of rejecting the commandment of God, in order to keep your tradition! For Moses said, 'Honor your father and mother'; and 'He speaks evil of father or mother, let him surely die'; but you say, 'If a man tells his father or his mother, What you would have gained from me is Corban' (that is given to God)—then you no longer permit him to do anything for his father or mother, thus making void the word of God through your tradition which you hand on. And many such things you do." (Mark 7:9–13)

How Did the Law of Moses Deal with the Poor?

"When you reap the harvest of your land, you shall not reap your field to its very border, neither shall you gather the gleanings after your harvest. And you shall not strip your vineyard bare, neither shall you gather the fallen grapes of your vineyard; you shall leave them for the poor and for the sojourner: I am the Lord your God." (Leviticus 19:9–10)

According to the Law of Moses, the poor were not allowed to steal, but they could glean, gather, and collect. Landowners were commanded to drop some ears of grain and leave some fruit on their trees for the needy, who could follow the harvesters and pick. This is what Ruth did for herself and her mother-in-law, Naomi. Boaz was generous and gave the widow from Moab a little more grain than she had gleaned (Ruth 2). The people who could no longer glean had their family members gather food for them. Everyone had to work and earn their bread. The disabled depended on alms and the generosity of the kind-hearted. Jesus encouraged almsgiving (Matthew 6:1–4). The government was not in the alms program, like ours is today.

Gathering Food after World War II

Tragically, someday we may go back to Moses's Law, like we had to at the end of World War II. People came from the cities into the fields and woods to gather whatever they could to eat. My mother and I also gleaned in the woods while we traveled by horse and wagon.

We traveled across much of Europe until we settled in the American Zone, across the river from where the railroad station was located in the British Zone. There was a small bridge, and the Americans had stationed some local German guards, who were not supposed to interfere with the people who crossed into the American Zone. We earned part of our bread in barter, by transporting starving people from the railway to towns where food was still available. I had no trouble taking the people where they wanted to go, but I often could not return them the same way. These same German guards began to confiscate food and prey on the misfortunate people for the guards' own benefit.

I started looking for alternative places where we could cross the river in secret. At the time, I was fifteen years old, and the German border police warned my parents. Therefore, I had to desist. Father decided to trade the younger horse for food, and shortly after, our older horse died. Those horses had provided us with a fair living, but now, we had to find other ways to earn our bread. Times were difficult. There was no work available. And there were no farms or orchards where gleaning was allowed.

How Does Grace Abound?

Where I come from, grace was not handed out in large bundles but in small crumbs that fell off someone's table. As I look back to the time when we were made homeless in the world, I am reminded of a mother who begged Jesus for some crumbs for her child.

> And Jesus went away from there and withdrew to the district of Tyre and Sidon. And behold, a Canaanite woman from the region came out and cried, "Have mercy on me, O Lord, Son of David; my daughter is severely possessed by a demon." But he did not answer her a word. And his disciples came and begged him, saying, "Send her away, for she is crying after us." He answered, "I was sent only to the lost sheep of the house of Israel." But she came and knelt before him, saying, "Lord, help me." And he answered, "It is not fair to take the children's bread and throw it to the dogs." She said, "Yes, Lord, yet even the

dogs eat the crumbs that fall from their masters' table."
Then Jesus answered her, "O woman, great is your faith!
Be it done for you as you desire." And her daughter was
healed instantly. (Matthew 15:21–28)

Let us continue this journey of grace in the next chapter with how our
needs were met.

SUMMARY

- God gave humankind the fullness of the earth to manage and use to sustain their well-being.
- We must rise, labor for our own bread, and feed ourselves.
- Jesus Christ set an example of how to live by God's law.
- Most of the time, grace comes in small crumbs, which often can fall from someone's table.

CHAPTER 11

Grace Comes in Small Portions

September 19, 2020

> And from his fullness have we all received, grace upon
> grace. For the law was given through Moses; grace and
> truth came through Jesus Christ. (John 1:16–17)

John tells us that Jesus was the fullness of grace, and he dispersed it in abundance. I believe this is true, and personally, I have experienced a jolt of grace many times on my journey, often in small doses, just when I needed it.

This Was How I Learned How Grace Works

Throughout much of the first fifteen years of my life, my parents were self-employed. They raised their own food and made their own bread. Even during the war, at times we appeared to have abundance; at other times, nothing at all. We went from feeling grace to having no knowledge of what grace was.

After the start of the war, our home was taken from us, and we were shipped to an indoctrination camp. Eventually, we ended up on a farm, where we spent most of the war producing food for the German army in western Poland. To feed ourselves and the people who worked for us, the army allowed us to butcher several hogs per year. At that time, the words of the apostle Paul meant nothing to me because I lacked his experience of the pinch of hunger.

> "My grace is sufficient for you, for my power is made perfect in weakness." I will all the more gladly boast of my weakness, that the power of Christ may rest upon me. (2 Corinthians 12:9)

> For I have learned, in whatever state I am, to be content. I know how to be abased, and I know how to abound; in any and all circumstances I have learned the secret of facing plenty and hunger, abundance and want. I can do all things in him who strengthens me. (Philippians 4:11b–13)

EVERYTHING CHANGED—AGAIN

In January 1945, once again the war took away our livelihood, and we discovered that grace was not guaranteed. As the German troops retreated, we were forced to leave everything behind and flee. We became less and less gracious because we had not stored enough to keep us supplied in the face of hunger.

We were homeless and workless but not hopeless. We were in our own farm wagon, traveling across what was left of Poland and Germany, seeking a place where we could settle from January through October 1945. We traveled under the Polish flag and did not disclose that we were a German family. After all, we were originally from southern Poland, where I was born (now Ukraine), and we spent the war in northern Poland; we were able to survive.

We were traveling in the American Zone, going south and then turning west into the French Zone, hoping to meet up with Father's youngest brother, who would be married upon our arrival.

In Frankfurt on the main road, our axle broke. A kind mechanic with a small torch spent two days welding it back together. People saw our predicament, and they took an interest in our baby brother, who was only four months old, and my two sisters, six and eight. Their hearts were filled with compassion, and they shared with us their apprehensiveness of our settling in the French Zone. These people had a bitter experience with the French after World War I. They pursued my parents, and we turned north and then west toward the British Zone.

I distinctly remember one day when we passed a potato field in bloom, and we were very hungry. My father sent me into the field and instructed me not to harm the plants but to find some larger potatoes. I was very careful. Amazingly, we were able to feed all eight of us hungry people. We also grazed our horses beside the roads long enough that they had strength to go on.

WE HAD A PLAN

The reason for going west through the British Zone was to eventually get to Holland, then to Canada, where we'd join up with Mother's brother in Manitoba. He had left Poland two years before I was born. My parents had visas, but our situation delayed their departure and Canadian immigration. This time, we were set on going to Holland.

HEAVEN FOR OUR HORSES

We passed through a town, and our father saw a machine shop; he needed something for our wagon. The owner was friendly and a blacksmith, like my father. In no time at all, he had my father working for him and offered free housing. There were three barracks in a huge meadow—a heaven for horses and a playground for us children. It was ideal at first, but we were foreigners here. Also, being Protestant, we were very lonely among strict Roman Catholics. The weather didn't help. While we stayed there, it poured rain every day for the whole month.

BACK ON THE ROAD

We were back on the road with our horses and wagon, and it would take several days for us to reach Cologne, where we could cross the River Rhine on our way to Holland. On one occasion, we did not find a place to observe curfew, and we were stranded in front of a small farm. A lady answered the door, but she refused to let us camp on her property. Fortunately, a British patrol forced her to give us shelter for the night. My parents understood her fear of immigrants like us, and they elected to stay in an empty pigpen in her stable. I didn't mind. Staying with the animals was warm, and we slept quite well on the straw. In the morning, we learned that our hostess, this same lady, had lost her husband and her sons in the war. She felt that the prisoners the war brought to help her take care of the farm were not trustworthy. When she learned about our plight, however, she became very hospitable. She brought milk for my baby brother and my sisters, and she even brought something for all eight of us to eat. We did not take up more of her time than needed, and we thanked her for her hospitality and kindness. We learned that being friendly, polite, and kind went a long way to getting people to help us where we were going (Ephesians 5:20).

GRACE KEPT TRAVELING A STEP AHEAD OF US

Our journey appeared as if it had been mapped out for us, as if we had no control. Again and again, unexpected events kept changing our plans. The adjustments we kept making to the life we were forced to live wore us down. If it had not been for the strong faith of my parents, I can only wonder where we would have ended. But somehow, these events shaped us into an enduring family that could face the worst that was yet to come. We had to start life over again, with nothing and from nothing. During the war, we were relocated to a farm to grow food, raise beef, milk cows, and so many other things that sustained us. Now, we had no jobs, no home, and no country. If we had been traveling in the American Zone, we would have been shipped back to Russia, because that was where our parents were born, and where I was born. Fortunately, we were traveling in the British Zone and the English troops did not send refugees back to Stalin and Russia.

GRACE HELPED US DEAL WITH THE UNEXPECTED

In my native German language, we say, "Man thinks, but God leads." In real life, as homeless refugees, we needed to believe that our lives were in the hands of a higher power. There was yet another time when our plans were changed. We were on our way to Holland when a car passed us on the road. My father recognized the men inside the car, and he was terrified. My father's face changed color, and fear was in his eyes. Without explaining, he made me turn the horses onto a small side road, which hid us from sight. Then he told us that he knew who the men were, and Father feared that they would come after him. Apparently, these men were Nazis. Fortunately, they did not see my father, and we were thankful that we were kept out of harm's way.

MANY SURPRISES

Life had many surprises, some good and some not to our liking. In spite of our ups and downs, we had to practice grace so we could deal with the unexpected. Up to the time we were crossing the Rhine on a pontoon bridge, we had met many gracious people, yet not the right kind for us to settle with. Our thoughts were still on Holland and Canada. When we were asked where we were going, our response made the English soldiers laugh out loud, as if we presumed that we could cross the ocean with horses and a wagon.

After several days toward Holland, we stopped at a Catholic manse, where three priests were reclining. We asked for rest for a night off the road, and they sent us to a huge farm, where they were harvesting at the time. The farmer needed help and treated us well. We spent two weeks setting up sheaves to dry before they could be thrashed. This too was a strong Catholic district, and we felt completely out of place, so we resumed our trip to Holland—but we did not get very far.

It happened again. A fast-approaching automobile with men in it frightened my father, and he made me turn off the main road onto a small road. This time, we stayed on that alternative road until we crossed the Rhine in Cologne again. My father had decided that he wanted us to find a Protestant area where we could settle for a longer period. After weeks of traveling, we ended up going along a river called Diemel, which separated the Catholic towns from the Lutheran towns and the British Zone from the American Zone. When we came to a guarded bridge, Father told me to turn right to visit this American town. We stopped in front of a large barn and hoped to stay the night. We stayed four years and began a new life.

A New Experience of Grace Was in the Making

The town was called Wrexen, and a handful of people welcomed us with a place to live and with work we could render with our horses, and they assisted us in establishing residence. For the first time, we felt wanted and needed by people with similar needs and ways to ours. They were similar but not like us in faith and customs. We were able to repair a rat-infested war-damaged place, which already had two bombed-out families living in it.

Looking back on it, I grew up in Wrexen. There, I met a lovely local girl. She had serious intentions, but I had nothing to offer her, so she promptly married another young man. Another young lady said a fortune teller predicted that I would marry her and that we would have four children. Fortunately, that didn't happen either. But we stayed there, and I was able to make friends.

Tragically, my brother died in the street in front of our home and Father's blacksmith shop. He was hit by an army truck and died in my arms. We were devastated. Throughout the entire war, we had survived together as a family, and now that it was over, this tragedy happened. It seemed senseless.

We decided to move again and found a farm not far from Wrexen that we were able to purchase from the government on a long lease and contract. This was a large farm that was being divided into six smaller farms, and six families were chosen to become the owners. One family had two boys my age, and we became friends. Another family had one boy, and we did OK, as long as the girls were not around. My interest was in a family that had five girls, and one in particular held my attention for a while. Her family was Roman Catholic, and we were Protestants. As far as I was concerned, our parents worried needlessly over us. We never became serious.

Besides, my mother was set on sending me to her brother in Canada, and I eventually followed my mother's advice and went. All along my journey, grace was in me and with me, and I did not even know it.

SUMMARY

- Grace is not guaranteed. We must practice it daily in our lives (Ephesians 5:20).
- Grace also helps us deal with the unexpected events and circumstances of life.

CHAPTER 12

GRACE OFFERS ENDLESS HOPE

SEPTEMBER 26, 2020

> Through him (Jesus) we have obtained access to his grace in which we stand, and we rejoice in our hope of sharing the glory of God. More than that, we rejoice in our suffering, knowing that suffering produces endurance, and endurance produces character, and character produces hope, and hope does not disappoint us, because God's love has been poured into our hearts through the Holy Spirit which has been given to us. (Romans 5:2–5)

The words of the apostle Paul very much depict my family's journey up to this point; we were a wonder to behold. Grace had sustained us through the war, as it was ending, and as we fled. For nearly ten months, all eight of us traveled from Poland through Germany by horse-drawn wagon in a motorized, mechanized, and war-torn part of the world. It was the tiny crumbs of grace that people shared with us that helped us keep going.

Four times, we were offered a place where we could stay, but my parents felt uneasy and out of place. Why were my parents so cautious where grace seemed abundant? They eventually chose Wrexen, where we had to start over with nothing but each other.

GRACE HAS A PRICE

Free grace is not free. Someone redeemed it and paid for it with their labor, their hard-earned money, or even with their very lives. As Christians, we believe that Jesus did exactly that for his followers. As his followers, now that we have been given grace, should we ask him what he requires of us? What can we give in return for the kindness, for the grace we enjoy and share?

Jesus spoke clearly about what he wants from his followers:

> As they were going along the road, a man said to him, "I will follow you wherever you go." And Jesus said to him, "Foxes have holes, and birds of the air have nests; but the Son of man has nowhere to lay his head." To another he said, "Follow me." But he said, "Lord, let me first go and bury my father." But he (Jesus) said to him, "Leave the dead to bury their own dead; but as for you, go and proclaim the kingdom of God." Another said, "I will follow you, Lord; but let me first say farewell to those at my home." Jesus said to him, "No one who puts his hand to the plow and looks back is fit for the kingdom of God." (Luke 9:57–62)

> And he said to all, "If any man would come after me, let him deny himself and take up his cross daily and follow me. For whoever would save his life will lose it; and whoever loses his life for my sake, he will save it. For what does it profit a man if he gains the whole world and loses or forfeits himself? For whoever is ashamed of me and of my words of him will the Son of man be ashamed when he comes in his glory and the glory of the Father and of the holy angels." (Luke 9:23–26)

> "Do not think that I have come to bring peace on earth; I have not come to bring peace, but a sword. For I have come to set a man against his father, and a daughter against her mother, and a daughter-in-law against her

mother-in-law; and a man's foes will be those of his own household. He who loves father or mother more than me is not worthy of me; and he who loves son or daughter more than me is not worthy of me; and who does not take his cross and follow me is not worthy of me. He who finds his life will lose it, and he who loses his life for my sake will find it." (Matthew 10:34–39)

Then Jesus said to the crowds and to his disciples. "The scribes and the Pharisees sit on Moses' seat; so practice and observe whatever they tell you, but not what they do; for they preach, but do not practice. They bind heavy burdens hard to bear, and lay them on men's shoulders; but they themselves will not move them with their finger. They do all their deed to be seen by men; for they make their phylacteries broad and their fringes long, and they love the place of honor at feasts and the best seats in the synagogues, and salutations in the market places, and being called rabbi by men.

"But you are not to be called rabbi, for you have one teacher, and you are all brethren. And call no man your father on earth, for you have one Father, who is in heaven. Neither be called masters, for you have one master, the Christ. He who is greatest among you shall be your servant; whoever exalts himself will be humbled, and whoever humbles himself will be exalted." (Matthew 23:1–12)

IN OUR LIVES TODAY, GRACE OPERATES IN A SIMILAR WAY

We lived in a war zone from 1939 to 1945. At times, our family was saved by men who gave their lives. Just to survive, we were dependent on the grace of others. We had moved in the heart of winter, in January 1940 and in January 1945. Both times, my mother was with child, and she gave birth, the first time to a baby girl in a German refugee camp. There, my newborn sister and fifteen other babies died. Then, in 1945, while we were running from the Russians, she gave birth to my brother, who did survive the war. Our time of desolation and suffering was what Jesus had predicted would happen to his followers. This war brought horrible devastation with the bombing and destruction of villages, homes, and land; the evil torturing of innocent people; and taking the lives of seventy million people.

We felt we were living in the times Jesus had spoken about.

> "But when you see the desolating sacrilege set up where it ought not to be (let the reader understand), then let those who are in Judea flee to the mountains; let him who is on the housetop not go down, nor enter his house, to take anything away; and let him who is in the field not back to take his mantle. And alas for those who are with child and for those who give suck in those days! Pray that it may not happen in winter. For in those days there will be such tribulation as has not been from the beginning of the creation which God created until now and never will be. And if the Lord had not shortened the days, no human being would be saved; but for the sake of the elect, whom he chose, he shortened the days. And then if any one says to you, 'Look, here is the Christ!' or 'Look, there he is!' do not believe it. False Christs and false prophets will arise and show signs and wonders, to lead astray, if possible, the elect. But take heed; I have told you all things beforehand." (Mark 13:14–23)

> Then he (Jesus) said to them, "Nation will rise against nation, and kingdom against kingdom; there will be great earthquakes, and in various places famines and pestilences; and there will be terrors and great signs from heaven. But before all this they will lay their hands on you and persecute you, delivering you up to the synagogues and prisons, and you will be brought before kings and governors for my name's sake. This will be a time for you to bear testimony. Settle it therefore in your minds, not to meditate beforehand how to answer; for I will give you a

mouth and wisdom, which none of your adversaries will be able to withstand or contradict. You will be delivered up even by parents and brothers and kinsmen and friends, and some of you they will put to death; you will be hated by all for my name's sake. But not a hair of your head will perish. By your endurance you will gain your lives." (Luke 21:10–19)

Unfortunately, this war was not the final work of evil, and its biggest evil is yet to come against what is good (Revelation 17–18; 2 Corinthians 5:10; Galatians 6:7–10).

WE USED GRACE TO HARVEST GRACE

From the time I was a child, I was taught a saying: "With my hat in my hand, I could cross the land." Meaning that by being gracious, kind, and polite, we could count on our days to be brighter.

We had followed the German soldiers all day and arrived in Breslau (Vrotslav) in a plaza at the bridge that crosses the Elbe River. The soldiers crossed the river and made camp. Our family stopped in the main town square. The city was already evacuated and seemed completely empty. It was late, the horses were tired, and the baby was crying. Seemingly out of nowhere, two people appeared, offering us hospitality and lodging for the night. While my father and I took care of the horses and unloaded the second smaller wagon to leave it behind, mother and my five siblings went with the old couple—they must have been in their seventies. That night, we enjoyed a good meal and a good sleep, provided by that gracious couple. With the help of our hosts, we were able to cross the river before the bridge was bombed.

As expected, we ended up on the same road we had left, following the soldiers. This time, however, we were not allowed to continue west. There was a roadblock, and we were told that we had to turn on a road that went south to Bohemia and Czech country. We turned down a small road, and we went down the hill with no brakes. There was snow on the road; my father took the reins and had the horses hold the wagon with two wheels on the pavement and two in the dirt on the side of the road. Somehow, we managed to get safely down that hill. It was wintertime, and this would not be the only time that we would have to drive on icy, hilly roads.

By nightfall, we came to a prosperous-looking, well-kept farm. Again, two older people were very cordial to us. My father was blessed with good charm and grace. He complimented this couple's remarkable accomplishment, which was in stark contrast to what we had left behind in Poland and what we had seen along the way. They shared with us that the war took the lives of their sons, and we sympathized with them. Our new friends treated us very well and even helped my father attach a brake to our wagon. Our brief stay with these people was mutually gracious.

As we left them, they told us how to get on the road to Dresden and from there to Riesa. Riesa was where the Germans had taken us to be indoctrinated at the start of the war, before they settled us on the Polish farm. It was in Riesa where my sister and fifteen other girls were born and died. They were all buried at the same time.

THE VERSATILE NATURE OF GRACE

We found the road to Dresden, and I learned something more about grace—how versatile it was. Our mother prayed a lot and put our safety in God's hands, and God put our care in our father's hands. My father had to "be as wise as serpents and innocent as doves" (Matthew 10:16). One time we were intercepted by two men in black jackets. These were Hitler's death squad, SS men. They asked very demanding questions of us. These men could shoot anyone under the slightest suspicion, and they were rewarded by the Nazi Party.

One asked, in a commanding, sharp voice, "Where are you going? Why are you not in uniform?" And then he looked up at me driving the horses. "Why is he not in the service?"

Our father was very tactful and said, "He is still a child, only fourteen." My father then said that he was taking the family to Riesa and leaving them with friends. And then, he would register with the authorities in Riesa. When the SS men saw my baby brother and my two little sisters, they mellowed and even smiled. They left us alone. I learned that even when we were in trouble, living in grace proved to be a very beneficial "living stream of the Holy Spirit" (John 7:38–39).

This was the second time in just a few days that my father used what he called a "white lie" to shelter his family. In both instances, my father had disobeyed orders. First, he was ordered to join the militia. At that time, he told the soldiers that he would do so after giving instructions to his family and getting me in the fields. I am certain that those soldiers did not believe our father, yet they did not have him arrested. These SS men let me go with my family. This was clearly an act of grace.

Two hours later, we were miles away from them and once again running from the Russians' advancing troops. When we were trying to travel west, it was an SS roadblock that made us go south. Now, two days later, we were back on the same road again, going west. This time, two different SS men showed us grace and let us continue west. That night, we camped in Dresden by the River Elbe with thousands of refugees who also were traveling west.

We traveled on; soon we would arrive in Riesa, like my father had said. But he did not keep his word to the SS men. We ended up staying with a very loyal Nazi family. They were very adamant about their faith in Adolf Hitler. It was very uncomfortable for us, but still, they were very gracious toward us.

> As Jesus once said, "If you then, who are evil, know how to give good gifts to your children, how much more will your Father who is in heaven give good things to those who ask him?" (Matthew 7:11)

SUMMARY

- Grace gives us hope not to surrender but to keep going.
- Grace is not free; it is paid with labor and sometimes even with our lives.
- War brings horrible devastation, destruction, and evil torturing of innocent people.
- To receive grace, we must practice grace.
- Sometimes, we must "be as wise as serpents and as innocent as doves" (Matthew 10:16).

CHAPTER 13

IS GRACE A GIFT, OR IS GRACE EARNED?

OCTOBER 3, 2020

Grace, as I was taught and also believed, is God's redemptive gift to let us back into his kingdom. In return, we are called to become vessels of grace and to distribute grace. How do we become these vessels of grace? Let me share how I became a member of the grace distribution team. It has taken me ninety years to understand my own journey of grace.

WHEN DID I BECOME AWARE OF THE NEED FOR GRACE?

Aware? Maybe it began when my mother dropped a hot lid from our stove, and I sat on it. I yelled and screamed, and my mother embraced me and treated my wound. Grace was in my mother's care and love for me. Or maybe it began when my parents were married. When I joined the family, I was taught right from wrong, and I learned to experience the good and the bad. I collected and stored all of these experiences and lessons in my own head and tried to use them. When I did something good, I was rewarded, and when I did something bad, I was punished. And the more good things I did, the more good things I received from others. My parents even insisted that I be good to those people who were not good to me. At times, this was humiliating and troubling, but that is how I was able to learn what grace was really about. For me, grace was a natural growing process without my even being aware of it. Grace was inherent in my upbringing, to grow in grace, in truth, and in knowledge. Grace in me matured like fruit.

JESUS BROUGHT GRACE TO EARTH

Luke shares that Jesus had a similar experience in growth (Luke 2:52). In the prologue of the Gospel of John (1:17), Jesus was the one who brought grace to earth. Jesus may have been the author of grace before he came to earth, but on earth, he had the mission of restoring grace into the heartless Law of Moses, which had been replaced by the traditions of the fathers (Matthew 5:17–18; Mark 7:9–13). The Jewish tradition did not allow their people to share grace with the Samaritans or other Gentiles (Luke 19:31–32). Jesus himself could only go to the lost sheep of Israel (Matthew 15:24). The Ten Commandments that Yahweh gave to Moses for Israel make no mention of love (Exodus 20; Deuteronomy 5), but in the application in their living, the word *love* was added (Deuteronomy 6:5). The Law protected the neighbor and the stranger. And Yahweh commanded the Israelites to love the neighbor as well as the stranger, just as much as they loved themselves (Leviticus 19:18, 33–34; 18:26; Exodus 12:49). The love for myself must equal the love for God, for the neighbor, and for the stranger.

> "Teacher, which is the greatest commandment in the law?" And he (Jesus) said to him, "You shall love the Lord your God with all your heart, and with all your soul, and with all your mind. This is the great and first commandment. And a second is like it, You shall love your neighbor as yourself. On these two commandments depend all the law and the prophets." (Matthew 22:36–40)

SHOWING GRACE AND LOVE

I learned to love by doing things for others and for myself. Therefore, what I did became deeds of grace for those I served. The simplest way for me to understand grace and love was to do the things that meant something good for others, and in return, I would experience grace for myself.

I began to collect and store good things in my heart, which I was hoping could gain favor with God and humankind (Luke 2:52).

Unfortunately, things did not always work out that way. I began to follow and copy people who were not doing what was right or true, and I too went off the straight and narrow road. I let bad thoughts and words into my heart and mind, for which I had to atone and apologize. Some of these people passed on before I could apologize. Although I have learned to put my failures into the hands of Christ our Lord, sometimes my conscience still rattles me with guilt (2 Corinthians 12:7).

I shall write about my conscience in this journey in a later chapter.

LASTING VALUES

Jesus had similar things on his mind regarding the storing of lasting values in our hearts that can help us be useful vessels in God's kingdom.

> "Either make the tree good, and its fruit good; or make the tree bad, and its fruit bad; for the tree is known by its fruit. You brood of vipers! how can you speak good, when you are evil? For out of the abundance of the heart the mouth speaks. The good man out of his good treasure brings forth good, and the evil man out of his evil treasure brings forth evil. I tell you, on the day of judgment men will render account for every careless word they utter; for by your words you will be justified, and by your words you will be condemned." (Matthew 12:33–37)

> And when he (Jesus) had entered the house, and left the people, his disciples asked him about the parable. And he said to them, "Then are you also without understanding? Do you not see that whatever goes into a man from outside cannot defile him, since it enters, not his heart but his stomach, and so passes on?" (Thus he declared all foods clean.) And he said, "What comes out of a man is what

defiles a man. For from within, out of the heart of man, come evil thoughts fornication, theft, murder, adultery, coveting, wickedness, deceit, licentiousness, envy, slander, pride, foolishness. All these evil things come from within, and they defile a man." (Mark 7:17–23)

He (Jesus) also told them a parable: "Can a blind man lead a blind man? Will they not both fall into a pit? A disciple is not above his teacher, but every one when he is fully taught will be like his teacher. Why do you see the speck that is in your brother's eye but do not notice the log that is in your own eye? Or how can you say to your brother, 'Brother, let me take out the speck that is in your eye,' when you yourself do not see the log that is in your own eye? You hypocrite, first take the log out of your own eye, and then you will see clearly to take out the speck that is in your brother's eye.

For no good tree bears bad fruit, nor again does a bad tree bear good fruit; for each tree is known by its own fruit. For figs are not gathered from thorns, nor are grapes picked from a bramble bush. The good man out of the good treasure of his heart produces good, and the evil man out of his evil treasure produces evil; for out of the abundance of the heart his mouth speaks." (Luke 6:39–45)

Now the parable (of the Sower) is this: The seed is the word of God. The ones along the path are those who have heard; then the devil comes and takes away the word from their hearts, that they may not believe and be saved. And the ones on the rock are those who, when they hear the word, receive it with joy; but these have no root, they believe for a while and in time of temptation fall away. And as for what fell among the thorns, they are those who hear, but as they go on their way they are choked by the cares and riches and pleasures of life, and their fruit does not mature. And as for that in the good soil, they are those who, hearing the word, hold it fast in an honest and good heart, and bring forth fruit with patience. (Luke 8:11–15)

WHAT DID I LEARN FROM JESUS'S TEACHINGS?

I dressed myself in Jesus's instructions to his disciples:

"But you are not to be called rabbi, for you have one teacher, and you are all brethren. And call no man father on earth, for you have one Father, who is in heaven. Neither be called masters, for you have one master, the Christ. He who is greatest among you shall be your servant; whoever exalts himself will be humbled, and whoever humbles himself will be exalted." (Matthew 23:8–12)

FIRST IS HUMILITY

The first virtuous quality of grace is humility. For me, humility has been the hardest and the most enduring lifelong discipline to learn. It was a grooming process of my whole self. At times, it was a delousing of critters that were damaging my image and would impair my usefulness to my fellow humans and God. At times, I had more than just a chip on my shoulder. If I were to compare myself with any of the characters of whom Jesus spoke, it would be the Pharisee who went up to the temple to pray and looked down on the tax collector.

"Two men went up to the temple to pray, one a Pharisee and the other a tax collector. The Pharisee stood and prayed thus with himself, 'God, I thank thee that I am not like other men, extortioners, unjust, adulterers, or even like this tax collector. I fast twice a week, I give tithes of all that I get.' But the tax collector, standing far off, would not even lift up his eyes to heaven, but he beat his breast, saying, 'God, be merciful to me a sinner!'" (Luke 18:10–13)

83

We Require Pruning

My life has been like a tree that had not enough pruning and trimming to keep the bugs from spoiling the fruit. My heart was not as open as it should have been, and my mouth did not restrain my tongue. I have much to regret and be disciplined for it, even at ninety years of age. I neglected to guard against things that tried to pervert my mind and my desire for forbidden fruit. Many times, I was tempted and pondered how it would feel. Like Cain of Genesis 4:7, sin was couching at my door. I am thankful that I resisted the temptation of the devil and that he did not have any power over me.

James, the brother of Jesus, has been very helpful in my life.

> Or do you suppose it is in vain that the scripture says, "He yearns jealously over the spirit which he has made to dwell in us?" But he gives more grace; therefore it says, "God opposes the proud, but gives grace to the humble." Submit yourselves therefore to God. Resist the devil and he will flee from you. Draw near to God and he will draw near to you. Cleanse your hands, you sinners, and purify your hearts, you men of double mind. Be wretched and mourn and weep. Let your laughter be turned to mourning and your joy to dejection. Humble yourselves before the Lord and he will exalt you." (James 4:5–10)

It's Not a Public Show

Humiliation is not an abasement or a demotion for public showing. Genuine humility is self-love and not self-praise. It made me aware of being a child of God, made in his image and in his likeness, fit to house the Spirit of God, and capable of doing the Lord's work on earth. Demeaning myself is an insult to God, my heavenly Father, who loved me so much that he sent his Son, Jesus, to save me and employ me as a vessel of grace. I must be cautious about whom I follow. I must avoid looking for faults in others and resist those who try to keep the word of truth from me.

In the world, I am a spiritual tree.

"For no good tree bears bad fruit, nor again does a bad tree bear good fruit; for each tree is known by its own fruit. For figs are not gathered from thorns, nor are grapes picked from a bramble bush. The good man out of the good treasure of his heart produces good, and the evil man out of his evil treasure produces evil; for out of the abundance of the heart his mouth speaks." (Luke 6:43–45)

SUMMARY

- Grace is God's redemptive gift to let us into his kingdom.
- We are called to become vessels of grace to distribute grace to each other.
- Jesus brought grace to earth!
- The love for myself must equal the love for God and for the neighbor (Matthew 22:36–40).
- Showing grace and love become deeds of grace for those we serve.
- We all need pruning to keep our hearts pure (James 4:4–10).
- Genuine humility is self-love and not self-praise to be a child of God and capable of doing the Lord's work on earth (Luke 6:43–45).

CHAPTER 14

GRACE HAS A HUGE, MERCIFUL HEART

OCTOBER 10, 2020

Grace is small enough to live in our hearts yet large enough to be shared with everyone. Most people practice some form of grace, but to those of us who follow Christ, the journey of grace is enduring sacrificial work.

Jesus, our Lord, commanded us to love even our unlovable enemies. Genuine, true grace is impartial and treats everyone equally and the same, as Jesus did, and so does God, our heavenly Father.

> "You have heard it said, 'You shall love your neighbor and hate your enemy.' But I say to you, Love your enemies and pray for those who persecute you, so that you may be sons of your Father who is in heaven; for he makes his sun rise on the evil and on the good, and sends his rain on the just and the unjust. For if you love those who love you, what reward have you? Do not even the tax collectors do the same? And if you salute only your brethren, what more are you doing than others? Do not even the Gentiles do the same? You, therefore, must be perfect, as your heavenly Father is perfect." (Matthew 5:43–48)

GRACE IS MANIFESTED IN GOOD MANNERS AND IN GOOD DEEDS

How do I know whether the grace of God is in me? Jesus gave us these manifestations and attributes of grace when he gave us the Beatitudes in the Sermon on the Mount:

> Blessed are the poor in spirit, for theirs is the kingdom of heaven.
> Blessed are those who mourn, for they shall be comforted.
> Blessed are the meek, for they shall inherit the earth.
> Blessed are those who hunger and thirst for righteousness, for they shall be satisfied.
> Blessed are the merciful, for they shall obtain mercy.
> Blessed are the pure in heart, for they shall see God.
> Blessed are the peacemakers, for they shall be called sons of God.
> Blessed are those who are persecuted for righteousness' sake, for theirs is the kingdom of heaven.
> Blessed are you when men revile you and persecute you and utter all kinds of evil against you falsely on my account. Rejoice and be glad, for your reward is great in heaven, for so men persecuted the prophets who were before you.
> You are the salt of the earth; but if salt has lost its taste, how shall its saltiness be restored? It is no longer good for anything except to be thrown out and trodden under foot by men.
> You are the light of the world. A city set on a hill cannot be hid. Nor do men light a lamp and put it under a bushel, but a stand, and it gives light to all in the house. Let your light so shine before men, that they may see your good works and give glory to your Father in heaven. (Matthew 5:3–16)

HOW CAN ONE BE BLESSED WHEN FACING PERSECUTION AND DEATH?

Persecution and death are no paradox to me, and neither were they to my parents. We survived the harshness of World War II in poor spirit. The words *poor in spirit* do not only mean destitution or dependence on divine providence; *poor in spirit* is an attitude of nonresistance, the willingness to avoid facing evil forces, and escaping. We were blessed because we found places where we were safe. During this time, we employed grace by being gracious to others; this helped us find safety.

JESUS HUMBLED HIMSELF

Jesus did not resist the evil leaders who wanted his life. Jesus let them have his life for the atonement of their sins (Matthew 20:28; Mark 10:45; 1 Timothy 2:5–6). And Jesus expected no less from his beloved disciples and from Peter (1 John 3:16; 1 Peter 3:17–18). Dying for what is right and just is dying for each other and for Christ. Those who do so do not even have to wait for the Resurrection; they are assured a place in heaven (Revelation 6:9–11).

For Jesus, death marked his departure from this earthly life and a return to his heavenly home. Jesus's followers are promised the same resting place and will receive blessings by leaving their marks of grace in the world. It is in this life that we can praise the name of Christ, and Christ alone can secure us an eternal residency for our spirits (Matthew 10:32; Luke 12:8; John 14:1–3). The apostle Paul wrote these words for us:

> Therefore, my beloved, as you always obeyed, so now, not only as in my presence but much more in my absence, work out your own salvation with fear and trembling; for God is at work in you, both to will and to work for his good pleasure. Do all things without grumbling or questioning, that you may be blameless and innocent, children of God without blemish in the midst of a crooked and perverse generation, among whom you shine as lights in the world, holding fast the word of life, so that in the

day of Christ I may be proud that I did not run in vain or
labor in vain. Even if I am to be poured as a libation upon
the sacrificial offering of your faith, I am glad and rejoice
with you all. Likewise you also should be glad and rejoice
with me. (Philippians 2:12–18)

WILL EVIL PEOPLE BE IMPRESSED WITH OUR GOOD DEEDS?

Jesus and Paul believed that the world would take notice and that some
people might appreciate the good deeds we do, but this will not always
be the case. You might experience what I have at times—being disliked
and even hated for having higher standards, trying to do a little better,
and resisting temptation. Even Christians can be envious and jealous
of each other. Unfortunately, I have had ill feelings for those who were
doing better; I was afraid that they would disturb my beliefs or upset my
perspective. No, the world may not look at us favorably for doing what we
believe or even for doing what is right, but the Lord will.

We now live in a world that may treat us very unkindly for what we
believe, but this is not new. My family lived under three regimes before
this, and we tried to live out the Sermon on the Mount many times, out
of necessity. It did prove very beneficial for our survival.

"You have heard that it was said, 'An eye for an eye and a
tooth for a tooth.' But I say to you, do not resist one who
is evil. But if anyone strikes you on the right cheek, turn
to him the other also; and if any one would sue you to take
your coat, let him have your cloak as well; and if any one
forces you to go one mile, go with him two miles. Give
to him who begs from you, and do not refuse him who
would borrow from you." (Matthew 5:38–42)

"Bless those who persecute you; bless and do not curse
them. Rejoice with those who rejoice, weep with those
who weep. Live in harmony with one another; do not be
haughty, but associate with the lowly; never be conceited.

Repay no one evil for evil, but take thought for what is noble in the sight of all. If possible, so far as it depends upon you, live peaceably with all. Beloved, never avenge yourselves, but leave it to the wrath of God; for it is written, 'Vengeance is mine, I will repay, says the Lord.' No, 'if your enemy is hungry, feed him; if he is thirsty, give him drink; for by doing so you will heap burning coals upon his head.' Do not be overcome by evil, but overcome evil with good." (Romans 12:14–21)

DURING VIOLENT TIMES, YOU MAY NEED TO BE SLOW ON GRACE

During World War II, we had to avoid being friendly or too kind to strangers. We had to be careful not to gather in groups, and we tried to avoid being suspected of subversive activity against the state. Even family gatherings were suspect and therefore suspended. Many people were taken away and put in jails and camps. It was dangerous to share your belief with anyone. The propaganda was everywhere, and the state told us what was true and who we couldn't trust. People turned on each other.

What I am seeing today in the Western world is all too familiar to my own eyes—the beginning of a similar trend. Christians are told to hide their beliefs and are banned from participating in the government of their countries. Friends shame each other for their beliefs; family disowns each other. Who would have ever thought that we would face another time when being gracious in the name of Christ would be banned? Be careful in thinking that we are immune to this and that we have evolved.

JESUS AND THE BANQUET GUESTS

He (Jesus) also said to the man who had invited him, "When you give a dinner or a banquet, do not invite your friends or your brothers or your kinsmen or rich neighbors, lest they also invite you in return, and be repaid. But when you give a feast, invite the poor, the maimed, the lame, the blind, and you will be blessed, because they cannot repay you. You will be repaid at the resurrection of the just."

When one of those who sat at table with him heard this, he said to him, "Blessed is he who shall eat bread in the kingdom of God!" But he said to him, "A man once gave a great banquet, and invited many; and at the time for the banquet he sent his servant to say to those who had been invited, 'Come; for all is now read.' But they all alike began to make excuses. The first said to him, 'I have bought a field, and I must go out and see it; I pray you, have me excused.' And another said, 'I have bought five yoke of oxen, and I go to examine them; I pray you, have me excused.' And another said, 'I have married a wife, and therefore I cannot come.' So the servant came and reported this to his master.

Then the householder in anger said to his servant, 'Go out quickly to the streets and lanes of the city, and bring in the poor and maimed and blind and lame.' And the servant said, 'Sir, what you commanded has been done, and still there is room.' And the master said to the servant, 'Go out to the highways and hedges, and compel people to come in, that my house may be filled. For I tell you, none of those men who were invited shall taste my banquet." (Luke 14:12–24)

SUMMARY

- Grace is small enough to live in our hearts yet large enough to be shared through our sacrificial work with everyone.
- Grace manifests in our good manners and deeds (Matthew 5:3–16).
- Dying for what is right and just is dying for each other and Christ.
- During violent times, you need to be slow on grace.

CHAPTER 15

QUENCHING THE SPIRIT IN US

OCTOBER 17, 2020

LEADERS WILL NOT QUENCH THEIR SPIRITS

But we beseech you, brethren, to respect those who labor among you and are over you in the Lord and admonish you, and esteem them very highly in love because of their work. Be at peace among yourselves. And we exhort you, brethren, admonish the idlers, encourage the fainthearted, help the weak, be patient with them all. See that none of you repays evil for evil, but always seek to do good to one another and to all. Rejoice always, pray constantly, give thanks in all circumstances; for this is the will of God in Christ Jesus for you. Do not quench the Spirit, do not despise prophesying, but test everything; hold fast to what is good, abstain from every form of evil. (1 Thessalonians 5:12–22)

So I exhort the elders among you, as a fellow elder and a witness of the sufferings of Christ as well as a partaker in the glory that is to be revealed. Tend the flock of God that is your charge, not by constraint but willingly, not for shameful gain but eagerly, not as domineering over those in your charge but being example to the flock. And when the chief Shepherd is manifested you will obtain the unfading crown of glory. Likewise you that are younger be subject to the elders. Clothe yourselves, all of you, with humility towards one another, for "God opposes the proud, but gives grace to the humble."

Humble yourselves therefore under the mighty hand of God, that in due time he may exalt you. Cast all your anxieties on him, for he cares about you. Be sober, be watchful. Your adversary the devil prowls around like a lion, seeking someone to devour. Resist him, firm in your faith, knowing that the same experience of suffering is required of your brotherhood throughout the world. And after you have suffered a little while, the God of all grace, who has called you to his eternal glory in Christ, will himself restore, establish, and strengthen you. To him be the dominion for ever and ever. Amen. (1 Peter 5:1–11)

WHAT IS THE SIGN OF A QUENCHED SPIRIT?

When I doubt that I can live out the Sermon on the Mount, the law of God, and the gifts of the Holy Spirit, I quench the spirit that God gave me. When I act helplessly, believing I am unable to live a godly life, I do it again. God created me and you and equipped us to run the world; insisting that we are incapable is absurd. I personally lost 75 percent of the use of my hands in my accident. I went through horrible pain and disabling suffering, yet I retrained myself and led a normal and productive life. Yes, I had to open up my spirit, and I worked hard. God did not keep me from what I could be or what might have been; I did.

I learned something else about myself from the apostle Paul, who also faced difficult physical problems, about which he wrote in Philippians:

I rejoice in the Lord greatly that now at length you have revived your concern for me; you were indeed concerned for me, but you had no opportunity. Not that I complain of want; for I have learned, in whatever state I am, to be content. I know how to be abased, and I know how to abound; in any and all circumstances I have learned the secret of plenty and hunger, abundance and want. I can do all things in him who strengthens me. (Philippians 4:10–13)

THE WORLD MAY HAVE ONE OVER US

Here is what I learned: worldly people may have one over me. They appear to be more prosperous without Christ than I am with Christ. They do not wait for God to come and assist them, but somehow, without knowing, they use the resources of God, and they may get what they want in this life. I, on the other hand, wait for the Lord to compel and show me where I should spend my time. In reality, I am no different, and I end up doing what so many good worldly people do. How, then, are we different? Worldly people do not blame their mistakes or bad deeds on God or the devil. We should take note of this.

When I make a mistake, it is my decision. I tried it and did what I thought I should do. Some things turned out right, and some turned out wrong. I need to correct the wrong and, at times, let someone else assist me and move on. We Christians differ in being responsible to God, while worldly people seem only to be responsible to their own kind. They, too, may work for God without being cognizant. With the way Christians participate in managing the world, it is not surprising that the unbelievers have control. These are similar times to when God handed Judea over to the Babylonians or to the Romans to do his work. The Jewish people simply were not doing it. Jesus gave this example to his disciples:

> "Then the king will say to those at his right hand, 'Come, O blessed of my Father, inherit the kingdom prepared for you from the foundation of the world; for I was hungry and you gave me food, I was thirsty and you gave me drink, I was a stranger and you welcomed me, I was naked and you clothed me, I was sick and you visited me, I was in prison and you came to me.' Then the righteous will answer him, 'Lord, when did we see thee hungry and

feed thee, or thirsty and give thee drink? And when did
we see thee sick or in prison and visit thee?' And the King
will answer them, 'Truly, I say to you, as you did it to
one of the least of these my brethren, you did it to me.'"
(Matthew 25:34–40)

WHAT DOES AN UNQUENCHED SPIRIT LOOK LIKE?

To begin with, as vessels of grace, we are expected to be leaders who
teach others how to retain membership in the kingdom of heaven on
earth. We are supposed to be living examples of grace, recognizable by our
conduct and service. The content of grace is filled with the Beatitudes. I
used to think these Beatitudes were only divine gifts, but Jesus insisted that
his followers were to grow such Beatitudes and be doers of the Beatitudes.

The Beatitudes are the tasks that the leaders must be able to perform
among their people. As refugees, my family and I needed all of the
Beatitude services. We had lost loved ones, experienced lowliness, longed
for justice, accepted mercy, bore no ill, were grateful for peace, and endured
abuse and even persecution. I also was given the opportunity to minister
to people with these needs. These are human needs, here on earth, where
God entrusted human beings to meet. And those who live and use the
Beatitudes are themselves blessed and feel fulfilled. That was why Jesus
used salt and light to demonstrate what the Beatitudes, in us, can and will
do when they are used and ignited by us (Matthew 4:4–16). That is how
an unquenched spirit behaves and acts (Acts 4:19–20).

In this world, we must do what Christ and God have entrusted us to
do until the end. Without the Beatitudes, what else can Christ's servants do
to serve their flocks? They set the followers of Jesus apart from the world.

THE RISEN CHRIST HANDED OVER
HIS WORK TO THE APOSTLES

This was the way Jesus did it; he handed over his work to his followers.
His Spirit empowered the spirits of his disciples. Jesus began to partner
with his followers, his servants, to reconcile the world to God. He also
did this with Paul, with Peter, and with all those who would follow him.

On the evening of the resurrection day, the first day of the week, the doors being shut where the disciples were, for fear of the Jews. Jesus came and stood among them and said to them, "Peace be with you." When he had said this, he showed them his hands and his side. Then the disciples were glad when they saw the Lord. Jesus said to them, "Peace be with you. As the Father has sent me, even so I send you." And when he had said this, he breathed on them, and said to them, "Receive the Holy Spirit. If you forgive the sins of any, they are forgiven; if you retain the sins of any, they are retained." (John 20:19–23)

All this is from God, who through Christ reconciled us to himself and gave us the ministry of reconciliation; that is, in Christ God was reconciling the world to himself, not counting their trespasses against them, and entrusting to us the message of reconciliation. (2 Corinthians 5:18–19)

When they had finished breakfast, Jesus said to Simon Peter, "Simon, son of John, do you love me more than these?" He said to him, "Yes Lord; you know that I love you." He said to him, "Feed my lambs." A second time he said to him, "Simon, son of John, do you love me?" He said to him, "Tend my sheep." He said to him the third time, "Simon, son of John, do you love me?" Peter was grieved because he said to him the third time, "Do you love me?" And he said to him, "Lord, you know everything; you know that I love you." Jesus said to him, "Feed my sheep. Truly, truly, I say to you, when you were young, you girded yourself and walked where you would; but when you are old, you will stretch out your hands, and another will gird you and carry you where you do not wish to go." (This he said to show by what death he was to glorify God.) And after this he said to him, "Follow me." (John 21:15–19)

"Let your loins be girded and your lamps burning, and be like men who are waiting for their master to come home from the marriage feast, so that they may open to him at once when he comes and knocks. Blessed are those servants whom the master finds awake when he comes; truly, I say to you, he will gird himself and have them sit at table, and he will come and serve them. If he comes in the second watch, or in third, and finds them so, blessed are those servants! But know this, that if the householder had known at what hour the thief was coming, he would not have left his house to be broken into. You also must be ready; for the Son of man is coming at an unexpected hour."

Peter said, "Lord, are you telling this parable for us or for all?" And the Lord said, "Who then is the faithful and wise steward, whom his master will set over his household, to give them their portion of food at the proper time? Blessed is that servant whom his master when he comes will find so doing. Truly, I tell you, he will set him over all possessions." (Luke 12:35–44)

SUMMARY

- God created me and you and equipped us to run, control, and manage the world.
- As vessels of grace, we are expected to be leaders who teach others how to retain membership in the kingdom of heaven on earth.
- Jesus insisted that his followers live and be doers of the Beatitudes.
- Jesus inspired and handed over his work to his followers to reconcile the world to God.

CHAPTER 16

Taking Grace for Granted

OCTOBER 24, 2020

Do I take grace for granted?

Will my Lord say to me, "Well done, good servant"? (Luke 19:17). For me, grace is the means and the way I serve Christ daily. Yet today, as I write this, I am ninety years old, and I still wonder if I am missing something that I must pass on. Have I been negligent in my duties, and have I taken grace for granted? Do I want to receive and be served, rather than give and serve? I recall a warning that Jesus issued:

> "But if that servant says to himself, 'My master is delayed in coming,' and begins to beat the (other servants,) and to eat and drink and get drunk, the master of that servant will come on a day when he does not expect him and at an hour he does not know, and will punish him, and put him with the unfaithful." (Luke 12:45–46)

WHAT DO WE THINK WE DESERVE?

"Will any one of you, who has a servant plowing or keeping sheep, say to him when he has come in from the field, 'Come at once and sit down at table'? Will he not rather say to him, 'Prepare supper for me, and gird yourself and serve me, till I eat and drink; and afterward you shall eat and drink'? Does he thank the servant because he did what was commanded? So you also, when you have done all that is commanded you, say, 'We are unworthy servants; we have only done what was our duty.'" (Luke 17:7–10)

TRY NOT TO BE A RECIPIENT BUT RATHER A SERVANT OF GRACE

Most of us want more for ourselves than we can give, which is not surprising. After all, we probably have not planted enough to harvest sufficiently for ourselves and others.

Jesus gave us such a lesson in one of his parables.

> And Jesus went about all the cities and villages, teaching in their synagogues and preaching the gospel of the kingdom, and healing every disease and every infirmity. When he saw the crowds, he had compassion for them, because they were harassed and helpless, like sheep without a shepherd. Then he said to his disciples, "The harvest is plentiful, but the laborers are few; pray therefore the Lord of the harvest to send out laborers into his harvest." (Matthew 9:35–38)

> "For it will be as when a man going on a journey called his servants and entrusted to them his property; to one he gave five talents, to another two, to another one, to each according to his ability. Then he went away. He who had received the five talents went at once and traded with them; and he made five talents more. So also, he who had the two talents made two talents more. But he who had received the one talent went and dug in the ground and hid his master's money. Now after a long time the master of those servants came and settled accounts with them. And he who had received the five talents came forward, bringing five talents more, saying, 'Master, you delivered to me five talents; here I have made five talents more.'

His master said to him, 'Well done, good and faithful servant; you have been faithful over a little, I will set you over much; enter into the joy of your master.' And he also who had the two talents came forward, saying 'Master, you delivered to me two talents; here I have made two talents more.' His master said to him, 'Well done, good and faithful servant; you have been faithful over a little, I will set you over much; enter into the joy of your master.' He also who had received the one talent came forward, saying, 'Master, I knew you to be a hard man, reaping where you did not sow, and gathering where you did not winnow; so I was afraid, and I went and hid your talent in the ground. Here you have what is yours.' But his master answered him, 'You wicked and slothful servant! You knew that I reap where I have not sowed, and gather where I have not winnowed? Then you ought to have invested my money with the bankers, and at my coming I should have received what was my own with interest. So take the talent from him and give it to him who has the ten talents. For to everyone who has will more be given, and he will have abundance; but from him who has not, even what he has will be taken away. And cast the worthless servant into the outer darkness; there men will weep and gnash their teeth.'" (Matthew 25:14–30)

WHAT DOES THIS PARABLE SAY TO ME?

This parable summarizes an organization, a large company with vast holdings and great wealth. It was established by Christ on earth, and it's called the kingdom of heaven. Jesus had to leave earth and return to heaven. And so, Jesus put the management of his organization into the hands of his disciples. Jesus gave them a mission. His instructions were,

Go therefore and make disciples of all nations, baptizing them in the name of the Father and the Son and the

Holy Spirit, teaching them to observe all that I have commanded you; and lo, I am with you always, to the close of the age. (Matthew 28:19–20)

To observe does not mean "to watch"; rather, it means "to take hold" (*terein*). We are to make it our own so that we have something to pass on. The disciples were with Jesus for three years, learning the meaning of grace and learning how to apply grace and pass it on to others. They were with him to observe so they could fulfill his command. Christ's commandments are wrapped in one word: love (*agape*), and the content of love is grace (*charis*).

GRACE IS THE CHARACTER AND THE NATURE OF CHRIST

Christ loved as he lived and showed us the meaning of grace. It is his example that I must follow. As I believe in him, I become a new creation and a vessel of grace.

Therefore, if anyone is in Christ, he is a new creation; the old has passed away, behold, the new has come. All this is from God, who through Christ reconciled us to himself and gave us the ministry of reconciliation. (2 Corinthians 5:17–18)

I had to assume that my nature would become a vessel of grace. It is my practice of grace that also prepares me for heaven. If I do not practice grace as I am commanded, then what right do I have? If I am not fit for the kingdom of heaven on earth, what right have I to be accepted in heaven? To my understanding, the kingdom of God was brought into the world so that I could prepare and learn the manners of heaven. God's love made this possible.

The book of Acts tells us that Barnabas was a man in whom and through whom grace was manifested at Antioch.

News came to the ears of the church in Jerusalem, and they sent Barnabas to Antioch. When he came and saw the grace (work) of God, he was glad; and exhorted them all to remain faithful to the Lord with steadfast purpose; for he was a good man, full of the Holy Spirit and of faith. And a large company was added to the Lord. So Barnabas went to Tarsus to look for Saul; and when he had found him, he brought him to Antioch. For a whole year they met with the church, and taught a large company of people; and in Antioch the disciples were for the first time called Christians. (Acts 11:22–26)

JESUS SAID WE MUST BE BORN ANEW

Jesus answered (Nicodemus), "Truly, truly, I say to you, unless one is born of water and the Spirit, he cannot enter the kingdom of God. That which is born of the flesh is flesh, and that which is born of the Spirit is spirit. Do not marvel that I said to you, 'You must be born anew.' The wind blows where it wills, and you hear the sound of it, but you do not know whence it comes or whither it goes; so it is with everyone who is born of the Spirit." (John 3:5–8)

WE ARE COMMANDED TO LOVE

"This is my commandment, that you love one another as I have loved you. Greater love has no man than this, that a man lay down his life for his friends. You are my friends if you do what I command you. No longer do I call you servants, for the servant does not know what his master is doing; but I have called you friends, for all that I have heard from my Father I have made known to you. You did not choose me, but I chose you and appointed you that you should go and bear fruit and that your fruit should abide; so that whatever you ask the Father in my name, he may give it to you. This I command you, to love one another. (John 15:12–17)

BECAUSE GOD LOVED US SO MUCH
||||||||||||||||||||||||||||||||

For God so loved the world that he gave his only begotten Son, that whosoever believes in him should not perish but have eternal life. For God did send his Son into the world, not to condemn the world, but that the world might be saved through him. He who believes in him is not condemned; he who does not believe is condemned already, because he has not believed in the name of the only Son of God. And this is the judgment, that the light has come into the world, and men loved darkness rather than light, because their deeds were evil. For every one who does evil hates the light and does not come to the light, lest his deeds should be exposed. But he who does what is true comes to the light, that it may be clearly seen that his deeds have been wrought in God. (John 3:16–21)

HOW AM I DOING?
||||||||||||||||||||||||||||||||

Paul writes that God knows exactly how much we can endure and carry.

No temptation has overtaken you that is not common to man. God is faithful, and he will not let you be tempted beyond your strength, but with the temptation will also provide the way of escape, that you may be able to endure it. (1 Corinthians 10:13)

Then how do I rate myself? Have I resisted temptation? What about the talents I have been given? Where do I place myself on a scale from one to ten? In the parable of the talents, Jesus used five, two, and one talent. To which group would I match up?

To those of us who measure up to only one talent, can we do sufficiently well to please him? The parable says we ought to give back our talent with interest. The five-pounder talent and the two-pounder talent of grace doubled their output. In the Lukan account, these faithful servants were rewarded and promoted, and they were given greater and better responsibilities (Luke 19:15–19). Even the world will choose such a laborer who works hard over one who only takes.

FAITHFUL IN MUCH OR LITTLE?

"He who is faithful in very little is faithful also in much; and he who is dishonest in very little is dishonest also in much. If then you have not been faithful in the unrighteous mammon, who will entrust to you the true riches? And if you have not been faithful in that which is another's, who will give you that which is your own? No servant can serve two masters; for either he will hate the one and love the other, or he will be devoted to the one and despise the other. You cannot serve God and mammon." The Pharisees, who were lovers of money, heard all this, and they scoffed at him. But he said to them, "You are those who justify yourselves before men, but God knows your hearts; for what is exalted among men is an abomination in the sight of God. The law and the prophets were until John; since then the good news of the kingdom of God is preached, and every one enters it violently. But it is easier for heaven and earth to pass away, than for one dot of the law to become void." (Luke 16:10–17)

MONEY RULES THIS WORLD

In this world, in our day and age, more now than ever, money controls everything. Mammon has the power, and even Christians depend as much on mammon as the world does. We need money to pay for our necessities, the things that sustain our bodies so our spirits can function and keep our world running. Even a reformed and reborn body and soul are subject to mammon and the workings of this world (John 3:5). To love our enemies (Matthew 5:44) is the same as the command to make friends with mammon (Luke 16:9). Being gracious can gain us some favor when such favor is needed to survive.

Jesus used this example:

> "There was a rich man who had a steward, and charges were brought to him that this man was wasting his goods. And he called him and said to him, 'What is this I hear about you? Turn in the account of your stewardship, for you can no longer be steward.' And the steward said to himself, 'What shall I do, since my master is taking the stewardship away from me? I am not strong enough to dig, and I am ashamed to beg. I have decided what to do, so that people may receive me into their houses when I am put out of the stewardship.' So, summoning his master's debtors one by one, he said to the first, 'How much do you owe?" He said, 'A hundred measures of oil.' And he said to him, 'Take your bill, and sit down quickly and write fifty.' Then he said to another, 'And how much do you owe?' He said, 'A hundred measures of wheat.' He said to him, 'Take your bill, and write eighty.' The master commended the dishonest steward for his prudence; for the sons of this world are wiser in their own generation than the sons of light. And I tell you, make friends for yourselves by means of unrighteous mammon, so that when it fails they may receive you into the eternal habitations." (Luke 16:1b–9)

SUMMARY

- Grace is the means and the way to serve Christ daily.
- Christ's commandments are wrapped in one word, love, and the content of love is grace.
- In Christ, we become a new creation.
- God's love makes it possible for us to understand, prepare, and learn the manners of the kingdom of heaven.
- Jesus said we must be born again!
- Jesus commanded us to love as he loves us (John 15:12–17).
- We all are subject to mammon and the workings of this world (Luke 16:9).

CHAPTER 17

AFRAID TO FAIL

OCTOBER 31, 2020

BEING AFRAID TO FAIL IS DETRIMENTAL

The fear of failing has always been very real to me, and I am not alone; it is the same for millions of people. When I was young, I lived in a world that taught me to fear. Our fears were very real; it was World War II. Although I tried very hard, I had difficulty in pleasing my parents and my teachers. Still, like most children, even children today, I was very dependent on others, even into my young adulthood. I worked hard on the farm, but I lived on what was provided for me. I was fortunate in that time. I looked up to others who appeared successful, and I tried following their example since they were in charge. This was the formula I used often, even as I began my formal training—following others who were successful.

DOING MY OWN WORK

It was not until I wrote my doctoral dissertation that one adviser plainly told me to stop following others, regardless of their noted accomplishments, and to do my own work. At that time, I had submitted my thesis, and it was rejected. This was a big failure for me and also an incredible lesson. I had to start all over on my thesis, and I was not confident that I could do it. But I went to work, and this time, following his advice, I found it much easier than I had believed it would be. I finished my work and passed, earning my doctorate.

How many millions of people are there in this world who are afraid to invest in themselves? Do they even begin? Do they try, even with the smallest start? To God and to Jesus, two copper coins from a widow drew their attention (Mark 12:42). Yet the man who did not invest the one pound lost it all and also himself (Matthew 25:24–30). How many never begin?

WE FAIL IF WE DO NOTHING

We fail when we do nothing or the wrong thing. Luke the evangelist found some additional things to this parable regarding the negligent servant and the steward.

> "Then another came, saying, 'Lord, here is your pound, which I kept laid away in a napkin; for I was afraid of you, because you are a severe man; you take up what you did not lay down and reap what you did not sow.' He said to him, 'I will condemn you out of your own mouth, you wicked servant! You knew that I was a severe man, taking up what I did not lay down and reaping what I did not sow? Why then did you not put my money into the bank, and at my coming I should have collected it with interest?' And he said to those who stood by, 'Take the pound from him and give it to him who has the ten pounds.' (And they said to him, 'Lord, he has ten pounds!') I tell you, that to everyone who has will more be given; but from him who has not, even what he has will be taken away. But as for these enemies of mine, who did not want me to reign over them, bring them here and slay them before me.'" (Luke 19:20–27)

The parable warns of a far more serious problem that lazy people cause. Jesus regarded such lazy, healthy individuals as enemies to the state, the community, and the family and as enemies to themselves. It is beyond our perception how much harm such people cause for those who faithfully fill their vessels. The earth, the country, the city, the village, and the family depend on our ability to re-create, reproduce, repair, restore, and numerous other things that survival demands. We are God's stewards and servants, charged with the management of the world (Genesis 1:2). Those who disobey that order and take part in the cycle of providing the substance, which continues to keep things running, are enemies of humanity and of God. These people—lazy people—were labeled selfish and greedy. Such people were to be stripped of their own property, and their property was to be given to those who were productive. Also, such lazy, selfish, and greedy people were not allowed to live. Paul ordered the Thessalonians not to feed such people (2 Thessalonians 3:10).

Jesus tried to solve a small problem for his people, but politicians used it to make it a world problem. By replacing the people who knew how to keep their countries productive and running, they set themselves up as the world's saviors. After the constant failure of their systems, they hope to make us respond, like Pavlov's dog, to the ringing of their bells. The global ruler and the second beast are a copy of the first beast that appeared in the world to dissect Christian unity and to deny the validity of the Christian Messiah. Revelation 13:16–17 is history in the making. The people who keep burying their pound are causing the fall of this proud nation. The world leader is already trained and prepared to take charge.

THE BEAST

Then I saw another beast which rose out of the earth; it had two horns like a lamb and it spoke like a dragon. It exercises all the authority of the first beast in its presence, and makes the earth and its inhabitants worship the first beast, whose mortal wound was healed. It works great signs, even making fire come down from heaven to earth in the sight of men; and by the signs which it is allowed to work in the presence of the beast, it deceives those who dwell on earth, bidding them make an image for the beast which was wounded by the sword and yet lived; and it was allowed to give breath to the image of the beast so that the image of the beast should even speak, and to cause those who would not worship the image of the beast to be slain. Also it causes all, both small and great, both rich and poor, both free and slave, to be marked on the right hand or the forehead, so that no one can buy or sell unless he has the mark, that is, the name of the beast or the number on its name. This calls for wisdom; let him who has understanding reckon the number of the beast, for it is human number, its number is six hundred and sixty-six. (Revelation 13:11–18)

NEGLECTING MY DUTY IS SELF-INCRIMINATING

Negligence, even if done in innocence, can be very detrimental. In my own life, many innocent mistakes have caused me serious harm. When I was little, my mother dropped a hot lid from our stove, and I sat on it. My mother was negligent in putting it on the floor, and I didn't know better. Another time, my father took a horse in payment for work he had done. He didn't know that this horse would not let anyone go behind it. When I was seven years old, I was left to watch the horse and two cows. When I went behind the horse, the horse kicked me, and I could not breathe. Thankfully, I recovered, but I was too embarrassed to tell my parents what I had done. When my father discovered the horse's behavior on his own, he traded it.

And it was an innocent fall that forever altered my life at that lumber camp. I slipped and fell, and two kerosene lamps set my body on fire. My life changed course after that moment.

NEGLIGENCE THAT IS DELIBERATE

In contrast, the one-pounder's choice was deliberate. He withheld his service with full intention because of his fear that he would not be able to produce anything. But there is more. Neither did he have any trust in the abilities of others. He was afraid that if he worked with someone else, and that person failed, he would be blamed and lose everything.

THE FEAR OF LOSING EVERYTHING

I understand this type of fear because we have experienced this in our lives. Our sons started a business and worked very hard for years to build it up. They had some success but needed financial help to continue to grow. We regarded it as our duty, so we put up all our savings and refinanced our home, taking on new debt to help them. In the end, this didn't save the business, and we lost everything. We went through this failure together, suffering and healing together along the way from our mistakes.

Another time, when my mother-in-law came to live with us, we had to move from a three-level to a one-level house to better accommodate her needs. This was at a time when mortgage rates were very high, and as I was a self-employed minister with a small salary, we could not qualify for a loan. The seller was willing to give us a short-term loan, but we still did not have enough. My mother-in-law liked the house very much, and to help us close the sale, she willingly offered her money from the sale of her own house. She really enjoyed that house.

In May 1985, my mother-in-law moved to her daughter in Edmonton, Alberta, Canada; within six months, she passed away. Turmoil and misunderstanding gave way for four of her children, and they immediately demanded their share of her estate. The real estate market was rough. There were no buyers; and we were unable to get any loans. We asked them to wait until our home sold, but they were unreasonable—they even threatened to take us to court. Fortunately, my parents came to our rescue. They sold their home in Canada and lent us the money we needed to satisfy our heartless relatives.

REFUSING TO HELP

The one-pound man did just the opposite. He refused to face the prospect of losing. People like him regard it as an imposition when someone asks them to take on added responsibility. It was an invasion of his privacy. He had no need for an additional pound to worry about, especially if he might have had to make up for its loss.

BEING IMPOSED UPON

I understand very much what this feels like—wanting to be left alone, wanting to be private. I also had those feelings and resented being imposed upon. Then, there came a time when I had no choice. I eagerly welcomed invaders into my life and regarded them as angels from heaven, for they eased my pain, treated my wounds, and helped me heal and recover. My accident kept me in hospital rooms and recovery centers for eighteen months without a break. Imagine how many people invested their "pounds" on me, and how many of them did this without hesitation. After that time, I would require assistance for the rest of my life. With these people—invaders in my life—I was able to develop new ways to make a living and, in return, help others. I have been doing this for nearly seventy years. By command, by law, I, too, have become a brother's keeper (Genesis 4:8–11; Matthew 22:39; Luke 10:33–37).

WHAT DID JESUS THINK OF PEOPLE WHO DO NOT ASSIST?

One of the multitude said to him (Jesus), "Teacher, bid my brother divide the inheritance with me." But he said to him, "Man, who made me a judge or divider over you?" And he said to them, "Take heed, and beware of covetousness; for a man's life does not consist in the abundance of his possessions. And he told them a parable, saying "The land of a rich man brought forth plentifully; and he thought to himself, 'What shall I do, for I have nowhere to store my crops?' And he said, 'I will do this: I will pull down my barns, and build larger ones; and there I will store all my grain and my goods. And I will say to my soul, Soul, you have ample goods laid up for many years; take your ease, eat, drink, be merry.' But God said to him, 'Fool! This night your soul is required of you; and the things you have prepared, whose will they be?" So is he who lays up treasure for himself, and is not rich toward God. (Luke 12:13–21)

"There was a rich man, who was clothed in purple and fine linen and who feasted sumptuously every day. At his gate lay a poor man named Lazarus, full of sores, who desired to be fed with what fell from the rich man's table; moreover the dogs came and licked his sores. The poor man died and was carried by angels to Abraham's bosom. The rich man also died and was buried; and in Hades, being in torment, he lifted up his eyes, and saw Abraham far off and Lazarus in his bosom. And he called out, 'Father Abraham, have mercy upon me, and send Lazarus to dip the end of his finger in water and cool my tongue; for I am in anguish in this flame.' But Abraham said, 'Son, remember that you in your lifetime received your good things, and Lazarus in like manner evil things; but now he is comforted here, and you are in anguish. And besides all this, between us and you a great chasm has been fixed, in order that those who would pass from here to you may not be able, and none may cross from there to us.' And he said, 'Then I beg you, father, to send him to my father's house, for I have five brothers, so that he may warn them, lest they also come into this place of torment.' But Abraham said, 'They have Moses and the prophets; let them hear them.' And he said, 'No, father Abraham; but if someone goes to them from the dead, they will repent.' He said to him, 'If they do not hear Moses and the prophets, neither will they be convinced if some one should rise from the dead.'" (Luke 16:19–31)

Do What Jesus Has Commanded

Jesus, the Son of God, returned from the grave. Jesus has declared, verified, and fulfilled the Law of Moses and the prophets, which can keep us out of hell. If we do not bear the fruit of grace, however, do not count on faith without deeds (James 2:18–26; Philippians 2:12).

Jesus says,

"Why do you call me Lord and do not what I tell you?
Everyone who comes to me and hears my words and does
them, I will show you what he is like: he is like a man
building a house, who dug deep, and laid a foundation
upon rock; and when the flood arose, the stream broke
against that house, and could not shake it, because it
had been well built. But he who hears and does not do
them is like a man who built a house on the ground
without a foundation; against which the stream broke,
and immediately it fell, and the ruin of that house was
great." (Luke 6:46–49)

"Not everyone who says to me, 'Lord, Lord,' shall enter
the kingdom of heaven, but he who does the will of my
Father who is in heaven. On that day many will say to me,
'Lord, Lord, did we not prophesy in your name, and cast
out demons in your name, and do many mighty works
in your name?' And then will I declare to them, 'I never
knew you; depart from me, you evildoers.'" (Matthew
7:21–23)

SUMMARY

- Being afraid to fail is detrimental.
- We fail if we do nothing.
- We are held responsible for our talents, even if it is just one pound.
People who keep their pound buried cause the fall of their nation.
- Negligence, even if done in innocence, can be very detrimental.
- Deliberate negligence, fear, and distrust in the abilities of others
cost the one-pounder everything.
- Jesus has declared, verified, and fulfilled the Law of Moses and the
prophets to keep us out of hell.

CHAPTER 18

BEWARE OF SELF-INCRIMINATION

NOVEMBER 7, 2020

The one-pound servant knew what he was supposed to do, yet he disobeyed. He was given a command and entrusted to do it. He knew what his master would do if he didn't do it, and he still failed to do it. How many of us do the same thing?

GREENER PASTURES

By our very nature as human beings, we know when we do what is right and what is wrong (Genesis 3:22; James 4:17). Even those who are not Christian, who are without the Law of Moses, the prophets, and Jesus Christ, know what is right and wrong. We all have a voice inside of us that tells us what we ought to do—but we do not always listen.

I have done it myself. Even though I was called to serve, I was lured away by greener pastures. As I rationalized taking the easier and better path, it seemed that my conscience was asleep. When it awoke, my spirit within me was struck with guilt, and I apologized. I received no additional confirmation, but that voice inside of me, my conscience, still bugs me, seventy years later.

114

WHAT DOES SCRIPTURE TELL ME?

In everyday life, I am told to let my conscience guide me and help others. By obeying my conscience, I keep my eyes on what I do. I have learned that the teachings of Jesus and his disciples assist my conscience. When I follow those teachings, I can and do trust my conscience, and it benefits me every day in my faith and in my work.

Paul teaches us in Romans,

> All who have sinned without the law will also perish without the law, and all who sin under the law will be judged by the law. For it is not the hearers of the law who are righteous before God, but the doers of the law who will be justified. When Gentiles who have not the law do by nature what the law requires, they are a law to themselves, even though they do not have a law. They show what the law requires is written on their hearts, while their conscience also bears witness and their conflicting thoughts accuse or perhaps excuse them on that day when, according to my gospel, God judges the secrets of men by Christ Jesus. (Romans 2:12–16)

And Jesus says,

> "If the world hates you, know that it has hated me before it hated you. If you were of the world, the world would love its own; but because you are not of the world, but I chose you out of the world, therefore the world hates you. Remember the word that I said to you, 'A servant is not greater than his master.' If they persecuted me, they would persecute you; if they kept my word, they will keep yours also. But all this they will do to you on my account, because they do not know him who sent me. If I had not come and spoken to them, they would not have sin; but now they have no excuse for their sin. He who hates me hates my Father also. If I had not done among them

the works which no one else did, they would not have sin; but now they have seen and hated both me and my Father. It is to fulfill the word that is written in their law, 'They hated me without a cause.' But when the Counselor comes, whom I shall send to you from the Father, even the Spirit of truth, who proceeds from the Father, he will bear witness to me; and you also are witnesses, because you have been with me from the beginning." (John 15:18–27)

Jesus continues,

"You search the Scriptures, because you think that in them you have eternal life; and it is they that bear witness of me; yet you refuse to come to me that you may have life. I do not receive glory from men. But I know that you have not the love of God within you. I have come in my Father's name, and you do not receive me; if another comes in his own name, him you will receive. How can you believe, who receives glory from one another and do not seek the glory that comes from the only God? Do you think that I shall accuse you to the Father; it is Moses who accuses you, on whom you set your hope. If you believed Moses, you would believe me, for he wrote of me. But if you do not believe his writings, how will you believe my words?" (John 5:39–47)

For we did not follow cleverly devised myths when we made known to you the power of the coming of our Lord Jesus Christ, but we were eyewitnesses of his majesty. For when he received honor and glory from God the Father and the voice was borne to him by the Majestic Glory, "This is my beloved Son with whom I am well pleased," we heard this voice borne from heaven for we were with him on the holy mountain. And we have the prophetic word made more sure. You will do well to pay attention to this as to a lamp shining in a dark place, until the day dawns and the morning star rises in your hearts. First of all you must understand this, that no prophecy of scripture is a matter of one's own interpretation, because no prophecy ever came by the impulse of man, but men moved by the Holy Spirit spoke from God. (2 Peter 1:16–21)

MY WORDS AND MY TONGUE BIND ME TO MY CONSCIENCE

I have learned to be careful of the promises I make. One time, when I was a student trying to gain entrance to the university, I attended a revival meeting. I was a very poor, hopeful student, with only a twenty-dollar allowance for the entire month. This revival meeting was at the beginning of the month, and the clever evangelist had me put my meal ticket on his offering plate. Imagine this—he made us take out our wallets and hold them up; then he said, "Show that you love the Lord more than your largest bill in your purse or wallet." Imagine what that did to me when I parted with my daily bread. This man did not exactly employ Jesus's method. I soon had nothing to live on. But I am thankful now because it taught me to slow down on making any promises. Does God really grade us by how much we give financially? Or is it more important what we say and do, each and every day? How do we speak?

"Beware of practicing your piety before men in order to be seen by them; for then you will have no reward from your Father who is in heaven. Thus, when you give alms, sound no trumpet before you, as the hypocrites do in the synagogues and in the streets, that they may be praised by men. Truly, I say to you, they have received their reward. But when you give alms, do not let your left hand know what your right hand is doing, so that your alms may be in secret; and your Father who sees in secret will reward you. And when you pray, you must not be like the hypocrites; for they love to stand and pray in the synagogues and at the street corners, that they may be seen by men. Truly, I say to you, they have received their reward. But when you pray, go into your room and shut the door and pray to your Father who is in secret; and your Father who sees in secret will reward you. And in praying do not heap up empty phrases as the Gentiles do; for they think that they will be heard for their many words. Do not be like them, for your Father knows what you need before you ask him. Pray then like this:

Our Father who art in heaven, Hallowed be thy name. Thy kingdom come, Thy will be one, on earth as it is in heaven. Give us this day our daily bread; and forgive us our debts, as we also have forgiven our debtors; and lead us not into temptation, but deliver us from evil. (Matthew 6:1–13)

My brethren, show no partiality as you hold the faith of our Lord Jesus Christ, the Lord of glory. For if a man with a gold ring and in fine clothing comes into your assembly, and a poor man in shabby clothing also comes in, and you pay attention to the one who wears the fine clothing and say, "Have a seat here, please," while you say to the poor man, "Stand there," or, "Sit at my feet," have you not make distinctions among yourselves, and become judges with evil thoughts? Listen, my beloved brethren. Has not God chosen those who are poor in the world to be rich in faith and heirs of the kingdom which he has promised to those who love him? But you have dishonored the poor man. Is it not the rich who oppress you, is it not they who drag you into court? It is not they who blaspheme the honorable name by which you are called? (James 2:1–7)

DO NOT SWEAR

"Again you have heard that it was said to the men of old, 'You shall not swear falsely, but shall perform to the Lord what you have sworn.' But I say to you, Do not swear at all, either by heaven, for it is his footstool, or by Jerusalem, for it is the city of the great King. And do not swear by your head, for you cannot make one hair white or black. Let what you say be simply, 'Yes' or "No'; anything more than this comes from evil." (Matthew 5:33–37)

WHAT HAPPENED TO ABIDE AS AGREED?

In all my years of service as a minister, I did not have written agreements on my responsibilities or duties. I had no set terms for any of my services. Our yeses were just that. In one place, I had to terminate my ministry when I was deceived. They did not live up to their part of our verbal agreement, so I had to shorten my ministry. Unfortunately, they were not very cordial—parishioners sliced my tires in the parking lot. It is hard to imagine that the church does such a thing, but that was the exception. Even with no set terms for any of my services, we enjoyed many successful years in ministry, and I have been called back to serve again at two churches.

Why can we not operate our earthly kingdom in a similar way, as Jesus did for his heavenly kingdom? I am troubled when good-hearted employers and providers are forced by the government to submit to the demands of labor, at a cost that closes down the providers' ability to operate. Why act surprised when companies close down and move elsewhere to do business? Why not take a hint from Matthew 20:1–16? It might help our consciences and revive a declining economy, which feeds the people of this and any other nation.

"For the kingdom of heaven is like a householder who went out early in the morning to hire laborers for his vineyard. After agreeing with the laborers for a denarius a day, he sent laborers for a denarius a day, he sent them into his vineyard. And going out about the third hour he saw others standing idle in the market place; and to them he said, 'You go into the vineyard too, and whatever is right I will give you.' So they went. Going out again about the sixth hour and the ninth hour, he did the same. And about the eleventh hour he went out and found others

119

standing; and he said to them, 'Why do you stand here idle all day?' They said to him, 'Because no one has hired us.' He said to them, 'You go into the vineyard too.' And when evening came, the owner of the vineyard said to his steward 'Call the laborers and pay them their wages, beginning with the last, up to the first.' And when those hired about the eleventh hour came, each of them received a denarius. Now when the first came, they thought they would receive more; but each of them received a denarius. And on receiving it they grumbled at the householder, saying, 'These last worked only one hour and you have made them equal to us who have borne the burden of the day and the scorching heat.' But he replied to one of them, 'Friend, I am doing you no wrong; did you not agree with me for a denarius? Take what belongs to you, and go; I choose to give to this last as I give to you. Am I not allowed to do what I choose with what belongs to me? Or do you begrudge my generosity?' So the last will be first, and the first last." (Matthew 20:1–16)

WHAT IS GRACE LIKE?

Describing grace is a mental exercise, but to apply grace is a way of living. To me, the householder in Jesus's parable is an example of true and active grace. In addition to being fair, generous, and a man of his word, the householder also was compassionate. He went out looking for people who might need help. There were workers who were not hired, and they had hungry families. This man went out six times and agreed to pay them all one denarius. He knew that he was generous and that he had the right to be so. Instead of being thankful to the householder for helping out their fellow men, they were greedy and heartless and forfeited their chance to work again for this man. Jesus used another parable to drive home the lack of grace.

I am reminded of a time when our family experienced the application of grace, just like the householder in the parable. The war had made us destitute and homeless. We were among strangers and had no income. My father had us make toys and trinkets that we could sell, but no one would buy them. Someone loaned my father a bicycle and a cart, and we put all the things we had made in the cart. We watched father ride off to a city, which was more than ten kilometers away. It was late that night when he came back, and there was so much joy in his eyes. After stopping at many stores, one merchant took everything and paid our father more than he had asked. He must have seen in our father's face the desperate need to feed his family. Well, a year later, we went back to thank the man, and there, in the window of his store, were our toys, still for sale. By then, they were more like a memorial to a needy family and a testament to a merciful man.

"Therefore the kingdom of heaven may be compared to a king who wished to settle accounts with his servants. When he began the reckoning, one was brought to him who owed him ten thousand talents; and as he could not pay, the lord ordered him to be sold, with his wife and children and all that he had, and payment to be made. So the servant fell on his knees imploring him, 'Lord, have patience with me, and I will pay you everything.' And out of pity for him the lord of that servant released him and forgave him the debt. But that same servant, as he went out, came upon one of his fellow servants who owed him a hundred denarii; and seizing him by the throat he said, 'Pay what you owe.' So his fellow servant fell down and besought him, 'Have patience with me, and I will pay you.' He refused and went and put him in prison till he should pay the debt. When his fellow servants saw what had taken place, they were greatly distressed, and they went and reported to their lord all that had taken place. Then his lord summoned him and said to him, 'You wicked servant! I forgave you all that debt because you besought me; and should not you have had mercy on your fellow servant, as I had mercy on you?' And in anger his lord delivered him to the jailers, till he should pay all his debt. So also my heavenly Father will do to every one of you, if you do not forgive your brother from your heart." (Matthew 18:23–35)

Summary

- When we follow Jesus's teachings, we can—and we do—trust our consciences; it benefits us every day in our faith and our work.
- Our words bind us to our consciences.
- We must be careful of the promises we make.
- We must not swear. There's no need for it.
- We must abide, as agreed.
- Applied grace is a way of living in all we do.

CHAPTER 19

CAN GRACE BEND THE LAW?

Grace does not do favors, nor does the law. The generous and compassionate householder satisfied both. He treated all his workers equally (Matthew 20:1–16).

The merciless servant begged his master for time to repay. His master was a gracious person. He had pity on his servant, released him, and canceled his debt. The same servant went to a fellow servant, who owed him a mere fraction. He demanded payment, and he did not free the debtor, nor did he forgive him. His actions forfeited his grace. And because he did not forgive his fellow servant, he himself did not deserve to be forgiven (Matthew 18:21:35). This was the law Jesus used (and still uses), and it is the way we earn our salvation. The heart of grace is forgiveness, and it is a condition that our heavenly Father requires from everyone.

> For if you forgive men their trespasses, your heavenly
> Father also will forgive you; but if you do not forgive
> men their trespasses, neither will your Father forgive your
> trespasses. (Matthew 6:14–15)

WHAT LAW MAKES GRACE POSSIBLE?

We are commanded to love, regardless of what and who the person is and regardless of whether we have to conduct business with the person.

What makes grace possible for me to receive? How do I receive such love?

Well, grace does not drop from heaven all at once. I have to decide to fill my heart with grace so that I can forgive and so I can be forgiven. It is my relationship with my fellow human beings that determines my standing with God. God loved me first and showed me grace, but then I am called to love, lest I end up like that wicked servant who forfeited the grace that was shown to him.

The apostle of love, John Zebedee, penned these words for us to follow:

> Beloved, let us love one another; for love is of God, and he who loves is born of God and knows God. He who does not love does not know God; for God is love. In this the love of God was made manifest among us, that God sent his only Son into the world, so that we might live through him. In this is love, not that we loved God but that he loved us and sent his Son to be the expiation for our sins. Beloved, if God so loved us, we also ought to love one another. No man has ever seen God; if we love one another, God abides in us and his love is perfected in us. By this we know that we abide in him and he in us, because he has given us of his own Spirit. And we have seen and testify that the Father has sent his Son as the Savior of the world. Whoever confesses that Jesus is the Son of God, God abides in him, and he in God. So we know and believe the love God has for us. God is love, and he who abides in love abides in God, and God abides in him. In this is love perfected with us, that we may have confidence for the day of judgment, because as he is so are we in this world. There is no fear in love, but perfect love casts out fear. For fear has to do with punishment, and he who fears is not perfected in love. We love, because he first loved us. If any one says, "I love God," and hates his brother, he is a liar; for he who does not love his brother whom he has seen, cannot love God whom he has not seen. And this commandment we have from him, that

he who loves God should love his brother also. (1 John 4:7–21)

WHAT IS THE RELATIONSHIP BETWEEN GRACE AND THE LAW?

The commandments of God and Christ serve to help keep me from judging and incriminating myself. The commandments direct me in what I ought to do and in avoiding what I must not do. The commandments also hold me accountable and responsible for what I do and for what I neglect to do.

Grace and the law are my partners in the Holy Spirit. Grace is found in the time God grants me and you to return to God and for us to resume obeying his laws and his ordinances in our daily lives. If we do not repent, if we do not live within the laws of God, and if we do not obey the words of Jesus the Christ, then we trample on God's grace and forfeit the grace God gave us.

When I do not obey the laws of God, I trample on grace. In so doing, I mock God, and I deprive myself of my own salvation. Therefore, when I enter the life of grace, I also must display grace in my conduct and in my deeds toward others. For grace to be instrumental, I must become an agent that dispenses grace. In grace, through me, God extends his arms of forgiveness toward others (Matthew 6:14–15).

THE TEN COMMANDMENTS

In the Ten Commandments, which Jesus restored, humankind has been given an idea of what they must do to qualify for the kingdom of heaven. The Ten Commandments are not just about believing in being righteous but in doing what is right. This is what Christ is looking for in all of us (Matthew 5:17–20).

What are we to do with the translator's rendition of Romans 10:4, "For Christ is the end of the law. That every one who has faith may be justified"? We must not presume that Paul would have dared to end the moral conduct of the law. We are not to live without morals. This is essential and universal for all humankind, to sustain life and relationships with each other, as we are all children of the Creator God, whether we are saints or sinners. Three problems face the idea that Christ ended God's law to give faith a chance.

First, the Greek word *telos* does not mean the end. Telos means the completion or fulfillment of something that was being temporarily used until Christ could come and pay the ultimate price of atonement for human beings' sins. The animals, the grains, and the rituals did not appease God.

Second, Jesus specifically came to fulfill God's law (*plerosai*). In fact, the word is to "set free from the law" (*katalusai*). Christ, however, did not set humankind free (katalusai) from God's law. We are not free to live without morals. Rather, Christ binds us closer to God's law. Grace does not operate without substance. Grace operates on the human response to the will of God (Matthew 7:21–23). It is God's law and our consciences that make us do what is right and just.

Third, faith by itself, without a rebirth and without a total transfer of allegiance from the world to Christ, will not justify or qualify anyone for the kingdom of heaven (John 3:3–7). To qualify and to remain in the kingdom of heaven and in the church (body) of Christ, we are to partner with the Holy Spirit (Ephesians 1:23).

Now, if Christ ended anything, then it was not the law. Jesus said that he came to fulfill the law. The law demanded that humankind do what was right. The Jewish traditions, however, had replaced the Law of Moses (Matthew 15:1–20) with their own agenda. The Jewish elders and Moses amended God's laws to please their people. They allowed men to dismiss their wives and to stone women on mere suspicion of infidelity. They did not hold children accountable for caring and honoring their parents, and they did not include outsiders in their second commandment of love.

On the Sabbath, no one could become ill, and if they were ill, they could not obtain help. No one could eat without washing their hands. Before entering the home of a Pharisee, one's feet had to be washed. Obligations and transgressions were remitted with gifts and offerings to the priests. Heavy iniquities were absolved with animal blood and sent into the desert with a goat. An elaborate and costly religious system with facilities, feasts, offerings, and daily sacrifices was designed to keep the Hebrews away from pagan shrines and from their gods. The tribes of Levi and of Moses were chosen to administer and enforce the demands of the system to the letter. All of this, Moses insisted, was from Yahweh and not of his own design, but Yahweh was (and is) very unintrusive in what humankind wills and does.

That also is the way that the Spirit of God works in my life. God has given me a free hand to do what I want, and that is why not all of my decisions have turned out right. I reap what I have sown. And I believe you do as well.

Paul put it eloquently:

> Do not be deceived: God is not mocked, for whatever a man sows, that he will also reap. For he who sows to his own flesh will from the flesh reap corruption; but he who sows to the Spirit will from the Spirit reap eternal life. And let us not grow weary in well-doing, for in due season we shall reap, if we do not lose heart. So then, as we have opportunity, let us do good to all men, and especially to those who are of the household of faith. (Galatians 6:7–10)

WHAT DOES GRACE CIRCUMVENT?

Grace does not replace good deeds because grace itself is the heart of good deeds and redemptive works. Grace does not accept or cover the traditions that seek the favor of God by their natural birth, religion, and tradition. In fact, many religious practices and traditions restrict the very nature of grace from functioning effectively. In the Jewish tradition of Jesus's day, the priest and the Levite could not serve the victim on the road to Jericho, but the Samaritan could (Luke 10:20–37). Their mercy did not extend to outsiders.

DO OUR TRADITIONS INCLUDE OR EXCLUDE OTHERS?

One morning, my sons and I went to a friend's church. When the minister served Communion, he had to break his vow to include us; we weren't the right type of Christians. When I retired from the ministry, I joined a church close by. Even there, I was not trusted with serving Communion. How many traditions do we have that exclude? Why do we judge so much?

But you are not in the flesh, you are in the Spirit, if the Spirit of God really dwells in you. Any one who does not have the Spirit of Christ does not belong to him. But if Christ is in you, although your bodies are dead because of sin, your spirits are alive because of righteousness. If the Spirit of him who raised Jesus from the dead dwells in you, he who raised Christ Jesus from the dead will give life to your mortal bodies also through his Spirit which dwells in you. (Romans 8:9–11)

But the fruit of the Spirit is love, joy, peace, patience, kindness, goodness, faithfulness, gentleness, self-control; against such there is no law. And those who are in Christ Jesus have crucified the flesh with its passion and desires. If we live by the Spirit, let us also walk by the Spirit. Let us have no self-conceit, no provoking of one another, no envy of one another. (Galatians 5:22–25)

All these fruits are deeds and works of grace, fostered and used by Jesus's followers and by people like you and me.

In one of my early churches, the phone rang in my office on a Sunday morning. When I answered, the person on the phone asked, "Is God there in your church?" I invited him to come and see, but I should have said, "If you do not bring him with you, you will not find him here."

God is Spirit. God does not live in buildings, or in rituals, or even in worship. God lives in the human hearts that allow him to live in them (John 14:23). It is when God's Spirit joins with my spirit and your spirit that grace redeems.

SUMMARY

- Grace does not do favors, nor does the law.
- Jesus teaches that the heart of grace is forgiveness (Matthew 6:14–15).
- Jesus commands us to love, regardless of who the person is.

- We must be willing to fill our hearts with grace so that we can forgive and be forgiven.
- The Ten Commandments hold us responsible for what we neglect to do.
- God extends his arms of forgiveness toward us when we become agents that dispense grace (Matthew 6:14–15).
- Jesus not only restored the Ten Commandments, but he came to fulfill God's law. We are not free to live without morals.
- Grace does not replace good deeds because grace by itself is the heart of good deeds and redemptive works.
- God lives in our human hearts when we allow him to live in us (John 14:23).

CHAPTER 20

How Is Grace Back to God?

NOVEMBER 21, 2020

To me, God and grace are one and the same. Without grace, the world would have fallen apart long ago. How, then, does the grace of God work? How does grace keep the world running?

GOD IS SPIRIT

Like God, who is Spirit, grace needs a body in which to live. The world itself is a body that the Spirit of God set in motion, with the ability to reproduce and renew itself. If God withdraws that energy, the world would return to a void—what it was before (Genesis 1:3). In a similar way, the Spirit of God made humankind and planted part of his breath/Spirit in his creation so that they can wrap themselves in the Spirit and grace of God (Genesis 2:7). The union and presence of Spirit and grace are best seen in the life and work of Jesus the Christ (John 1:14–17). Christ is best seen and manifested in you and me, who believe and do what Jesus commanded (John 15:5–10; 17:20–26).

> "I am the vine; you are the branches. He who abides in me and I in him he it is that bears much fruit; for apart from me you can do nothing. If a man does not abide in me, he is cast forth as a branch and withers; and the branches are gathered, thrown into the fire and burned. If you abide

130

in me, and my words abide in you, ask whatever you will, and it shall be done for you. By this my Father is glorified, that you bear much fruit, and so prove to be my disciples. As the Father has loved me, so have I loved you; abide in my love. If you keep my commandments, you will abide in my love, just as I have kept my Father's commandments and abide in his love." (John 15:5–10)

GOD CHOSE TO WORK THROUGH MAN

God did not withdraw from the world when he handed the world over to humankind (Genesis 1:26–31). God secured his place in the spirit and breath of man (Genesis 2:7). The Creator endowed each of us with a will, a conscience, and the ability to choose what we think is best. Adam and Eve learned, by their mistake, that what God wanted for them was in their own interest (Genesis 3).

Mistakes are our first teachers, and they are not the end of our life journeys. Rather, they are the beginning of our learning how to live. To help us overcome our stumbling, the heavenly Father sent his Spirit to enlighten some of his children. Not many of the children, however, were able to help their fellow individuals correct their bad choices. So God sent his only begotten Son. Yet his own chosen people disposed of Jesus, the Christ (Hebrews 1:1–4; Matthew 21:33–43).

When God the Father needed to manifest his love, he sent Jesus (John 3:16), and God had Jesus show us how to love by giving his life for his own (John 15:13). Jesus illustrated how love must be applied to anyone in need (Luke 10:29–37). Jesus showed us how to forgive our enemies (Luke 23:34). Jesus taught us how to pray (Matthew 6:7–16). And Jesus taught us how to behave in public and in the world (Luke 14:10–11; Matthew 5:16; 7:1–2, 12). We must be wrapped in grace and act like our Lord, with poise and truth (Luke 6:36; Matthew 5:48). To Jesus, his followers were quite capable of outdoing their Lord because of his limited stay on earth (John 14:12).

The Jews questioned Jesus's being the Son of God. Therefore, Jesus told them that man himself can be a "little god." Humankind has the ability and the skill to do anything they want. In fact, humankind has been entrusted with God's work and with the redemptive work of God's Son (John 17:1–26; 20:22–23). Everything that God has to do in the world, humankind can do, and that is the reason why humankind will represent themselves on Judgment Day, and their deeds will either defend or condemn them (2 Corinthians 5:6–10; Revelation 20:12).

WHAT KIND OF A PERSON DID JESUS HAVE IN MIND?

On the Feast of Dedication, Jesus had gone to Jerusalem and offered to the Jews what only God would do—Jesus was sent to do God's will as the Son of God. On earth, God the Spirit works through humankind. To communicate with God's Spirit, humans bear God's image and likeness and house God's breath and God's Spirit. This was incomprehensible to the Jews! This concept continues to be incomprehensible to us as well. Then how did Jesus face the puzzled people?

> It was the feast of dedication in Jerusalem; it was winter, and Jesus was walking in the temple, in the portico of Solomon. So the Jews gathered round him and said to him, "How long will you keep us in suspense? If you are Christ, tell us plainly." Jesus answered them, "I told you, and you do not believe. The works that I do in my Father's name, bear witness to me; but you do not believe, because you do not belong to my sheep. My sheep hear my voice, and I know them, and they follow me. I give them eternal life, and they shall never perish, and no one shall snatch them out of my hand. My Father, who has given them to me, is greater than all, and no one is able to snatch them out of the Father's hand. I and the Father are one."
>
> The Jews took up stones again to stone him. Jesus answered them, "I have shown you many good works from the Father; for which of these do you stone me?" The Jews answered him, "It is not for a good work that we stone you but for blasphemy; because you, being a man, make yourself God." Jesus answered them, "Is

it not written in your law, 'I said, you are gods'? If he called the gods to whom the word of God came (and scripture cannot be broken), do you say of him whom the Father consecrated and sent into the world, 'You are blaspheming' because I said, 'I am the Son of God'? If I am not doing the works of my Father, then do not believe me; but if I do them, even though you do not believe me believe the works, that you may know and understand that the Father is in me and I am in the Father." Again they tried to arrest him, but he escaped from their hands. (John 10:22–39)

EQUIPPED TO MANAGE

God has created us, as human beings, equipped to manage ourselves, the earth, and what is on the earth. Humans are even able to conquer gravity and reach into space. God has made a good person and filled him or her with good seeds.

Where, then, do the weeds come from that have filled the world and hurt life's existence? What has become of humans who were made in the image and likeness of God? Humans are God's incarnation of the divine, and Jesus Christ is the sublime evidence. God has incarnated humans with his Spirit. Life, in any form, would not exist without the breath and the Spirit of God. Only the body and the flesh of a human being is carnal, but the soul and the spirit are eternal. Like the Son of God, a human too is an offspring of God. At conception, the soul and the Spirit of the Son of God assumed a physical body to become the Son of man.

Likewise, every soul or spirit at conception takes on a physical body that is intended to be productive in this world for humankind and God. Woe be to those souls or spirits that deprive the unborn of the right to live. All souls and spirits do not die when they leave their earthly bodies; they go to paradise or to the place of the dead, and they await their day of reckoning (Luke 23:39–43; 16:19–31; 1 Peter 3:18–22).

ALL THE DEPARTED RESPONDED
TO THE VOICE OF CHRIST
||||||||||||||||||||||||||||||||||||

Jairus's daughter heard Jesus and came back from her sleep (Mark 5:35–43), and so did the widow's son of Nain (Luke 7:11–17), and so did Lazarus (John 11:38–44). Jesus shared some specific things that he had to do before his departure and what he would do during his absence. He did everything by his own choice. Before Jesus returned to be with his Father, Jesus spent three days and three nights with my ancestor in Valhalla. And then, Jesus spent forty days with his disciples (Acts 1:1–11).

> "For this reason the Father loves me, because I lay down my life, that I may take it again. No one takes it from me, but I lay it down on my own accord. I have power to lay it down, and I have power to take it again; this charge I have from my Father." (John 10:17–18)

> And he began to teach them that the Son of man must suffer many things, and be rejected by the elders and the chief priests and the scribes, and be killed, and after three days rise again. (Mark 8:31)

> It was about the sixth hour, and there was darkness over the whole land until the ninth hour, while the sun's light failed; and the curtain in the temple was torn in two. Then Jesus, crying with a loud voice, said, "Father, into thy hands I commit my spirit!" And having said this he breathed his last. (Luke 23:44–46)

> For Christ also died for sins once for all, the righteous for the unrighteous, that he might bring us to God, being put to death in the flesh but made alive in the spirit; in which he (Jesus) went and preached to the spirits in prison, who formerly did not obey, when God's patience waited in the days of Noah, during the building of the ark, in which a few, that is, eight persons, were saved through water. (1 Peter 3:18–20)

> "Truly, truly, I say to you, the hour is coming, and now is, when the dead will hear the voice of the Son of God, and those who hear will live. For as the Father has life in himself, so he has granted the Son also to have life in himself, and has given him authority to execute judgment, because he is the Son of man. Do not marvel at this; for the hour is coming when all who are in the tombs will hear his voice and come forth, those who have done good, to the resurrection of life, and those who have done evil, to the resurrection of judgment." (John 5:25–29)

WHAT HAS BECOME OF GRACE AND TRUTH?

Grace and truth were brought into the world by Jesus Christ (John 1:17). Who has Jesus entrusted with passing on grace and truth?

Theologians led me to believe that God kept grace and that God is handing it out as a free gift of salvation to whoever believes in Jesus, regardless of what the person has done (Ephesians 2:8–9). But is that all there is to the story? Are we not supposed to do something?

GOD NEEDS US TO SPREAD GRACE

> But how are men to call upon him in whom they have not believed? And how are they to believe in the one of whom they have never heard? And how are they to hear without a preacher? And how can men preach unless they are sent? As it is written: "How beautiful are the feet of those who preach good news!" But they have not all heeded the gospel; for Isaiah says, "Lord, who has believed what he has heard from us?" So faith comes from what is heard and what is heard comes by the preaching of Christ. (Romans 10:14–17)

According to Jesus's prayer in John 17, God the Father gave Jesus's disciples grace and truth, and they received it from their Lord. The disciples passed grace and truth to their disciples, who handed down grace and truth from disciple to disciple into our time. We, too, are the heirs of grace and truth, and that is why our fellow human beings need to find their way back to God. I am to become like Christ, a way of grace and truth that leads to salvation for me and for others (John 20:21–23; Matthew 28:18–20).

A Way to Contentment and Peace

When I began to manifest grace and truth in my life, my conscience found contentment and peace. Before I could sow and harvest grace, however, I had to acquire grace and grow grace, and then I had to learn how to use grace. I acquire grace through my belief in Jesus Christ, and I grow grace by practicing grace toward others, by practicing what Jesus taught us to practice, and by living the way Jesus taught his disciples to live.

Summary

- God is Spirit.
- The Spirit made humankind, and God planted part of his breath and Spirit in humankind, so that God did not withdraw from the world.
- God chose to work through humankind.
- God endowed us (humankind) with a will, a conscience, and the ability to choose what we think is best.
- God sent Jesus to help humankind correct their bad choices.
- Life, in any form, does not exist without God's breath and the Spirit of God.
- We, too, are the heirs of grace and truth, and that is why our fellow individuals need to find their way back to God.
- We acquire grace through our faith in Jesus Christ by practicing grace toward others—what Jesus taught us.

CHAPTER 21

PRACTICE MADE GRACE REAL

I was born into a multicultural environment, where we exchanged favors without having anything in common. In school, I was able to do favors for my classmates, who I thought were my friends, but when rumors of war came, these friends became my enemies. Their parents were in power, and I had to continue to do favors for them against my will. In my heart, I built an intense dislike for these false friends, but I could not afford to show any animosity against them. It was a very racism-charged environment, and I was different from them. It didn't matter that I had grown up with them; I was now the same race as the enemy. Imagine how I felt when I had to swallow my pride to avoid getting my family into trouble? At that time, I did not realize that I was learning what *grace* meant.

MY CHILDHOOD UNDERSTANDING OF GRACE

To me, grace was not a gift from heaven. Grace was a skill and a tool that I learned to use from my parents and grandparents. It was the skill of grace that kept me out of trouble, which during the war could have led to harm and even death. Grace didn't mean gaining favors; grace meant giving favors to those who had the power to exterminate us.

When Germany invaded Poland, our people were incarcerated. My father had to report to his Polish army unit. My mother took us three boys into hiding until the Soviets rescued us. Yet my people feared the Russians more than they feared the Poles or the Germans. During the First World War, my grandparents had a taste of Siberia. When we were loaded into boxcars and shipped to Germany, our people regarded being sold to the Germans as a blessing from heaven.

ART OF DIPLOMACY

Even as a nine-year-old boy, I managed to get along with friends and hostile people by being someone they could depend on for favors. It did not take long to discover that the use of grace was necessary to survive, and I had to learn the art of diplomacy.

In that sense, I was truly blessed from heaven with the ability to prepare myself. I had to learn early not to offend anyone or to stand out by volunteering answers or skills that would embarrass my friends or my foes.

On one occasion, I did embarrass myself. A German officer in a shiny uniform came to our school, looking for recruits. He asked what anyone would like to become. Foolishly, I raised my hand and proudly said, "An officer!" The Nazi leader was ready to take me with him to enroll. My father had to intervene and rescue me. After this incident, my fellow classmates became merciless, saluting me with raised hands and standing at attention. This experience taught me to be more careful with what I said.

I was not an outgoing boy who would try pushing ahead of others, and while under the Nazi way of life, that was against me. Nevertheless, a classmate of mine, who also was my neighbor, got himself promoted to be our area scout leader. He put me in charge of two of the groups of scouts who were between ages ten and fourteen. At fifteen, the lads became Hitler Jugend (HJ). After a year of running these two groups, the head leader suggested that I go for ten days to the Nazi training center in western Poland. I went with two of my friends. It was a rigid military experience, and we barely survived. We simply were not aggressive and mean enough to become leaders in the Third Reich. Yet we were tough enough to pass our tests, and back home, our teachers and students welcomed us with acclamation. We were not being brought up in the fear of the Lord God but in the fear of *Der Fuehrer* Adolf Hitler. It was a marvel that we turned out the way we did.

FOR ME, GRACE WAS A GROWING PROCESS

I did not wake up one morning and find myself full of grace; rather, I found that every day, I had to use a little more grace to make it through the day. As I look back to my youth, adulthood, and even my ministry, the words of the apostle Peter and Jesus's parable of the fig tree in need of care come to mind:

> But grow in the grace and knowledge (truth) of our Lord and Savior Jesus Christ. (2 Peter 3:18a)

> And Jesus told this parable: "A man had a fig tree planted in his vineyard; and he came seeking fruit on it and found none. And he said to the vinedresser, 'Lo, these three years I have come seeking fruit on this fig tree, and I find none. Cut it down; why should it use up the ground?' And the answered him, 'Let it alone, sir, this year also, till I dig about it and put on manure. And if it bears fruit next year, well and good; but if not, you can cut it down.'" (Luke 13:6–9)

In a way, I was arrogant—a wild and fruitless fig tree—and it was my own doing. Physically, I turned out quite handsome, and so did my pride. Mentally, I adapted easily to the requirements that life demanded. Morally, my conscience kept me decent, kind, polite, and friendly when needed. I behaved and displayed good manners, which were resented by boys my age. To their parents, however, I was what they hoped their sons would be.

I once attended a party and danced with a young lady. One of the more popular boys bad-mouthed me while his father was watching. His father stopped him and reprimanded him in front of me. The next day, my father met the father of the boy who had insulted me, and again he praised me for being such a well-mannered young man. Later, when my father spoke to me about it, he broke down in tears and asked, "Why would you even consider going to a place where you would cause disharmony between a father and a son over a dance?"

Something good came out of the incident but not good enough for my father. The young man who insulted me also changed and became friendlier toward me; he wanted me on his soccer team. I had yet to learn to weigh my intentions before I acted.

I Blundered Much

I turned fifteen several months before World War II ended. During the next six years, I grew physically into manhood but not mentally. I blundered too much and made too many mistakes to claim that stature. During that time, I was totally oblivious to the idea that I was being protected by someone who had a higher purpose for me. In addition to being snatched from death four times (that I know of), my conscience kept me from completing actions and intentions that could have caused me irreversible harm. I was also led to believe that I was being punished by heaven for my mistakes, when, in fact, heaven, through my conscience and heart, was showing me how to minimize my bad behavior and to have manners to improve my standing before God and others.

I did not see myself as a fruitless fig tree in those days, and no one around me thought of fertilizing or properly grooming me so that I could have become a more productive person. I learned—much later in my journey of grace—that it was not their fault. They had not been fertilized or properly groomed. They did to me what was done to them.

Guilty and Lost

What I had been taught made me feel very guilty and lost. Their prescription was to repent, pray, and believe in Jesus, and he would take care of my guilt and make me into a new person. At first, it appeared to work. I was baptized, joined the church, attended study groups, and surprised people with my Bible knowledge. I was not surprised because I'd had eighteen months in the hospital after my accident, when I was recovering and reading the Bible. And while I was in the hospital, a minister felt that I belonged in the ministry, and I decided to follow his lead.

When I was discharged, I joined a German-speaking church, and the pastor knew of a Bible school that helped people like me to prepare for college and seminary. The school had daily chapel services. Different speakers came and roasted us on the altar of guilt. Students confessed to bad things and broke down in tears and mumbling. To them, that was a sign that they were touched by the Holy Spirit, but I could only marvel that I did not have that experience. One time, I stood up and forced myself to say something about the Spirit, and a voice in me said, *Sit down. I said nothing to you!* Guilt persisted in making me even more miserable.

HOW DID GRACE AFFECT MY LIFE?

God is grace, and God is Spirit. How can God serve me? I'd heard it enough and taught it myself that Jesus takes care of that service. But when Jesus left this earth to go back to God, his Father, to whom did he charge with that service?

After a long stretch of guilt, I met a man who helped me. My parents had a boarder renting a room, and he took me to see a man who showed me how Jesus could change my problem of guilt. The man invited us for lunch, and in a timid and humble way, he told us what he had to do to allow the peace of Christ to enter his heart. He was in charge of his own redemption. To make things right with his others, he had to remove all the obstacles that were in the way of his conscience—and that cleared the way to God and to Jesus Christ.

What did this good man do? He made things right with the people he had hurt and insulted. It was not just feeling remorse and offering an apology but repairing and reimbursing for the losses people had, due to his mistakes. While he spoke, my conscience sent me home to my father, and he was surprised that I had not felt right toward him. I made things right with apologies, letters, and even money where I could have acted properly but didn't.

At once, a river of peace came into my life. And I, too, like that fig tree, with the help of the vinedresser, began to live and bear the fruit of grace. Making things right with my fellow individuals opens the way to our heavenly Father, who is the Father of us all.

> You have heard that it was said to the men of old, 'You shall not kill; and whoever kills shall be liable to judgment.' But I say to you that every one who is angry with his brother

shall be liable to judgment; whoever insults his brother shall be liable to the council, and whoever says, 'You fool!' shall be liable to the hell of fire. So if you are offering your gift at the altar, and there remember that that your brother has something against you, leave your gift there before the altar and go; first be reconciled to your brother, and then come and offer your gift. Make friends quickly with your accuser while you are going with him to court, lest your accuser hand you over to the judge, and the judge to the guard, and you be put in prison; truly, I say to you, you will never get out till you have paid the last penny. (Matthew 5:21–26)

SUMMARY

- Grace is a skill that we learn to keep us out of trouble and that, at times, is necessary to survive.
- Grace is a growing process (2 Peter 3:18).
- Grace provides a way to live to bear fruit by making things right with our fellow individuals, which opens the way to our heavenly Father (Matthew 5:21–26).

CHAPTER 22

HAS GRACE FREED ME FROM SINNING?

DECEMBER 5, 2020

Oh, how I wished it were so! I am in a body of flesh and blood, however, that does not stop craving things that are harmful. I can and do taste what is harmful, but if I swallow it, I end up with indigestion. Then, if I continue with this deception, it becomes my master, and I, its slave.

I was six years old when I nearly choked on a cigarette, and I never smoked again. I was sixteen or seventeen when a neighbor gave me a harmless mickey, and it knocked me out for hours. After that, I would spit out the poison, and my companions wondered why I did not become intoxicated. When I was old enough to date, I was often tempted, but someone kept me from making a fool of myself. I was not any better or smarter than the other lads my age, but I had parents who prayed for me and warned me of the consequences that promiscuity causes. Someone was answering my mother's prayers, and that kept me from engaging in worldly pleasures.

The same temptations continued when I became a Christian by definition, a pastor by training and ordination, and a retiree with time on my hands to get into mischief. The belief that Christ paid for all sins has led many to fall for Adam's apple, which cost Adam his expulsion from Eden. It is no different from trampling on the kingdom of God here on earth.

WHO SETS ME FREE FROM SINNING?

Early in my life, I learned that I was getting into things all by myself and that I also managed to get out of my troubles that I had caused. There were times when I had to turn to my parents for help, and my mother was more gracious than my father. Mistakes became valuable lessons for my future actions. I seldom escaped punishment for my harmful misbehavior. Mistakes are sins, and they are costly and even embarrassing. I had to take control of myself! I had to stop my mind from wandering after the forbidden fruit, of which the world has so much (Matthew 5:27–30).

Being a Christian and even a minister, I kept making mistakes. I also hoped and prayed that the Lord would come to my aid. He sent Paul to give me this answer: "You are reaping what you sowed" (Galatians 6:7). God, the heavenly Father, sent Jesus, his Son, to show me that God cannot leave his holiness and follow his child who deliberately muddied himself in the world. The prodigal son had to come back to his own father, and he also had to accept his father's way of receiving him back into the family (Luke 15:11–24). This parable has been especially meaningful to my ministry. I, too, was dependent on people like the older brother, who kept the churches intact for the delinquents to come back to. I, too, once belonged to the people of the good son, and I could help others in need.

Then World War II stripped us of our source of bread, and we became like the prodigal, only we could not go back home! We had to restart our lives among strangers. It was while I lived among these strangers that I needed a moral harness to protect my life. There is no doubt, in my mind that I had help from heaven (James 4:1–10; Ephesians 6:10–20).

WHILE I AM IN THE BODY, I AM
RESPONSIBLE FOR WHAT I DO

Sin is no mystery, nor is evil! I was not born with sin, nor was sin handed down to me by Adam and Eve or by my parents. Sin began in me when my heart and my mind began to concoct ways and means to satisfy my desire. I decided whether to do good or evil, no one else! That was what the Lord (Yahweh) said to Cain—and to me and to you. It was what Jesus said to his disciples, and so did his brother James, his disciple John, and his apostle Paul.

> "If you do well, will you not be accepted? And if you do not do well, sin is couching at the door; its desire is for you, but you must master it." (Genesis 4:7)

> "But I say to you that everyone who looks at a woman lustfully has already committed adultery with her in his heart." (Matthew 5:28)

> "For out of the heart come evil thoughts, murder, adultery, fornication, theft, false witness, slander. These are what defile a man (person)." (Matthew 15:28–29; Mark 7:20–23)

> Blessed is the man who endures trial, for when he has stood the test he will receive the crown of life which God has promised to those who love him. Let no one say when he is tempted, 'I am tempted by God'; for God cannot be tempted with evil and he himself tempts no one; but each person is tempted when he (she) is lured and enticed by his (her) own desire. Then desire when it has conceived gives birth to sin; and sin when it is full-grown brings forth death. (James 1:12–15)

> This is the message we have heard from him (Jesus) and proclaim to you, that God is light and in him is no darkness at all. If we say we have fellowship with him while we walk in darkness, we lie and do not live according to the truth; but if we walk in the light, as he is in the light, we have fellowship with one another, and the blood of Jesus his Son cleanses us from all sin. If we say we have no sin, we deceive ourselves, and the truth is not in us. If we confess our sins, he is faithful and just, and will forgive our sins and cleanse us from all unrighteousness. If we say we have not sinned, we make him a liar, and his word is not in us. (1 John 1:5–10)

Put to death therefore what is earthly in you: immorality, impurity, passion, evil desire, and covetousness, which is idolatry. On account of these the wrath of God is coming. In these you once walked, when you lived in them. But now put them all away: anger, wrath, malice, slander, and foul talk from your mouth. Do not lie to one another, seeing that you have put off the old nature with its practices and have put on the new nature, which is being renewed in knowledge after the image of its creator (Christ). (Colossians 3:5–10)

Let not sin therefore reign in your mortal bodies, to make you obey their passions (desires). Do not yield your members to sin as instruments of wickedness, but yield yourselves to God as men who have been brought from death to life, and your members to God as instruments of righteousness. For sin will have no dominion over you, since you are not under the law but under grace. (Romans 6:12–14)

WHO HAS DOMINION OVER MY SINS?

Sin is a product of humankind, and humankind must control their desire to sin. Grace is like a double-edged sword.

The time that has been granted to me to live on this planet is a gift of grace from the Creator, but to live and to build relationships on earth, which will count in heaven, I must equip myself with grace. Grace is the most powerful agent to control sin. Grace offers a lifestyle that nips sin in the bud whenever sin begins to show its ugly head. Grace does not condemn a person who stumbles; rather, grace seeks to restore the sinner from falling. I do not live under grace, but I live in grace, with one eye on my behavior toward sin and with the other eye on my neighbor's condition. The law (the Ten Commandments) keeps me from transgressing, and grace helps when I do. That was why Paul quickly added an explanation regarding living under grace. Under the law, I (we) obey, but under grace, I (we) do what needs to be done and become a law unto myself (ourselves).

What then? Are we to sin because we are not under the law but under grace? By no means! Do you not know that if you yield yourselves to any one as obedient slaves, you are slaves of the one whom you obey, either of sin, which leads to death, or of obedience, which leads to righteousness? But thanks be to God, that you who were once slaves of sin have become obedient from the heart to the standard of teaching to which you were committed, and, having been set free from sin, have become slaves of righteousness. I am speaking in human terms, because of your natural limitations. For just as you once yielded your members to impurity and to greater and greater iniquity, so now yield your members to righteousness for sanctification. (Romans 6:15–19)

Now this I affirm and testify in the Lord, that you must no longer live as the Gentiles do, in the futility of their minds; they are darkened in their understanding, alienated from the life of God because of the ignorance that is in them, due to their hardness of heart; they have become callous and have given themselves up to licentiousness, greedy to practice every kind of uncleanness. You did not so learn Christ!—assuming that you have heard about him and were taught in him, as the truth is in Jesus. Put off your old nature which belongs to your former manner of life and is corrupt through deceitful lusts, and be renewed in the spirit of your minds, and put on the new nature, created after the likeness of God in true righteousness and holiness. Therefore, putting away falsehood let everyone speak the truth with his neighbor, for we are members one of another. Be angry but do not sin; do not let the sun go down on your anger, and give no opportunity to the devil. Let the thief no longer steal, but rather let him labor, doing honest work with his hands, so that he may be able to give to those in need. Let no evil talk come out of your mouths, but only such as is good for edifying, as fits the occasion, that it may impart grace to those who hear. And do not grieve the Holy Spirit of God, in whom you were sealed for the day of redemption. Let all bitterness and wrath and anger and clamor and slander be put away from you, with all malice, and be kind to one another, tenderhearted, forgiving one another, as God in Christ forgave you. (Ephesians 4:17–32)

SUMMARY

- We reap what we sow (Galatians 6:7).
- Just like the prodigal son, we, too, must come back to the Father and accept the Father's way of receiving us back into the family (Luke 15:11–24).
- Sin is no mystery, nor is evil.
- Grace is like a double-edged sword.
- The time we have to live on this planet is a gift of grace from God, the Creator.
- Grace offers us a lifestyle that nips sin in the bud when sin shows its ugly head.
- We do not live under grace, but we live in grace.
- Grace does not condemn a person who stumbles; rather, grace seeks to restore the sinner from his falling.

CHAPTER 23

How Do I Stay Saved?

DECEMBER 12, 2020

For me to stay saved means to stay and live in grace and practice grace in my daily living. It also means to live in Christ and do what he has commanded. One of Christ's commands was that if I do not forgive, I forfeit my right to be forgiven. Forgiveness itself is a lifelong task, and so is staying saved. Jesus says,

> "I am the true vine, and my Father is the vinedresser. Every branch of mine that bears no fruit, he takes away, and every branch that does bear fruit he prunes, that it may bear more fruit. You are already made clean by the word which I have spoken to you. Abide in me, and I in you. As the branch cannot bear fruit by itself, unless it abides in the vine, neither can you, unless you abide in me. I am the vine, you are the branches. He who abides in me, and I in him, he it is that bears much fruit, for apart from me you can do nothing. If a man does not abide in me, he is cast froth as a branch and withers; and the branches are gathered, thrown into the fire and burned. If you abide in me, and my words abide in you, ask whatever you will, and it shall be done for you. By this my Father is glorified, that you bear much fruit, and so prove to be my disciples. As the Father has loved me, so have I loved

you; abide in my love. If you keep my commandments, you will abide in my love, just as I have kept my Father's commandments and abide in his love. These things I have spoken to you, that my joy may be in you, and that your joy may be full." (John 15:1–11)

WHAT KIND OF FRUIT WILL KEEP ME IN CHRIST?

My fruit is summarized by two words: grace and truth. I must guard against being a disciple of Christ by misrepresenting him with my deeds, my behavior, and my presumption of what God will do for us. We have far too many prophets who predict what God will do in our time when history records the exact opposite of what the prophets in the past predicted (Deuteronomy 8:20–22). Hence, Jesus gave us this warning that we can use to judge ourselves:

"Beware of false prophets, who come to you in sheep's clothing but inwardly are ravenous wolves. You will know them by their fruits. Are grapes gathered from thorns, or figs from thistles? So, every sound tree bears good fruit, but the bad tree bears evil fruit. A sound tree cannot bear evil fruit, nor can a bad tree bear good fruit. Every tree that does not bear good fruit is cut down and thrown into the fire. Thus you will know them by their fruits.

Not everyone who says to me, 'Lord, Lord,' shall enter the kingdom of heaven, but he who does the will of my Father who is in heaven. On that day many will say to me, 'Lord, Lord, did we not prophesy in your name, and cast out demons in your name, and do many mighty works in your name?' And then will I declare to them, 'I never knew you; depart from me, you evildoers.'

Every one then who hears these words of mine and does them will be like a wise man who built his house upon the rock; and the rain fell, and the floods came, and the winds blew and beat upon that house, but it did not fall, because it had been founded on the rock. And every one who hears these words of mine and does not do them will be like a foolish man who built his house upon the sand; and the rain fell, and the floods came, and the winds blew and beat against that house, and it fell; and great as the fall of it.

And when Jesus finished these sayings, the crowds were astonished at his teaching for he taught them as one who had authority, and not as their scribes." (Matthew 7:15–29)

HOW WILL MY LIFE (HOUSE) HOLD UP IN A STORM?

In Christ's kingdom, there are no lords and ladies; there are only brothers and sisters, slaves and servants, where the least among us is equal to the highest among us. It is a community in which we are good at saving others but not so good at saving ourselves. That was the issue Jesus was accused of (Mark 15:31–32). While Jesus, the Son of God, was in the flesh, the people who hung him on a cross also had to take him down, and so it was with Jesus's followers. What must I do to stay in the race to be crowned with the cross? How did the apostle Paul perceive himself? Paul also remembered the time when Moses's people tested the Lord:

Do you not know that in a race all the runners compete, but only one receives the prize? So run that you may obtain it. Every athlete exercises self-control in all things. They do it to receive a perishable wreath, but we for an imperishable. Well, I do not run aimlessly, I do not box as one beating the air; but I pommel my body and subdue it, lest after preaching to others I myself should be disqualified. (1 Corinthians 9:24–27)

We must not put the Lord to the test, as some of them did and were destroyed by serpents; nor grumble, as some of them did and were destroyed by the Destroyer. Now these things happen to them as a warning, but they were written down for our instruction, upon whom the end of the ages has come (the end of Israel—Judah as nations).

Therefore let any one who thinks that he stands take heed lest he fall. No temptation has overtaken you that is not common to man. God is faithful, and he will not let us be tempted beyond our strength, but with the temptation will also provide the way of escape, that you may be able to endure it. (1 Corinthians 10:9–13)

WHAT MUST I DO TO STAY IN CHRIST?

I already know that God has made me with physical strength to compensate and replace the loss of my hands and the scars on my body. But how did I deal with the moral and spiritual hurdles and obstacles during this long period? What can I recommend to those who are on a similar spiritual journey? I am not as certain as Paul was, who said, "Be imitators of me, as I am of Christ" (1 Corinthians 11:1).

Paul did not have the four Gospels to read, but he had his own gospel that could not be compared (Galatians 1:6–9). He did not even have his own writings to look upon. He lived in a dual world of Jews and Gentiles. I live in a world where there is goodness and kindness among the believers and the unbelievers in God. Had I lived in Jesus's day, the Jewish priest and the Levite could not save me from drowning, from the fire, or from cancer because I was not of their race (Luke 10:29–37). The people who saved my life were total strangers; without identifying themselves, they saved me because of their attitude to do what is right, regardless of who I was. To me, these people were like the Good Samaritan and the sheep; they did what was needed out of the goodness of their hearts (Matthew 25:34–40).

The examples Jesus used were applications of grace that qualified these people for his kingdom. Jesus told these stories to inspire us to do good deeds. Their deeds kept them in the race to earn the prize. Even a cup of water to a thirsty stranger will not escape notice (Mark 9:41).

I began my ministry in small churches, and my ministry ended in small churches. I retired twenty-eight years ago without any notoriety. In retrospect, I could have been like the one-pound man, who buried that one pound, afraid of losing it (Matthew 25:24–30). In my mid-sixties, polymyalgia rheumatica (PMR) hit my muscles with pain and made me immobile, and next, I was diagnosed with cancer. I became very depressed, and I felt defeated. As I sat in the urologist's office, I was entertained by a cheerful ninety-year-old Christian man who talked about going to heaven. It was right there and then that I realized that I was not behaving like a Christian and that I had to change my attitude by driving out those evil spirits that were robbing me of my hope and my joy (Luke 11:24–26; Matthew 12:43–45).

I cleaned my house, my life, from time to time, but I never really understood how to fortify myself on the inside. God, the Son, and the Holy Spirit existed and lived outside of me, and they only seemed available to people with divine function. Like most of us human beings, I too sang along, begging the Holy Spirit to fill my life, my church, my home, my country, and much more. Yet my prayers and wishes were not answered. God, the Son, and the Holy Spirit do not live in material structures and in man-made idols or even in faith that is supposed to move mountains. Where does the Trinity live? The Trinity lives in my inner being, which we know as spirit, soul, heart, and mind. My body is only a housing, and to be a temple, it too has to be sanctified. And what is made holy must not be trampled on. This is what Jesus himself told his disciples.

> Judas (not Iscariot) said to Jesus, "Lord, how is it that you will manifest yourself to us, and not to the world?" Jesus answered him, "If a man loves me, he will keep my word, and my Father will love him, and we will come to him and make our home with him." (John 14:22–23)

> "Do not give dogs what is holy; and do not throw your pearls (life) before swine, lest they trample them underfoot and turn to attack you." (Matthew 7:6)

> Do you not know that you are God's temple and that God's Spirit dwells in you? If anyone destroys God's temple, God will destroy him. For God's temple is holy, and that temple you are. (1 Corinthians 3:16–17)

> But he who is united to the Lord becomes one Spirit with him. Shun immorality. Every other sin which a man commits is outside the body; but the immoral man sins

against his own body. Do you not know that your body is a temple of the Holy Spirit within you, which you have from God? You are not your own; you were bought with a price. So glorify God in your body. (1 Corinthians 6:17–20)

So then you are no longer strangers and sojourners, but you are fellow citizens with the saints and the members of the household of God, built upon the foundation of the apostles and prophets, Christ Jesus himself being the chief cornerstone, in whom the whole structure is joined together and grows into a holy temple in the Lord; in whom you also are built into it for a dwelling place of God in the Spirit. (Ephesians 2:19–22)

CHOSEN BEFORE I WAS BORN TO GLORIFY GOD ON EARTH

My life has been so bombarded that I should not have survived and lasted this long. Someone had to have a hand in pulling me through the many intrusions I faced. I was preserved for a reason—and I did not arrive here accidentally. The apostle Paul has shown me why:

Blessed be the God and Father of our Lord Jesus Christ, who has blessed us in Christ with every spiritual blessing in the heavenly places, even as he chose us in him before the foundation of the world, that we should be holy and blameless before him. He destined us in love to be his sons through Jesus Christ, according to the purpose of his will, to the praise of his glorious grace which he freely bestowed on us in the Beloved. In him we have redemption through his blood, the forgiveness of our trespasses, according to the riches of his grace which he lavished upon us. For he has made known to us in all wisdom and insight the mystery of his will, according to his purpose which he set forth in Christ as a plan for the fullness of time, to unite all things in him, things in heaven and things on earth. In him, according to the purpose of him who accomplishes all things according to the counsel of his will, we who first hoped in Christ have been destined and appointed to live for the praise of his glory. In him you also, who have heard the word of truth, the gospel of your salvation, and have believed in him, were sealed with the promised Holy Spirit, which is the guarantee of our inheritance until we acquire possession of it, to the praise of his glory. (Ephesians 1:3–14)

I am not saved to stay saved. I am saved to do God's good work in this world. The Greek writer used *peripatesomen*, and it means that we are chosen to carry out God's purpose and God's will. We are not just here to be saved; we are here to implement Christ's salvation on earth.

For we are his workmanship, created in Christ Jesus for good works, which God prepared beforehand, that we should walk in them. (Ephesians 2:10)

SUMMARY

- To stay saved, we need to live and practice grace in our daily living, love God with all our beings, and love our neighbor as ourselves.
- In Christ's kingdom, there are no lords and ladies; there are only brothers and sisters, slaves and servants.
- The least among them is equal to the highest among them.
- Even a cup of water to a thirsty stranger will not escape notice (Mark 9:41).
- When we follow Christ, the Trinity can live in our inner beings that we know as spirit, soul, heart, and mind.
- And what is made holy, must not be trampled on, Jesus said, "Do not give dogs what is holy; and do not throw your pearls (life) before swine, lest they trample them underfoot and turn and attack you" (Matthew 7:6).
- We are saved not to stay saved; we are saved to do God's good work in this world, to carry out God's purpose and God's will, and to implement Christ's salvation on earth.

CHAPTER 24

WHY AM I IN THIS WORLD?

DECEMBER 19, 2020

The reason for my being here is you. I cannot get into Christ's kingdom without making things right with you. God made us keepers of each other, and we are responsible for each other's salvation (Genesis 4:9–11; Ezekiel 3:17–21; John 20:22–23; Matthew 6:14–15; James 5:19–20). All these references stress one thing: that you and I can ascertain our redemption together but not alone.

Here I am, ninety-plus years later, with experience and insight that is out of the ordinary for those who want God to do everything. To give us more confidence in ourselves, I have chosen some encounters that Jesus had with his disciples, which have been helpful to me on my journey of grace. The Spirit of the Lord has partnered with my spirit to fill my heart with grace that enables me to love and forgive. And this is my prayer and wish for everyone.

HUMANKIND IS GOD'S INSTRUMENT OF SAVING HUMANKIND

God in Christ became a man to work in and through his Son to save and lead humankind back to him. Just as God the Father sent his Son, Jesus, into the world, so the Son sent his followers into the world to continue his redemptive work, until Jesus, the Son, returns to finish his mission. This was and is the way the Holy Spirit manifested himself in

Jesus, in Paul, and in all of those who believe that Jesus was the Son of God in the flesh (1 John 4:1–6).

> "I do not pray that thou shouldest take them away from the world, but that thou shouldest keep them from the evil one. They are not of the world, even as I am not of the world. Sanctify them in the truth; thy word is truth. As thou didst send me into the world, so I have sent them into the world. And for their sake I consecrate myself, that they also may be consecrated in truth. I do not pray for these only, but also for those who believe in me through their word, that they may all be one; even as thou, Father, art in me, and I in thee, that they also be in us, so that the world may believe that thou hast sent me. The glory which thou hast given me I have given to them, that they may be one even as we are one, I in them and though in me, that they may become perfectly one, so that the world may know that thou sent me and hast loved them even as thou hast loved me. Father, I desire that they also, whom thou hast given me, may be with me where I am, to behold my glory which thou hast given me in thy love for me before the foundation of the world. O righteous Father, the world has not known thee, but I have known thee; and these know that thou hast sent me. I made known to them thy name, and I will make it known, that the love with which thou hast loved me may be in them, and I in them." (John 17:15–26)

But how are men to call upon him in whom they have not believed? And how are they to believe in him of whom they have never heard? And how are they to hear without a preacher? And how can men preach unless they are sent? As it is written, "How beautiful are the feet of those who preach good news!" But they have not all obeyed the gospel; for Isaiah says, "Lord, who has believed what he has heard from us?" So faith comes from what is heard,

and what is heard comes by the preaching of Christ.
(Romans 10:14–17)

Therefore, if anyone is in Christ, he is a new creation;
the old has passed away, behold, the new has come. All
this is from God, who through Christ reconciled us to
himself and gave us the ministry of reconciliation; that is,
God was in Christ reconciling the world to himself, not
counting their trespasses against them, and entrusting to
us the message of reconciliation. So we are ambassadors
for Christ, God making his appeal through us. We
beseech you on behalf of Christ, be reconciled to God.
For our sake he made him to be sin who knew no sin, so
that in him we might become the righteousness of God.
(2 Corinthians 5:17–21)

MAN, NOT GOD, FORGIVES SINS ON EARTH

I was born into a family that believed God was the only one who could
forgive sins. Yet when something happened that made people angry and
hurt, they made every effort to restore their relationships. As a pastor, for
a long time I, too, held that individuals were saved by grace alone, and
then I went on to tell the people what they had to do to maintain a godly
relationship. That view still is heard from pulpits today, and so it was in
Jesus's day in their synagogues.

One day, Jesus showed up in Capernaum, and while he was healing
and teaching, four men brought in a paralytic on a stretcher through the
roof. In addition to Mark 2:1–12, the incident was also reproduced in
Matthew 8:1–8 and in Luke 5:17–26. The man on the stretcher reminded
me of when I was on a stretcher on a train, which took me five hundred
miles to Toronto General Hospital, where I was healed and where I decided
to become a servant of redemption to myself and to others. It took six
people to get me transferred. Now, what did Jesus teach by doing? Before
Jesus returned to the Father, he delegated forgiveness to his disciples and
his leadership to Peter (John 20:19–23; 21:15–17).

And when Jesus returned to Capernaum after some days, it was reported that he was at home. And many were gathered together, so that there was no longer room for them, not even about the door; and he was preaching the word to them. And they came, bringing to him a paralytic carried by four men. And when they could not get near him because of the crowd, they removed the roof above him and when they had made an opening, they let down the pallet on which the paralytic lay. And when Jesus saw their faith, he said to the paralytic, "My son, your sins are forgiven." Now some of the scribes were sitting there, questioning in their hearts, "Why does this man speak thus? It is blasphemy! Who can forgive sins but God alone?" And immediately Jesus, perceiving in his spirit that they thus questioned within themselves, said to them, "Why do you question thus in your hearts? Which is easier, to say to the paralytic, 'Your sins are forgiven,' or to say, 'Rise, take your pallet and walk'? But that you may know that the Son of man has authority on earth to forgive sins"—he said to the paralytic—"I say to you, rise, take up your pallet and go home." And he rose immediately took up the pallet and went out before them all; so that they were all amazed and glorified God, saying, "We never saw anything like this!" (Mark 2:1–12)

On the evening of that day, the first day of the week, the doors being shut where the disciples were, for fear of the Jews, Jesus came and stood among them and said to them, "Peace be with you." When he had said this, he showed them his hands and his side. The disciples were glad when they saw the Lord. Jesus said to them again, "Peace be with you. As the Father has sent me, even so I send them." And when he had said this, he breathed on them, and said to them, "Receive the Holy Spirit. If you forgive the sins of any, they are forgiven; and if you retain the sins of any, they are retained." (John 20:19–23)

159

When they had finished breakfast, Jesus said to Simon
Peter, "Simon, son of John, do you love me more than
these?" He said to him, "Yes Lord; you know that I love
you." Jesus said to him, "Feed my lambs." A second time
Jesus said to him, "Simon, son of John, do you love me?
Peter replied, "Yes Lord; you know that I love you." Jesus
said to him, "Tend my sheep." Then, Jesus said to Peter the
third time, "Simon, son of John, do you love me?" Peter
was grieved because Jesus asked him the third time, "Do
you love me?" And he answered him, "Lord, you know
everything; you know that I love you." Jesus said to him,
"Feed my sheep." (John 21:15–17)

HUMANKIND CAN EARN FORGIVENESS

Jesus was a guest at a Pharisee's home, and a sinful woman bowed
at Jesus's feet. She wetted his feet with her tears, dried his feet with her
hair, and anointed his feet with her costly oil. While the Pharisee mused,
Jesus gave an example of how a disgraced person can find forgiveness
for a gracious act of kindness. Forgiveness is not an option! Forgiveness
is a necessity among men and women to gain favor with God. Another
example that earned forgiveness was Zacchaeus (Luke 19:1–10).

"If this man were a prophet, he would know who and
what sort of woman this is who is touching him, for
she is a sinner." And Jesus said to him, "Simon, I have
something to say to you." And he answered, "What is it
Teacher?" Jesus put forth and example, "A certain creditor
had two debtors; one owed five hundred denarii, and the
other fifty. When they could not pay, he forgave them
both. Now which of them will love him more?" Simon
answered, "The one, I suppose, to whom he forgave more."
And he said to him, "You have judged rightly." Then
turning toward the woman he said to Simon, "Do you see
this woman? I entered your house, you gave me no water
for my feet, but she has wet my feet with her tears and

wiped them with her hair. You gave me no kiss, but from the time I came in she has not ceased to kiss my feet. You did not anoint my head with oil, but she has anointed my feet with ointment. Therefore I tell you, her sins, which are many, are forgiven for she loved much; but he who is forgiven little, loves little." And he said to her, "Your sins are forgiven." Then those who were at table with him began to say among themselves, "Who is this, who even forgives sins?" And he said to the woman, "Your faith has saved you; go in peace." (Luke 7:39b–50)

He (Jesus) entered Jericho and was passing through. And there was a man named Zacchaeus; he was a chief tax collector, and rich. And he sought to see who Jesus was, but could not, on account of the crowd, because he was small of stature. So he ran on ahead and climbed up into a sycamore tree to see him, for Jesus was to pass that way. And when Jesus came to the place, he looked up and said to him, "Zacchaeus, make haste and come down; for I must stay at your house today. So he (Zacchaeus) made haste and came down, and received Jesus joyfully. And when they (Pharisees) saw it, they all murmured, "He has gone in to be a guest who is a sinner." And Zacchaeus stood and said to the Lord, "Behold, Lord, half of my goods I give to the poor; and if I have defrauded any one of anything, I restore it fourfold." And Jesus said to him, "Today salvation has come to this house, since he also is a son of Abraham. For the Son of man came to seek and to save that which was lost." (Luke 19:1–10)

"You have heard that it was said to the men of old, 'You shall not kill; and whoever kills shall be liable to judgment.' But I say to you that every one who is angry with his brother shall be liable to judgment; whoever insults his brother shall be liable to the council, and whoever says, 'You fool!' shall be liable to the hell of fire. So if you are offering your gift at the altar, and remember that your brother has something against you, leave your gift there before the altar and go; first be reconciled to your brother, and then come and offer your gift. Make friends quickly with your accuser, while you are going with him to court, lest your accuser hand you over to the judge, and the judge to the guard, and you be put in prison; truly, I say to you, you will never get out till you have paid the last penny." (Matthew 5:21–26)

WE CAN SAVE OURSELVES BY SAVING OTHERS

The sin against God (Spirit) is unforgivable because there is no one who can forgive the sin against God (Matthew 12:31–32; Mark 3:28–29; Luke 12:8–10). The sin against others is committed against each other, and therefore, it must be released by us. Jesus was very outspoken about human transgressions in his words and his parables.

"Take heed to yourselves; if your brother sins, rebuke him, and if he repents, forgive him; and if he sins against you seven times in a day, and turns to you seven times, and says, 'I repent,' you must forgive him." (Luke 17:3–4)

Then Peter came up and said to Jesus, "Lord, how often shall my brother sin against me, and I forgive him? As many as seven times?" Jesus said to him, "I do not say to you seven times, but seventy times seven." (Matthew 18:21–22)

"For if you forgive men their trespasses, your heavenly Father also will forgive you; but if you do not forgive men their trespasses, neither will your Father forgive your trespasses". (Matthew 6:14–15)

"Whoever causes one of these little ones who believe in me to sin, it would be better for him if a great millstone were hung around his neck and he were thrown into the sea. And if your hand causes you to sin, cut it off; it is better for you to enter life maimed than with two hands to go to hell, to the unquenchable fire. And if your foot causes you to sin, cut it off; it is better for you to enter life lame than with two feet to be thrown into hell. And if your eye causes you to sin, pluck it out; it is better for you to enter the kingdom of God with one eye than with two eyes to be thrown into hell, where their worm does not die, and the fire is not quenched. For every one will be salted with fire. Salt is good; but if salt has lost its saltiness, how will you season it? Have salt in yourselves, and be at peace with one another." (Mark 9:42–50)

"Therefore the kingdom of heaven may be compared to a king who wished to settle accounts with his servants. When he began the reckoning, one was brought to him who owed him ten thousand talents; and as he could not pay, the lord ordered him to be sold, with his wife and children and all that he had, and payment to be made. So the servant fell on his knees imploring him, 'Lord, have patience with me, and I will pay you everything.' And out of pity for him the lord of that servant released him and forgave him the debt. But that same servant, as he went out, came upon one of his fellow servants who owed him a hundred denarii; and seizing him by the throat he said, 'Pay what you owe.' So his fellow servant fell down and besought him 'Have patience with me, and I will pay you.' He refused and went and put him in prison till he should pay the debt. When his fellow servants saw what had taken place, they were greatly distressed, and they went and reported to their lord all that had taken place. Then his lord summoned him and said to him, 'You wicked servant! I forgave you all that debt because you besought me; and should not you have had mercy on your fellow servant, as I had mercy on you?' And in anger his lord delivered him to the jailers, till he should pay all his debt. So also my heavenly Father will do to every one of you, if you do not forgive your brother from your heart." (Matthew 18:23–35)

SUMMARY

- God made us keepers of each other, and we are responsible for each other's salvation.
- God in Christ became a man to work in and through Jesus, his Son, to save and lead humankind back to God.
- Humankind and not God forgives the sins of our fellow individuals on earth so that God can forgive us.
- Before Jesus returned to God, his Father, he delegated forgiveness to his disciples and his leadership to Peter (John 20:19–23; 21:15–17).
- Forgiveness is not an option. Forgiveness is a necessity among men and women to gain favor with God (Luke 7:39–50).
- We can save ourselves by saving others!

CHAPTER 25

MY LOSS OF SELF-CONFIDENCE

DECEMBER 27, 2020

In seconds, I became physically and mentally helpless, useless, and confined to seclusion. I also came from a background that regarded my accident as a divine act of correction and punishment. My conscience agreed with that belief, and it plagued me for years to come. Nevertheless, this accident also revived my faith.

I began to read the Bible and seek the company of like-minded people. During this time, I had very low self-confidence, and I wondered what I could do in this new life that I was facing. How was I to prepare to function in the world with my injuries? I needed help in restoring my self-confidence.

MY CONFIDENCE IN MYSELF WAS VERY LOW

During my seclusion from the outside world, I became acquainted with the Bible and found much comfort. It told me that I was in the world but not *of* the world (John 17:15–17). God sent confidence-builders into my life, and three of the people were ministers.

The first minister put value into my life and helped me believe that I was in God's hands. The second minister helped me decide to become a servant of Christ, and although that required a lot on my part, he saw me serving in the pastorate before he entered eternity. The third pastor took me into his church family and found a place where I could prepare for my long

165

journey to be a minister of the gospel. Before I could serve the Lord with my heart and mind, however, my body had to heal and be repaired from the fire accident. It took twenty skin grafts and reconstruction surgery and eighteen months of hospital and rehabilitation confinement before I was able to be discharged to be on my own.

In addition to what had happened to me, I also was a displaced war victim who spoke no English and had only six years of elementary education in Polish and German. Because my body was 70 percent disabled by the fire accident, I thought I had a future as a freak clown in a circus. One young Christian man looked at me and said, "Put on horns, and you'll look like the devil." How much self-confidence do you think I had left?

My problem was that I needed ten years of education to qualify as a minister. To the denominational leaders and the counselor from the Worker's Compensation Board, it was inconceivable that I could ever reach that goal. Nevertheless, the counselor promised that if I could get into college, the Worker's Compensation Board would pay for my tuition. In seven and one-half years, I made it into college, and I graduated from the North American Baptist Seminary in Sioux Falls, South Dakota, with the second-best grade in my class. Now my ego had grown a bit too fast.

My search for a church to serve dashed my ego somewhat. Smart handicapped ministers were not in demand. To many lay leaders, I was too well educated to be listening to the Holy Spirit. According to them, I could not preach or teach that the Lord had revealed any additional insight on the scriptures to me.

ON TO OKLAHOMA

One church in Oklahoma heard of me and invited me to be their pastor. The people were very good to us, but I felt inadequate, unfulfilled, and lonely. I decided to further my education so that I could teach in a seminary. A German church in New York City needed a minister who could speak their language, and they took us on faith. They allowed me to study, and I earned a post-seminary degree from Biblical Seminary, which was an accredited seminary. Therefore, I was accepted at the University of Toronto, where I earned a doctorate in theology. Sioux Falls Seminary was not accredited, but the New York Biblical Seminary allowed me to prove myself on probation. Toronto also required some qualifying, and at the end of the first year, I was advised to pursue my studies in the biblical field.

I took a two-year break to relocate my New York church and merged it with a church on Long Island, which became the Alden Terrace Baptist Church. During this time, I also read extensively and prepared for my final year in Toronto. In Toronto, I took courses in four religious institutions, and I also taught a subject at an Evangelical Baptist school. Then, I became the pastor of the Central Baptist Church in Buffalo, New York. In Buffalo, I began to write over four hundred pages on "A Setting for the Son of Man."

When I was on my way to take these bulky manuscripts to my supervisor in Toronto to be reviewed for my defense, the Canadian customs mistook them to be contraband, and they were ready to confiscate them. It took some time to explain to them that my manuscript was my work for my doctoral degree before they let me continue on to Toronto.

I HAD TO LEARN MORE LESSONS ON CONFIDENCE

Inadvertently, I had become overconfident in my preaching, teaching, and counseling. I had a chip on my shoulder, and I did not even know it. At that time, I felt equipped to defend and represent the Evangelical way, but that was not what the Toronto seminaries were looking for in my dissertation. A liberal breeze was plastering major schools that were looking for students with new insight. My supervisor, who was an Oxford man, would have let me pass, as would have the examiner from the Pontifical Institute of Rome, but the man from Harvard was disturbed and even insulted that I had dared to defend 150 Evangelical experts for my thesis. He was rude and insisted that I go back home and show him what I could do without the assistance of these people, whom he disliked. He then calmed down and became soft and made me feel that I had the making of an independent scholar. He did not fail me, but he marked my work as being incomplete, and he expected me back with a revised thesis so that I would not be forgotten.

My ego was hurt, and I was sold on evangelicalism. My wife also felt disappointed because she had done all my typing by hand on our old typewriter and had left spaces for the foreign words, which had to be filled in by hand. Yet we did not give up, and I began to do my own reconstruction to see where I would end up. At this point, I had no confidence that this Harvard scholar would accept my work. My supervisor also was cautious and reminded me in a note, "You are going into a lion's den a second time."

I did tremble the second time, but the Harvard man greeted me with a smile, congratulated me with praise, and urged me to publish my work in their journals, and he added this comment that has rung in my ears for over fifty years: "We will hear from you." My load of failing fell off my shoulders like lead, and my ego began to celebrate. At last, the chancellor of Victoria University of Toronto knighted me with the sword and bestowed on me, "Sir Daniel A. Kolke," the degree of doctor of theology.

I was the only one receiving that degree. My supervisor was pleased and apologized for being so hard on me. A dream had come true, and my ego was raised higher than it should have been. Of course, the degree affected my preaching, teaching, and writing. I was turning the pulpit into a classroom with heavy lectures, and I was totally oblivious to what was happening around me. Again, it would take years before I would identify the breeze that was swiping by me.

IT STILL WAS TIME FOR ANOTHER LESSON ON MY SELF-CONFIDENCE

Reaching the doctoral academic level in Christianity added to my ego and self-confidence. The State University at Buffalo hoped to add a religious branch. In addition to serving the Central Baptist Church, I was teaching two historical subjects on "Jesus and the Origin of Christianity." The expected financial support, however, was assigned to Long Island, New York, and so we had to disband. During this time, I also applied to seminaries and colleges for a teaching position, but they all regretted that their financing was drying up, and they had to lay off teachers. Denominations were shrinking and splintering, and that caused the loss of financial aid to operate.

The war had reawakened the need for God, and a swift emotionalism, which appeared godly, swept the nation. Seemingly overnight, huge mega-churches sprang up, and the evangelists with psychic compulsions impressed the public, and many people were converted. I longed for such an experience, which never happened. These people became the Evangelicals who would separate themselves from their social and political duties to the nation and allow liberal secularism to take over the nation, the schools, and even many churches. When this movement realizes its blundering, will it be too late to save this nation?

While this was going on, I had buried myself in the Gospels and wrote a book on the walls that churches built to survive, and I kept delivering sound biblical sermons. My church held its own, and we even added new members. Our denominational press was not interested in my work, so I published my own book. I was asked to write about racism, social injustice, women's rights to abortion, and enjoying other liberties. Our denomination head, who oversaw over New York State with some four hundred churches, became curious and friendly with me, and he requested that I send him one of my sermons. I was elated that he showed such interest in me, my family, and my work.

He did not take long to hand down his analysis of my wisdom. I felt a little insulted, but my ego needed to be halted from moving up too fast. It was brief: "Your lecture put me to sleep. Break it up, and put some humor in your sermons." I do not recall what else he said, for this was enough for my wife and me to digest. I took his advice to heart, shortened the biblical content, and enhanced it with illustrations and humor. To my surprise, my new style made me more popular, and never again was I rejected at a first job interview. I believe that I thanked him. I served three churches under this leader and assisted in teaching some of his leaders in Buffalo, Ilion, and Fulton. During my last church in Fulton, I wrote an article for the local paper titled "Stop and Think," and this theme became my hobby blog in retirement.

CHANGE AFFECTED MY CONFIDENCE

Things happened too quickly, and we had no control over anything, except the choice to follow. At this time, we were pleased with where we were. Our oldest son was on a five-year region's scholarship from the New York State University, and he had just finished his first year. The scholarship paid us to house and feed our son because he was close enough to live at home. Then my father became ill and required life-threatening surgery in West Vancouver, British Columbia, Canada. To be near our parents and to give my wife and our three sons a chance to get to know my parents, their grandparents, we decided to leave a comfortable church in Fulton, New York, and moved to Gorst, Washington.

My father recovered, and we had more than fifteen years with him and more than twenty with my mother. With time on my hands in a small church, I helped out at a denominational college and in a seminary. During this time, my wife's mother was losing her sight and became less mobile. Her second husband brought her to us and then deserted her. She stayed with us for three and one-half years, mostly in my care. Our sons were all in school, and my wife, Selma, went back to college, where she qualified to go back to work.

Two years later, we moved to Edmonds, Washington (two hours closer to our parents in Canada). The search committee of Edmonds First Baptist Church liked my Bible preaching but not my emphasis on spirituality. I did not have any special revelations but the Bible. The attempt, by some members to replace me failed, and they left the church. Even so, the Lord added new people, and I stayed until I retired, twelve and one-half years later. We had an associate who could not take over, and I was called back until they found a pastor to their liking.

Some charismatic members had stayed with me all these years, and some new ones had joined. At this time, they saw an opportunity to bring their kind of man from the Pentecostal Bible School in Kirkland, Washington, who filled their wishes. He begged me not to visit his church, which I had no interest in doing because we were moving away. Apparently, most of the people were leaving, including his friends, and he blamed it all on my family. He also took the church out of the denomination, and he ended up with only eleven people on Sundays; in his anger, he left the church. Another independent Baptist group came in, and the church grew to three worship services on Sundays and on other days.

IT WAS HARD TO HANG ON TO MY CONFIDENCE

In my pursuit of the best education, I must have lived in a cocoon. I was unaware that a degree from Toronto would not be acceptable to the Conservatives, Charismatics, and Evangelicals. It did not matter to these people that I had two degrees from conservative schools. Within the liberal movement, I was tolerated but not endorsed. When Seattle tried to open a liberal seminary, I was invited to teach two subjects that I soon learned would not alter their perceptions. I withdrew because I did not fit in with their program. It was Toronto that was the best for me because the teachers did not force their views on me. They accepted and respected every paper I wrote in our seminars, as were the papers of the other candidates. However, when I used the prevailing Evangelical conservative experts to substantiate my position on the Son of man, the liberal examiners saw me as being unfaithful to myself. These scholars were not pushing their views but the ability for me to reach my own conclusion based on the scriptures.

OUR FAILURE TO FORGIVE EACH OTHER

From that day on, I was faithful to the Word of the Lord for over fifty years. I am more convinced than ever that our failure to forgive each other and do what is right, before God can forgive us, is the reason why we do not get into Christ's kingdom (Matthew 6:14–15; 18:23–35; John 20:21–23). Jesus is the Savior, not Paul or even one of his disciples.

I retired at age sixty-two and a half, and my wife retired several years later due to ill health. We bought a little country place and assumed we were set for the rest of our days. We hoped to divide the land with our sons and help them build their own homes, but the county laws had other plans. It would become a development with over thirty homes. Meanwhile, we had other surprises.

With time on my hands, I tried to take part in revivals, but the evangelists had no place for my schooling, and the Charismatics disagreed with my spirit. So, we tried to go on vacation to visit some of our relatives. As my wife and I were in our car going north, my PMR suddenly struck my muscles with unbearable pain, and I could not move. Prednisone relieved me of the pain and time did some of the healing. I had two more attacks of PMR, one that lasted a year. Before the second bounce, I also was diagnosed with prostate cancer, with a PSA count of 129. The urologist no longer could operate, but he did inject me with hormones. The oncologist used over thirty radiations and concluded I was incurable.

While I wallowed in my misery in the urologist's office, a man in his nineties walked in, singing cheerfully about heaven. I felt ashamed, and right there, I turned cheerful and put my trust in the Lord. We had people working, praying, and laying their hands on me. Instantly, I felt my self-confidence returning—that was twenty-three years ago. I have written much since then, and my blog and the internet have extended my journey as a vessel of grace for my Lord Jesus Christ.

SUMMARY

- We can overcome inconceivable obstacles through our confidence in ourselves and with God's help.
- Change can affect our confidence for the better.

CHAPTER 26

WHAT HAS SELF-CONFIDENCE DONE FOR ME?

JANUARY 2, 2021

In the previous chapter, I shared how my self-confidence resembled a thermometer—accidents, mistakes, unpleasant surprises, health problems, and many other troubling things dropped and raised my confidence. My confidence, however, never fell below a level where I could not come back and rebuild it. In retrospect, I am convinced that my Lord did not let Satan bury me in my miseries! Therefore, the Lord also kept whatever confidence I had alive in me (Luke 22:31–32; 1 Corinthians 10:13; Matthew 28:20; Psalm 27:10). The words of King David are on my mind, and so is the promise of that our Lord made:

> Whither shall I go from thy Spirit? Or whither shall I flee from thy presence? If I ascend to heaven, thou art there! If I make my bed in Sheol, thou art there! If I take the wings of the morning and dwell in the uttermost parts of the sea, even there thy hand shall lead me, and thy right hand shall hold me. If I say, "Let only darkness cover me, and the light about me be night," even the darkness is not dark to thee, the night is bright as the day; for darkness is as light with thee.

173

For thou didst form my inward parts, thou didst knit me together in my mother's womb. I praise thee, for thou art fearful and wonderful. Wonderful are thy works! Thou knowest me right well; my frame was not hidden from thee, when I was being made in secret, intricately wrought in the depths of the earth. Thy eyes beheld my unformed substance; in thy book were written, every one of them, the days that were formed for me, when as yet there was none of them. How precious to me are thy thoughts, O God! How vast is the sum of them! If I would count them, they are more than the sand. When I awake, I am still with thee. (Psalm 139:7–18)

It was the feast of Dedication in Jerusalem; it was winter, and Jesus was walking in the temple, in the portico of Solomon. So the Jews gathered round him and said to him, "How long will you keep us in suspense? If you are Christ, tell us plainly." Jesus answered them, "I told you, and you do not believe. The works that I do in my Father's name, they bear witness to me; but you do not believe, because you do not belong to my sheep. My sheep hear my voice, and I know them, and they follow me; and I give them eternal life, and they shall never perish, and no one shall snatch them out of my hand. My Father, who has given them to me, is greater than all, and no one is able to snatch them out of the Father's hand. I and the Father are one." (John 10:22–30)

Judas (not Iscariot) said to him, "Lord, how is it that you will manifest yourself to us, and not to the world?" Jesus answered him, "If a man loves me, he will keep my word, and my Father will love him, and we will come to him and make our home with him. He who does not love me does not keep my words; and the word which you hear is not mine but the Father's who sent me." (John 14:22–24)

How Do I Maintain Self-Confidence in God?

According to the apostle Paul, I am a temple of the Holy Spirit (1 Corinthians 6:19). With Christ and God, the Spirit living in me, I can stop living in sin (Romans 6:12–14). The apostle John agreed with Jesus that if we let Jesus live in us, we will stop sinning and do what is right to survive in the world as Christ's servants and Christ's witnesses (John 8:34–47; 15:1–27; Matthew 7:21–29).

> No one who abides in him (Jesus) sins; no one who sins has either seen him or known him. Little children, let no one deceive you. He who does right is righteous, as he is righteous, as he is righteous. He who commits sin is of the devil; for the devil has sinned from the beginning. The reason the Son of God appeared was to destroy the works of the devil. No one born of God commits sin; for God's nature abides in him, and he cannot sin because he is born of God. By this it may be seen who are the children of God, and who are the children of the devil: whoever does not do right is not of God, nor he who does not love his brother. (1 John 3:6–10)

> Jesus answered them, "Truly, truly, I say to you, everyone who commits sin is a slave to sin. The slave does not continue in the house forever; the son continues forever. So if the Son makes you free, you will be free indeed. I know that you are the descendants of Abraham; yet you seek to kill me, because my word finds no place in you. I speak of what I have seen with my Father, and you do what you have heard from your father." (John 8:34–38)

> "For no good tree bears bad fruit, nor again does a bad tree bear good fruit; for each tree is known by its own fruit. For figs are not gathered from thorns, nor are grapes picked from the bramble bush. The good man out of the good treasure of his heart produces good, and the evil

man out of his evil treasure produces evil; for out of the abundance of the heart his mouth speaks.

Why do you call me 'Lord, Lord' and do not do what I tell you? Every one who comes to me and hears my words and does them, I will show you what he is like: he is like a man building a house, who dug deep, and laid a foundation upon rock; and when the flood arose, the stream broke against that house, and could not shake it, because it had been well built. But he who hears and does not do them is like a man who built a house on the ground without a foundation; against which the stream broke, and immediately it fell, and the ruin of that house was great." (Luke 6:43–49)

WHO IS MAINTAINING MY CONFIDENCE?

I turned my life over to Christ, my Lord, seventy-some years ago, but who has maintained my life all these years? From a physical perspective, I had only 30 percent of my body left to work with, but regarding my mental capability, the Lord must have increased it to 130 percent.

To keep the Lord and the Holy Spirit comfortable in my life, I constantly have to clean my own house and keep the things out that defile my body and my temple. And my body ought to house the Holy Spirit and God, who is Spirit. I have not always been free of temptations, bad thoughts, or using bad words. I have not used surgery on myself, but my conscience has helped me resist enticements, which would have dishonored my faith, my family, and myself. Nevertheless, I had many small infractions that kept the Lord, God, and the Holy Spirit outside my door. There were times when I was afraid to open the door too far and be sprayed with a hefty dose of holiness. At least, this was my perception at one time of how the Holy Spirit and God worked in my life. That perception has taken on a more realistic approach to how the Holy Trinity functions in the world.

I have come to believe that God has stopped waiting for us to become perfect or holy before we can be used to accomplish his redemptive purpose. The Son of God came into the world to make up for our shortcomings. Jesus gave us the reason why we must believe and follow him to reach redemption ourselves and help others to attain the same. It is while we are being redeemed that we become the instruments of redemption for others. We are being redeemed by assisting in the redemption of our fellow individuals. Redemption is a lifelong process, and we do not get crowned until we leave this world (Philippians 2:12).

> Brethren, if a man is overtaken in any trespass, you who are spiritual should restore him in the spirit of gentleness. Look to yourself, lest you be tempted. Bear one another's burdens, and so fulfill the law of Christ. For if any one thinks he is something, when he is nothing, he deceives himself. But let each one test his own work, and then his boast will be in himself alone and not in his neighbor. For each man will have to bear his own load. (Galatians 6:1–5)

> My brethren, if any one among you wanders from the truth and some one brings him back, let him know that whoever brings back a sinner from the error of his way will save his soul from death and will cover a multitude of sins. (James 5:19–20)

> This is the message we have heard from him (Jesus) and proclaim to you, that God is light and in him is no darkness at all. If we say we fellowship with him while we walk in darkness, we lie and do not live according to the truth; but if we walk in the light, as he is in the light, we have fellowship with one another, and the blood of Jesus his Son cleanses us from all sin. If we say we have no sin, we deceive ourselves, and the truth is not in us. If we confess our sins, he is faithful and just, and will forgive our sins and cleanse us from all unrighteousness. If we say we have not sinned, we make him a liar, and his word is not in us. (1 John 1:5–10)

> Then let us no more pass judgment on one another, but rather decide never to put a stumbling-block or hindrance in the way of a brother. I know and am persuaded in

the Lord Jesus that nothing is unclean in itself; but it is unclean for anyone who thinks it unclean. If your brother is being injured by what you eat, you are no longer walking in love. Do not let what you eat cause the ruin of one for whom Christ died. So do not let your good be spoken of as evil. For the kingdom of God is not food and drink but righteousness and peace and joy in the Holy Spirit; he who thus serves Christ is acceptable to God and approved by men. Let us then pursue what makes for peace and for mutual upbuilding. Do not, for the sake of food, destroy the work of God. Everything is indeed clean, but it is wrong for any one to make others fall by what he eats; it is right not to eat meat or drink wine or do anything that makes your brother stumble. The faith that you have, keep between yourself and God; happy is he who has no reason to judge himself for what he approves. But he who has doubts is condemned, if he eats, because he does not act from faith; for whatever does not proceed from faith is sin. (Romans 14:13–23)

We who are strong ought to bear with the failings of the weak, and not to please ourselves; let each of us please his neighbor for his good, to edify him. For Christ did not please himself; but, as it is written, "The reproaches of those who reproached thee fell on me." For whatever was written in former days was written for our instruction, that by (our) steadfastness and by the encouragement of the scriptures we might have hope. (Romans 15:1–4)

SELF-CONFIDENCE HELPED ME ENDURE AND PERSEVERE

During my ninety years of grace, these words of our Lord reverberated often:

"In the world you have tribulation; but be of good cheer, I have overcome the world." (John 16:33b)

"By your endurance you will gain your lives." (Luke 21:19)

"But he who endures to the end will be saved." (Mark 13:13b)

Thus far, I have yet to overcome the world, and at this stage in my life, my journey of grace can still be damaged and interrupted. Hence, I, too, like the writer of Hebrews, regard my trials and tribulations as heavenly discipline and training for my day of departure from this world.

Therefore, since we are surrounded by so great a cloud of witnesses, let us lay aside every weight, and sin which clings so closely, and let us run with perseverance the race that is set before us, looking to Jesus the pioneer and perfecter of our faith, who for the joy that was set before him endured the cross, despising the shame, and is seated at the right hand of the throne of God.

Consider him who endured from sinners such hostility against himself, so that you may not grow weary or fainthearted. In your struggle against sin you have not yet resisted to the point of shedding your blood. And have you forgotten the exhortation which addresses you as sons? "My son, do not regard lightly the discipline of the Lord, nor lose courage when you are punished by him. For the Lord disciplines him whom he loves and chastises every son whom he receives."

It is for discipline that you have to endure. God is treating you as sons; for what son is there whom his father does not discipline? If you are left without discipline, in which all have participated, then you are illegitimate children and not sons. Besides this we have had earthly fathers to discipline us and we respected them. Shall we not much more be subject to the Father of spirits and live? For they disciplined us for a short time at their pleasure, but he disciplines us for our good, that we may share his holiness. For the moment all discipline seems

179

painful rather than pleasant; later it yields the peaceful fruit of righteousness to those who have been trained by it. (Hebrews 12:1–11)

Jesus said,

"If the world hates you, know that it has hated me (Jesus) before it hated you. If you were of the world, the world would love its own; but because you are not of the world, but I have chosen you out of the world, therefore the world hates you. Remember the word I said to you, 'A servant is not greater than his master.' If they persecuted me, they will persecute you; if they kept my word, they will keep yours also. But all this they will do to you on my account, because they do not know him who sent me. If I had not come and spoken to them, they would not have sin; but now they have no excuse for their sin. He who hates me hates my Father also. If I had not done among them the works which no one else did, they would not have sin; but now they have seen and hate both me and my Father." (John 15:18–24)

I (Jesus) have said all this to you to keep you from falling away. They will put you out of their synagogues (churches); indeed, the hour is coming when whoever kills you will think he is offering service to God. And they will do this because they have not known the Father, nor me. But I have said these things to you, that when the hour comes you may remember that I told you of them. (John 16:1–4)

SUMMARY

- With Christ living in us, humankind can stop living in sin (Romans 6:12–14).
- To maintain our confidence, we need to constantly clean our own houses (bodies, temples) to keep out that which defiles our bodies and our temples.

- Redemption is a lifetime process (Philippians 2:12).
- Self-confidence and faith are twins.
- The world God made re-creates and sustains itself, and so does humankind, whom God put in charge (Genesis 1:26–30).
- Our conscience is God's voice, and his Word fervently vibrates when we stray off his path (Ephesians 6: 10–17).
- Forgiveness frees humankind to follow and obey Jesus's command, "Rise up."

CHAPTER 27

LOSING CONFIDENCE IN FAITH

The writer of Hebrews 11:6 made this statement:

> And without faith it is impossible to please him (God).
> For whoever would draw near to God must believe that
> he exists and that he rewards those who seek him.

It is not just the invisible that requires faith but also the visible and the unexpected accidents and incidents that disrupted and crippled my life. It's where and when faith—in me or in myself—had to step up and pull me through my stretch of difficulties. Even as a handicapped person, I had to make choices, seek answers, and apply myself and restore my life so I could serve God and humankind. You may think me unorthodox, but at times, I did feel that God and Christ were going with me, instead of me going with God and Christ. I believed that whatever I was doing, I would succeed, and I did succeed. I could not sit back and wait for someone to come and improve my life. Our Lord made this suggestion:

> "Ask, and it shall be given you; seek, and you will find; knock, and it will be opened to you. For every one who asks receives, and he who seeks finds, and to him who knocks it will be opened. Or what man of you, if his son asks him for a loaf, will give him a stone? Or if he asks

for a fish, will he give him a serpent? If you then, who are evil, know how to give good gifts to your children, how much more will your Father who is in heaven give good things to those who ask him? So whatever you wish that men would do to you, do so to them; for this is the law and the prophets." (Matthew 7:7–12)

JUST HOW IMPORTANT IS FAITH IN MYSELF?

To me, self-confidence and faith are twins. With regard to faith in God, even creation demands that I believe in a superior intelligence, energy, and force (Psalm 19:1–6), defined in the scriptures as "Spirit and breath of God" (Genesis 1:11–12; John 4:24). In relationship to me, God made me in his image and in his likeness with his breath and his Spirit (Genesis 1:26; 2:7), before the world was created (Ephesians 1:4). And I was predestined to enter the world through my parents, to be one of his servants in the Christian year AD 1930. The world God made re-creates and sustains itself and so does humankind, whom God put in charge (Genesis 1:26–30). And then, God retired to give humankind and the world a chance (Genesis 2:1–3). And then, at the end of time, humankind will appear before God (2 Corinthians 5:10; Revelation 20:11–15). With all this in mind, I understand why God does not interfere in the affairs of humans, regardless of how bad they become. (I will discuss this further in other chapters.)

HOW DOES THIS SPIRIT TALK TO ME?

How did the Spirit and God talk to me? I must have been six years old when my conscience began to fear and sweat whenever I had an accident or did something wrong. I was told, by my adults, that God would punish me for the bad I did and reward me for the good I did. Unfortunately, there was more wrong than right, but God never showed up.

God, however, sent my father to discipline me and then teachers, preachers, and many others that I needed. When I was drowning, a Pole, who was an enemy, saved me. When I was burning alive, an Italian and a German, two army vets, saved me. Then, when I was dying of cancer, an army of people helped me rebuild my body, mind, and spirit. Now, I believe this, for that is the way God speaks with me and works through me. My conscience is his voice, and his words fervently vibrate when I stray off his path. The Lord has been playing with my conscience all my life and has kept me from yielding to the wiles of the devil.

> Finally, be strong in the Lord and in the strength of his might. Put on the whole armor of God, that you may be able to stand against the wiles of the devil. For we are not contending against flesh and blood, but against the principalities, against the powers, against the world rulers of this present darkness, against the spiritual hosts of wickedness in the heavenly places. Therefore take the whole armor of God, that you may be able to withstand in the evil day, and having done all to stand. Stand therefore, having girded your loins with truth, and having put on the breastplate of righteousness, and having shod your feet with the equipment of the gospel of peace; besides all these, taking the shield of faith, with which you can quench all the flaming darts of the evil one. And take the helmet of salvation, and the sword of the Spirit, which is the word of God. (Ephesians 6:10–17)

IT IS IN THIS LIFE THAT MY FAITH AND MY CONFIDENCE NEED TO BE ARMED

For me, the possible realm in which I live has been a struggle and a battle against the forces that diminished my faith and my self-confidence. The words and examples of Jesus have become my armor, and they have rebuilt my faith and self-confidence more than once. After the fire disabled me, I could have ended my life, like the man who waited thirty-eight years for someone to put him in the pool of Bethzatha in Jerusalem. He needed someone to tell him, "Get up, take your stretcher, and walk." Jesus told him exactly that, and he obeyed and walked. Later on, the Lord told him to stop sinning and prevent more suffering (John 5:1–9, 14).

Like the paralytic, I also could have depended on others to care for me. Four men, with faith in themselves and in Jesus, brought the paralytic, with no faith in himself, to Jesus (Mark 2:1–12). When they could not find any access to Jesus, they opened the roof and let their friend down in front of Jesus. Jesus saw the faith of the four men and not the faith of the paralytic. Sin was in the way of the paralyzed man's faith. Sin made him sicker than he was. The first thing Jesus said was, "Son, your sins are forgiven." Forgiveness freed his faith in himself, and he could obey Jesus's next command: "Rise, take up your pallet, and go home." So he did and amazed the public.

I was on my recovery bed in the hospital when a man of God told me that I would be a minister for Christ. That comment brought hope and purpose into my life. Like the little lady who used all her strength to get through the crowd to touch Jesus's hem, so I, too, had to pass a jungle of thinking to reach Christ. I am so much more blessed than that lady, who had to go to Jesus in her condition. When I began to believe and practice God's Word by distributing his grace, Jesus's Spirit, God the Spirit, and the Holy Spirit's love began to reside in me (John 14:23–24). The Holy Trinity manifests itself in who we are, how we live, and in what we do (Matthew 5:16).

One of Jesus's most moving encounters was the touch of faith by a nameless woman who had suffered for twelve years (Mark 5:25–34). Crowds surrounded Jesus. And Jesus was on his way to save a little girl. Suddenly, Jesus halted his movement. Jesus broke the silence by asking, "Who touched me?" In spite of her weakness, this woman had managed to get close to Jesus. By stretching her arms and reaching out with her hands, the woman was able to brush the hem of Jesus's garment. Jesus's question stunned most of the people. Many people were thronging around Jesus. How could Jesus know that someone had touched him? How could Jesus possibly detect a single person's touch? We are told that Jesus knew the touch because this woman's faith sapped Jesus's energy. Jesus did not move on until the woman came forward and confessed what she had done.

Then, Jesus publicly recognized her by saying to her, "Daughter, your faith has saved you. Go in peace and be free from your infirmity" (Mark 5:34). We must note that her faith not only healed her but also saved her. Peace and healing were added blessings. Her real benefit was that she was saved and that she was delivered from whatever sickness plagued her. We only can guess that it might have been bitterness and disappointment against those who used her and those who could not help her. We gather this from the statement she made—that she had spent all she had on doctors who could do nothing for her.

It is important for us to recognize that salvation must precede our physical problems. It is when our faith boosts our souls that our bodies also will reap the benefits. Faith is powerful enough to sap energy from Jesus, our Lord, and it can also release some of our faith to others in need. But how much more can God do if we allow him to live in us?

READING JESUS'S WORDS, I HEAR HIM AND GOD THE FATHER

Jesus told Judas, not the traitor, "The word which you hear is not mine but the Father's who sent me" (John 14:24). To the disciples, Jesus said, "If they kept my word, they will keep yours also" (John 15:20).

And Jesus prayed,

> "I do not pray for these only (his disciples), but also for those who are to believe in me through their word (us, you, and I), that they all be one; even as thou, Father, art in me, and I in thee, that they also may be in us, so that the world may believe that thou has sent me. The glory which thou hast given to me I have given to them, that they may be one even as we are one, I in them and thou in me, that they may become perfectly one, so that the world may know that thou hast sent me and hast loved them even as thou hast loved me." (John 17: 20–23)

The Word of Christ is the Word of God and that Word the Holy Spirit reproduced in the New Testament, and no one can alter or omit it (John 1:1). Luke recorded Jesus's conclusion:

> "The law and the prophets were until John (the Baptist): since then the good news of the kingdom of God is preached, and every one enters violently. But it is easier

for heaven and earth to pass away, than for one dot of the law to become void." (Luke 16:16–17; Matthew 5:17–18; Mark 13:30–31)

Jesus used a Roman officer to demonstrate how powerful his word and the word of the Father in heaven is. As to the faith regarding a Roman officer, Jesus declared, "I tell you, I have not found such great faith even in Israel" (Luke 7:9b). The Jewish leaders had sent a delegation to Jesus, begging him to come and heal the centurion's servant. They told Jesus that this man deserved to be visited because he had done a number of things for the people. Jesus responded, and while he was on his way, a second delegation came with a new request. Their message was that their master did not see himself as worthy to receive Jesus. Their master believed that all Jesus had to do was to speak the word of healing, and his servant would get well. This Roman did not need Jesus's presence because, to him, Jesus's words were sufficient to verify his faith and his request. The incident reminds us of Thomas, who had to see in order to believe. And for all our sakes, Jesus obliged him.

> Eight days later, his (Jesus') disciples were again in the house, and Thomas was with them. The doors were shut, but Jesus came and stood among them, and said, "Peace be with you." Then he said to Tomas, "Put your finger here, and see my hands; and put out your hand, and place it in my side; do not be faithless, but believing." Thomas answered him, "My Lord and my God!" Jesus said to him, "Have you believed because you have seen? Blessed are those who have not seen and yet believe." (John 20:26–29)

WHAT AM I DOING WITH MY FAITH AT NINETY?

I still depend on myself. Nearly seventy years ago, the fire put me out of manual labor. To help me become dependent on public help, they gave me a small disability, that was just not enough to live on. I could have remained uneducated, unmarried, and a burden to my family. I would not have become a minister, teacher, writer, or a publisher. When I disclosed my intentions to reach for that goal, most of the listeners dismissed me as being overly pretentious. What could become of a twenty-one-year-old who could not complete his elementary education because of the war, and then a fire robbed him of his physical ability? I was a badly hurt person—that was all I was at that time—but I had an irreversible spark of faith in myself and a trust in Jesus, my Lord, which helped me see only my goals ahead.

If I were to compare myself to any of Jesus's subjects, I would be the man with the one pound (Matthew 25:14–30). Instead of burying my pound, however, I reinvested it over and over until I reached my ninetieth year. When I retired from the pastorate and was diagnosed with cancer, I began publishing my Bible studies on the internet, titled, "Stop and Think."

I am at an age when I am supposed to wait on the Lord to take me home, but it appears that the Lord is waiting on me to finish a task, which never gets done. It took me many years to realize what the task was. And here it is—even as a handicapped person, I was endowed with sufficient faith and energy to get me where I wanted to go and do what I wanted to do. Imagine if I had begun waiting on the Lord seventy years ago. I would be sitting in a wheelchair, preventing people from doing what they were intended to do for themselves and for others. If I had stopped using the faith I had, I would very likely have become the biggest failure to myself and an immense burden to others.

With regard to my fellow human beings, I do not imagine it because too many people are waiting for God to come and even vote for them and clean up the world. That is not what will happen because God put humankind in charge when he made the world and humankind (Genesis 1:26–2:3). How much faith did God give to humankind to manage the world or solve personal problems? The disciples of Jesus asked that question, and the Lord gave them this answer: "No larger than a mustard seed!"

> Then the disciples came to Jesus privately and said, "Why could we not cast it out?" Jesus said to them, "Because of your little faith. For truly, I say to you, if you have faith as a grain of mustard seed, you will say to this mountain, 'Move hence to yonder place,' and it will move; and nothing will be impossible to you." (Matthew 17:19–21)

I vividly remember that I had no faith when I was drowning, and then I was burning alive, but the men who saved me had enough faith to keep me alive, and they were total strangers. Their impulsive moves were deeds of their faith that saved me. When I regained consciousness in the hospital, the tiny mustard seed of faith helped me unbury myself from the huge mountain that had fallen on me and all the other obstacles that stood in the way of becoming a small tree myself, where some birds can find nests.

Friends, if your faith does not move you, then remember the ten spies who died with their people in the wilderness (Numbers 13:30–33). Faith without deeds is not only dead, but it also kills those who trust in you (James 3:14–28). Faith is serious business. (We will continue in the next chapter.)

SUMMARY

- It is impossible to please God without faith.
- It is in this life that our faith and our confidence need to be armed and anchored.
- The words and examples of Jesus can become our armor to rebuild our faith and self-confidence.

CHAPTER 28

ELEMENTARY FAITH IS BASIC

JANUARY 16, 2021

For me, faith began as a mustard seed that I had to put into the ground (into my heart). Then I had to care for it so that God's Spirit could make it grow. Growth itself requires constant attention to keep faith on track. We must partner with the Spirit of God to build and maintain faith in ourselves before we can be of any use to anyone else. In this world, we do not give orders; we carry them out. Our orders come from Jesus in Luke 17:5–6 and from Paul in 1 Corinthians 3:5–9, in Matthew 13:24–30, and again in Luke 22:24–30.

> The apostles said to the Lord, "Increase our faith!" And the Lord said, "If you had faith as a grain of mustard seed, you could say to this sycamine tree, 'Be rooted up, and be planted in the sea,' and it would obey you." (Luke 17:5–6)

> What then is Apollos? What is Paul? Servants through whom you believed, as the Lord assigned to each. I planted, Apollos watered, but God gave the growth. So neither he who plants nor he who waters is anything, but only God who gives the growth. He who plants and he who waters are equal, and each shall receive his wages according to his labor. For we are fellow workmen for God; you are God's field, God's building. (1 Corinthians 3:5–9)

Another parable Jesus put before them, saying, "The kingdom of heaven may be compared to a man who sowed good seed in his field; but while men were sleeping, his enemy came and sowed weeds among the wheat, and went away. So when the plants came up and bore grain, the weeds appeared also. And the servants of the householder came and said to him, 'Sir, did you not sow good seed in your field? How then has it weeds?' He said to them, 'An enemy has done this.' The servants said to him, 'Then do you want us to gather them?' But he said, 'No; lest in gathering the weeds you root up the wheat along with them. Let both grow together until the harvest; and at harvest time I will tell the reapers, Gather the weeds first and bind them in bundles to be burned, but gather the wheat into my barns.'" (Matthew 13:24–30)

A dispute also arose among them, which of them was to be regarded as the greatest. And he (Jesus) said to them, "The kings of the Gentiles exercise lordship over them; and those in authority over them are called benefactors. But not so with you; rather let the greatest among you become as the youngest, and the leader as one who serves. For which is the greater, one who sits at the table, or one who serves? Is it not the one who sits at the table? But I am among you as one who serves. You are those who have continued with me in my trials; as my Father appointed a kingdom for me, so do I appoint for you that you may eat and drink at my table in my kingdom, and sit on twelve thrones judging the twelve tribes of Israel." (Luke 22:24–30)

FAITH COMES IN SMALL SERVINGS; NEVERTHELESS, IT IS ENOUGH TO KEEP US GOING

There is no doubt that most of us have little faith and that we are weak in our knees. And the problem is doubt. Like Peter, we seem to undertake the impossible. In order to get to Jesus, we want to walk on water. Why do we always seek the more difficult road? Do we all have to walk on water to get to the Lord? Each one of us has to answer that question for ourselves. But if we do venture out on a risky stretch of road, we should take faith with us, not doubt. If we set out with doubt, we are certain to sink at the first wave of trouble. As in the case of Peter, Jesus will not be there in human form to pull us out of trouble. Jesus's words to Peter were, "You of little faith, why did you doubt?" (Matthew 14:28–31).

We are not called upon to take unnecessary risks. There are enough troublesome waters in life that we have to cross. These troubled waters of life scare us to the point that we practically become spiritual invalids. As for the disciples, it was fear that drove them to desperation. Jesus had to calm the storm. Jesus also had to calm their hearts. Jesus said to them, "Why are you afraid, O men of little faith?" (Matthew 8:26b). Fear is the product of our doubts, and faith is there to counter fear. Jesus had these words for his people: "Fear not little flock, it is the Father's will to give you the kingdom" (Luke 12:32).

For the worst part, fear has many advocates, and doubt always lingers in its shadow. When Jairus, the ruler of the synagogue, was told not to bother Jesus, the teacher, after his daughter had died, Jesus encouraged Jairus, saying, "Do not fear, only believe" (Mark 5:36). Jairus believed, and his daughter lived. Faith knows that the one who cares for the birds and the flowers shall do more than supply the needs of his children (Matthew 6:25–34). Someone once said, "When fear knocks at the door, send faith to open it, and you will find that there is no one there."

WE ARE NOT BORN WITH FAITH

We have to acquire faith. And with most of us, faith increases. But faith also can decrease. The disciples of Jesus knew this. That is why they asked their Lord to increase their faith (Luke 17:5). It was not just faith in God but also faith in other human beings and, foremost, faith in themselves—particularly those who are prone to sin and stand in need of forgiveness. Yes! Forgiveness! Forgiving—and then not just once or twice but seven times seventy per day. This endless forgiveness requires a lot of faith in order that these people will change for the better. Faith also requires faith on the part of those who forgive. If they do not forgive, then they have to live with a guilty conscience. In that sense, faith helps us to clear our consciences and calm our eternal souls. We have faith that in forgiving others, we ourselves are forgiven (Matthew 6:12–15).

Perhaps a noteworthy example was the relationship between Jesus and Peter. The boastful Peter declared himself willing to die with Jesus, his teacher. Jesus told Peter that he would deny him three times before the cock crowed. In that connection, the Lord said to his brave disciple, "Simon, Simon, watch out. Satan has sought to sift you as wheat, but I have prayed for you so that your faith may not fail. And when you come back, strengthen your brethren" (Luke 22:31–32; writer's own translation).

During the arrest of Jesus, the disciples all fled, except Peter. Peter even struck Malchus's ear with his sword. Then Peter followed Jesus, his Lord, at a distance. Inside the courtyard, Peter began to disown Jesus, his master. At the third denial, Peter caught the eyes of Jesus looking at him with pity and with forgiveness. Peter's conscience awakened at the moment Peter's eyes met Jesus's eyes. Jesus's look of pity and forgiveness revived Peter's memory of what Jesus had told him. Peter was overwhelmed with remorse and guilt! Peter went outside and wept bitterly (Luke 22:60–62). And that prayer revived Peter. Peter gathered the other followers of Jesus, and he strengthened his brethren.

FAITH, SMALL AS A CRUMB, CAN BECOME A MIRACLE

Jesus had left the region, and he traveled in the area of Sidon and Tyre. A native or Canaanite woman ran after Jesus, and she cried out, "Have mercy on me, Lord, son of David. My daughter is demonized by evil" (Matthew 15:22; writer's own translation). Jesus, who normally responded to such pleading, refused to answer. She became so annoyed that the disciples begged Jesus to send her away. Instead, however, Jesus indicated that this woman was not his responsibility because he only was sent to the lost sheep of Israel.

That did not stop the Canaanite woman. She knelt down before Jesus and pleaded, "Lord help me!" Then, Jesus made a remark, which remains a puzzle today.

"It is not right to take bread from the children and throw it to the dogs." The woman was equal to the challenge. She replied, "Yes Lord, but the dogs do eat the crumbs that fall off their master's table." Jesus acknowledged her faith and said, "Woman, great is your faith. Be it unto you as you wish." The recorder added, "Her daughter was healed that same hour." (Matthew 15:21–28; writer's own translation)

Faith must not be taken for granted. It requires determination and persistence, and persistence in faith will be rewarded. Above all, faith requires extreme humility. This woman did not mind being compared to dogs, just as long as her daughter was helped. The Canaanite woman did not ask for a whole meal, just for some crumbs. Even the crumbs of the Lord are sufficient for our healing and our needs. What, then, was so great in this woman's faith? It appears to be that even a crumb from the Lord was enough to free her daughter from the mental oppression of the demons. It is this writer's conviction that Jesus deliberately traveled to that region to meet this woman, so that Jesus could teach his followers the real meaning of little faith.

Faith Can Do Things That Count Much

Jesus was an unwelcome guest in Simon's home, a Pharisee. This incident, however, allowed a woman of ill repute to enter Simon's home, and she dishonored Jesus by wetting his feet with tears, wiping them with her hair, and anointing Jesus's feet with costly ointment. In Simon's mind, Jesus could not be a prophet and allow such a person to touch him.

And Jesus answering said to him, "Simon, I have something to say to you." And he answered, "What is it, Teacher?" And Jesus continued, "A certain creditor had two debtors; one owed five hundred denarii, and the other fifty. When they could not pay, he forgave them both. Now which of them will love him more?" Simon answered, "The one, I suppose, to whom he forgave more." And Jesus said to him, "You have judged rightly." Then turning toward the woman he said to Simon, "Do you see this woman? I entered your house, you gave me no water for my feet, but she has wet my feet with her tears and wiped them with her hair. You gave me no kiss, but from the time I came in she has not ceased to kiss my feet. You did not anoint my head with oil, but she has anointed my feet with ointment. Therefore I tell you, her sins, which are many, are forgiven, for she loved much; but he who is forgiven little, loves little. And he said to her, "Your sins are forgiven." Then those who were at table with him began to say among themselves, "Who is this, who even forgives sins?" And he said to the woman, "Your faith has saved you; go in peace." (Luke 7:40–50)

On the way to Jerusalem Jesus was passing along between Samaria and Galilee. And as he entered a village, he was met by ten lepers, who stood at a distance and lifted up their voices and said, "Jesus, Master, have mercy on us." When he saw them he said to them, "Go and show yourselves to the priests." And as they went they were cleansed. Then one of them, when he saw that he was healed, turned back, praising God with a loud voice; and he fell on his face at Jesus' feet, giving him thanks. Now he was a Samaritan. Then Jesus said, "Were not ten cleansed? Where are the nine? Was no one found to return and give praise to God except this foreigner?" And he said to the one, "Rise and go your way; your faith has made you well." (Luke 17:11–19)

And while Jesus was at Bethany in the house of Simon the leper, as he sat at table, a woman came with an alabaster jar of ointment of pure nard, very costly, and she broke the jar and poured it over his (Jesus') head. But there were some who said to themselves indignantly, "Why was the ointment thus wasted? For this ointment might have been sold for more than three hundred denarii, and given to the poor." And they reproached her. But Jesus said. "Let her alone; why do you trouble her? She has done a beautiful thing to me. For you always have the poor with you, and whenever you will, you can do good to them; but you will not always have me. She has done what she could; she has anointed my body beforehand for burying. And truly, I say to you, wherever the gospel is preached in the whole world, what she has done will be told in memory of her." (Mark 14:3–9)

THESE EXAMPLES HAVE HELPED ME IN MY JOURNEY OF GRACE

All of these incidents and lessons are based on two things Jesus emphasized:

"He who is faithful in very little is faithful also in much; and he who is dishonest in very little is dishonest also in much. If then you have not been faithful in the unrighteous mammon, who will trust you with the true riches? And if you have not been faithful in that which is another's, who will give you that which is your own? No servant can serve two masters; for either he will hate the one and love the other, or he will be devoted to the one and despise the other. You cannot serve God and mammon." (Luke 16:10–13)

And one of the scribes came up and heard them disputing with one another, and seeing that Jesus answered them well, asked him, "Which commandment is the first of all?" Jesus answered, "The first is, 'Hear, O Israel: The Lord our God, the Lord is one; and you shall love the Lord your God with all your heart, and with all your soul, and with all your mind, and with all your strength.' The second is this, 'You shall love your neighbor as yourself.' There is no other commandment greater than these." And the scribe said to him, "You are right, Teacher; you have truly said that he is one, and there is no other but he; and to love him with all the heart, and with all the understanding, and with all the strength, and to love one's neighbor as oneself, is much more that all whole burnt offerings and sacrifices." And when Jesus saw that he answered wisely, he said to him, "You are not far from the kingdom of God." (Mark 12:28–34)

In this life and in this world, I must mold my faith to serve and treat others as I want to be served and treated. It is not my faith that puts me close to God but what I do for others (Matthew 25:40). In fact, my service can gain respect from saints and sinners. We are in the world. "Behold, I send you out as sheep in the midst of wolves; so be wise as serpents and innocent as doves" (Matthew 10:16). We need to learn from this parable of Jesus:

"There was a rich man who had a steward, and charges were brought to him that this man was wasting his goods. And he called him and said to him, 'What is this that I hear about you? Turn in the account of your stewardship, for you can no longer be steward.' And the steward said to himself, 'What shall I do, since my master is taking the stewardship away from me? I am not strong enough to dig, and I am ashamed to beg. I have decided what to do, so that people may receive me into their houses when I am put out of the stewardship.' So, summoning his master's debtors one by one, he said to the first, 'How much do you owe my master?' He said, 'A hundred measures of oil.' And he said to him, 'Take your bill, and sit down quickly and write fifty.' Then he said to another, 'And how much do you owe?' He said, 'A hundred measures of wheat.' He said to him, 'Take your bill, and write eighty.' The master commended the dishonest steward for his prudence; for the sons of this world are wiser in their own generation than the sons of light. And I tell you, make friends for yourselves by means of unrighteous mammon, so that when it fails they may receive you into the eternal habitations." (Luke 16:1b–9)

SUMMARY

- Humankind must partner with the Spirit of God to build and maintain faith in ourselves before we can be of any use to anyone else.
- Fear is the product of our doubts, and our faith is there to counter fear so that our faith can increase.
- Faith and forgiveness help us clear our consciences and calm our eternal souls (Matthew 6:12–15).
- If we don't forgive, we live with our guilt.
- Faith requires determination, persistence, and extreme humility.
- We must mold our faith to serve others as we want to be served and treated (Matthew 25:40).

CHAPTER 29

HOW DID I KEEP BELIEVING?

JANUARY 24, 2021

In reviewing my life, I see that prayer and faith illuminated my journey. There were many times when my faith was smaller than a mustard seed, and the hurdles were insurmountable, but Jesus, who promised to be with me, strengthened my little faith, which kept me moving past the unexpected gigantic problems (Philippians 4:13). At least, that was what I was led to believe.

My accident became a plausible example for faith to go into action and restore me to my former physical condition. All I had to do was believe, and Jesus would restore me. When things did not happen, I was dismissed as an unbeliever and as a person with insufficient faith. Jesus had not turned me into a superman with divine powers to accommodate misguided earthlings like me. I was too blind to see that I had become a profound miracle of faith that overcame the impossible for a human being. Jesus, my Lord and your Lord, was answering prayer after prayer, while I continued to endure and even improve my circumstances in this world. I was experiencing what the apostle Paul experienced, only I was not aware of it.

But I refrain from it, so that no one may think more of me than he sees in me or hears from me. And to keep me from being too elated by the abundance of revelations, a thorn was given me in the flesh, a message of Satan, to harass me, to keep me from being too elated. Three times

I besought the Lord about this, that it should leave me; but he said to me, "My grace is sufficient for you, for my power is made perfect in weakness." I will all the more gladly boast of my weakness, that the power of Christ may rest upon me. For the sake of Christ, then, I am content with weakness, insults, hardships, persecutions, and calamities; For when I am weak, then I am strong. (2 Corinthians 12:6b–10)

MY FAITH RESTRAINED ME FROM
USING MY INJURIES FOR GAIN

It took ten years for many people to bring me back physically, mentally, and spiritually. In addition to healing my body, I coped with English and schooling to qualify for college and seminary. It was in my second year in seminary that I braved myself to ask a young lady whether she would consider going out with me. She presumed that I meant marriage and promptly announced that we were getting engaged, and so, we did. Nine months later, we were married, and that is now over sixty years ago.

Especially after our marriage, I did not feel right in using my injuries as means to attract people to the kingdom of God. To enlighten people of their need to prepare for salvation, I completely relied on my understanding of the Gospels. Now that I am no longer able to stand in a pulpit and have you look at me, I dare to challenge you with my experience and insight to follow the Lord yourself, not at the apron strings of someone else. I recommend that you ascertain everything you hear and read with Jesus, the only authority on our redemption.

Far too many of us have taken liberties on grace alone as the means of our salvation. In order to qualify for receiving grace, I only have tried to point out some things that we need. While I was waiting for God's grace to fill me, I remained empty—until I met another traveler on the narrow road who showed me how to plant a tiny seed of grace in my heart and spirit, and let it grow large enough that I, too, could share grace with others on the narrow road. I had yet to learn that for God to distribute grace, God has to use a human being, filled with grace, to pass it on to other human beings.

God is Spirit, and so is Jesus, the Christ. Now, the only way the Three-in-One functions in the world is through Spirit-filled human beings. While I was traveling on the narrow road, grace did not exempt me from earthly trials and tribulations. These trials and tribulations, however, were enough for fellow travelers who urged me on, and most of them were equipped to help me deal with myself and with my problems (Galatians 6:1–5). I met many wonderful people, and I did not ask them whether they were of a similar faith because their deeds and sacrifices for me profoundly humbled me (Matthew 25:34–40).

DIFFICULT TIMES

Perhaps the most difficult time in my life was when an ultrasound revealed that Benjamin, one of our grandchildren, was internally totally deformed. I begged the Lord not to let him live as handicapped, as I had to. Against all the prayers and wishes of my family, the Lord did set our little boy free. It was the hardest thing I have ever asked the Lord to do for the precious little boy, and not for me. And it was prayer that gave me the wings of understanding why God answers those prayers that will not hurt us.

Our grandson was not the first to be with the Lord. While living in a refugee camp in Germany, I was ten years old when my baby sister and fifteen other babies were taken to the cemetery on the same day. And I was fifteen years old when I watched my ten-year-old brother, who was hit by a truck, die in my arms, while looking at me with his big eyes and smiling. I buried both of my parents in their nineties, lost another brother fifteen years younger than I when I turned eighty-nine, and another sister thirteen years younger when I was ninety. In addition to living with a major disability, I also had heart problems and painful frozen muscles. I had to carry a soft pillow for some time so I could sit, and I also have cancer hanging over my head since. The cancer was discovered, fully grown, to 129 PSA twenty-three years ago.

Looking back at some of these difficult times, it seems impossible that I carried these burdens alone. Like the apostle Paul, I had a thorn in my flesh (2 Corinthians 12:7), but I also had the Lord keeping Satan from crushing me with his temptations (1 Corinthians 19:13). The promise of Jesus was very real during such times:

And if the Lord had not shortened the days, no human being would be saved. For the sake of the elect, whom he chose, he shortened the days (Mark 13:20).

HOW MUCH IMPACT DID JESUS HAVE ON MY FAITH?

I had the desire to be like Jesus, but Jesus wanted me to be like me, merely human. The New Testament writers tried to elevate Jesus above human abilities and powers, but Jesus refused to use them while he was a man. Instead, Jesus empowered people with faith to perform miracles, and people who had some faith were healed and could walk and carry their stretchers. At least, that was what I heard and also believed, but I certainly did not have a faith that could instantly raise me up.

At the time of my accident, I was put in the complete care of skillful people who did everything humanly possible to help me recover, but they left the reconstruction of my body to a skin specialist and my healing to the Lord and to me. At this time, it also became apparent to me that I could never be put back together as I was before and that I had to learn to live with my new self. Overnight, I began to worry how I could make a living in my handicapped condition. A minister resolved my dilemma by urging me to embark on being a servant of Christ in God's kingdom. My decision to follow the clergyman's advice freed my spirit from my misery and endowed me with a reason to live. I was going to work for Jesus, and peace entered my heart that I had never known existed.

Toronto would become a world metropolis and the center of learning, where universities and seminaries cooperated in advanced education and where I would earn a doctor of theology degree eighteen years later. After my hospital days, there was no study available for me to get into a college. I joined a church, and the pastor knew of a Bible school in Edmonton, Alberta, that had a licensed department from the province, where adults could take subjects and qualify for higher education. The congregations of the churches I attended in Toronto were quite conservative-mannered believers. Even the largest Evangelical, mission-minded congregation was spellbound by their minister but not with emotions. The people in

Edmonton were mostly immigrants like myself, who had lost everything they had, including loved ones, and were emotionally charged. They experienced all kinds of miracles and had revelations they believed came from the Lord. I, of course, did not have that gift. While I attended chapel, I, too, tried to come up with a revelation, but the spirit in me said, *Sit down. I did not speak to you.* I had heard that voice when I was drowning and again when I was being consumed by fire. *You are lost!* I knew exactly what these words meant, and I stopped loving the world and began loving the Lord.

I had yet to meet someone who really could explain to me why I did not feel saved or freed from my guilt feelings. So far, all I'd heard and was taught was that I had to repent and feel sorry for my sins, and Christ would take care of everything. Only the grace of God could save me from my total human depravity. Nothing in me was good enough to be worth saving.

An evangelist was invited to hold a large outdoor tent meeting, and he was an expert on roasting sinners over the fires of hell. He ignited my guilt, and it began to consume me. I consulted the experts, but all they said was, "Pray, brother, pray!" I took that guilt home to Winnipeg for the summer. My mother's boarder took me to his friend, who felt the need to explain to us what Jesus meant by repentance. While he spoke, guilt began to leave my tortured soul, and I knew what I had to do—and it became the path I followed into my nineties.

WHAT PRECISELY DID JESUS DO AND TEACH?

Salvation is a human act. It is a path of recovery, restoration, reconciliation, reparation, restitution, and many other things that I carelessly incurred on my journey. Even when I began my new life as a Christian, I was saying things and doing things that were unbecoming of a follower of Jesus. In fact, I took for granted that my careless liberties were covered by the redemptive work of Christ (1 Corinthians 8:8–13; 10:23–11:1). Even the powerful chapter on grace in Ephesians 2:10 has a payback for what Christ has done for me and you, and it is similar to what Paul the apostle was to face (Acts 9:15–16). Thus, that stranger who had us over for lunch on a Sunday after church service during the summer of 1954 sent me back to do what Jesus commanded, and that brought peace into my heart and conscience. Whatever I could and when I remembered, I went to people and apologized and begged to be forgiven. I wrote letters of apology and forgiveness, and I included money where I had taken some wood from the forest to heat our stove for a meal without permission. While I was doing my reconstruction on myself, my heart began to rejoice. This process of healing my soul has continued into my ninetieth year. One of my strongest supporters for my reconstruction and redemption was the man who believed that he was saved by grace alone. Salvation, if it is not cared for like a plant or a fig tree, will wither and die (Ephesians 4:1–5:20; Mark 11:12–14, 20–25; Philippians 2:12).

Being a disciple of Jesus is a busy, hard, and dangerous life. There are many believers, but not everyone is or can be a disciple. The disciples became the apostles Jesus sent out into the world as witnesses of Christ and God's kingdom. But before they could do this, they needed a solid base of believers to support the apostles in the world. Jesus promised his disciples that would happen, and it did happen on Pentecost. The Holy Spirit delivered thousands of witnesses, which made it possible for the apostles to go into the world and make more disciples (Acts 1:1–8; 2:1–47; Matthew 28:16–2). That is when the believers in Jerusalem sent their apostles to Samaria, Antioch, and other places. And that was when the first Christians in Antioch authorized Paul, Barnabas, John Mark, and Silas to spread the kingdom of heaven in the Roman Empire and outside (Acts 13:2, 13; 15:36–41). In our time, pastors, teachers, and Christian leaders are the disciples in the process of becoming Jesus's apostles. And what must they face?

CAN MY FAITH KEEP UP WITH JESUS'S DEMANDS?

Then Jesus told his disciples, "If any man would come after me, let him deny himself and take up his cross and follow me. For whoever would save his life will lose it, and whoever loses his life for my snake will find it. For what will it profit a man, if he gains the whole world and forfeits his life? Or what shall a man give in return for his life? For the Son of man is to come with his angels in the glory of his Father, and then he will repay every man for what he has done. Truly, I say to you, there are some standing here who will not taste death before they see the Son of man coming in his kingdom." (Matthew 16:24–28)

"Whoever does not bear his own cross and come after me, cannot be my disciple. For which of you, desiring to build a tower, does not first sit down and count the cost, whether he has enough to complete it? Otherwise, when he has laid a foundation, and is not able to finish, all who see it begin to mock him, saying, 'This man began to build, and was not able to finish.' Or what king, going to encounter another king in war, will not sit down first and take counsel whether he is able with ten thousand to meet him who comes against him with twenty thousand? And if not, while the other is yet a great way off, he sends an embassy and asks terms of peace. So therefore, whoever of you does not renounce all that he has cannot be my disciple." (Luke 14:27–33)

"Behold, I send you out as sheep in the midst of wolves; so be wise as serpents and innocent as doves. Beware of men; for they will deliver you up to councils, and flog you in their synagogues, and you will be dragged before governors and kings for my sake, to bear testimony before them and the Gentiles. When they deliver you up, do not be anxious how you are to speak or what you are to say; for what you are to say will be given to you in that hour; for it is not you who speaks, but the Spirit of your Father speaking through you. Brother will deliver up brother to death, and the father his child, and children will rise against their parents and have them put to death; and you will be hated by all for my name's sake. But he who endures to the end will be saved. When they persecute you in one town, flee to the next; for truly, I say to you, you will not have gone through all the towns of Israel, before the Son of man comes. A disciple is not above his teacher, nor a servant above his master; it is enough for the disciple to be like his teacher, and the servant like his master. If they have called the master of the household Beelzebul, how much more will they malign those of his household." (Matthew 10:16–25)

Friend, saint or sinner, what kind of a world do we live in now?

SUMMARY

- Prayer and faith illuminate our journeys.
- Jesus alone is the only authority of our salvation and redemption.
- It is our prayers that give us the wings to understand why God does or does not answer our prayers.
- Jesus refused to be elevated above human abilities and powers while he was a man.
- Jesus empowered people with faith to perform miracles, and people who had some faith were healed.
- Jesus taught that salvation is a human act, and it requires a path of recovery, restoration, reconciliation, reparation, restitution, and many other things that we incur on our journeys (Mark 11:12–14, 20–25).
- Being a disciple of Jesus is a busy, hard, and dangerous life (Matthew 10:16–25).

CHAPTER 30

The Apostles' Manual

January 31, 2021

Jesus delivered the Sermon on the Mount verbally, in person, to his disciples, whom he had appointed as apostles to spread the good news of the kingdom of God. According to John Mark, Jesus went up into the hills to pray, where he called his disciples to be with him, and then he appointed them as his apostles. According to Matthew, it was on a mountain where Jesus showed his apostles what they had to do to become a blessing to themselves and to their fellow human beings. Ten men were Galileans, one was a Canaanite, and only one was a Jew and a traitor.

> And Jesus went up into the hills, and called to him those whom he desired; and they came to him. And he appointed twelve to be with him, and to be sent out to preach and have authority to cast out demons: Simon whom he surnamed Peter; James the son of Zebedee and John the brother of James, whom he surnamed Boanerges, that is, sons of thunder; Andrew, and Philip, and Bartholomew, and Matthew, and Thomas, and James the son of Alphaeus, and Thaddaeus, and Simon the Cananaean, and Judas Iscariot, who betrayed Jesus. (Mark 3:13–19)

> Seeing the crowds, Jesus went up on the mountain, and when he sat down his disciples came to him. And he

opened his mouth and taught them, saying: "Blessed are the poor in spirit, for theirs is the kingdom of heaven. Blessed are those who mourn, for they shall be comforted. Blessed are the meek, for they shall inherit the earth. Blessed are those who hunger and thirst for righteousness, for they shall be satisfied. Blessed are the merciful, for they shall obtain mercy. Blessed are the pure in heart, for they shall see God. Blessed are the peacemakers, for they shall be called sons of God. Blessed are those who are persecuted for righteousness' sake, for theirs is the kingdom of heaven. Blessed are you when men revile you and persecute you and utter all kinds of evil against you falsely on my account. Rejoice and be glad, for your reward is great in heaven, for so men persecuted the prophets who were before you." (Matthew 5:1–12)

WHAT WAS JESUS DOING FOR THE DISCIPLES?

Jesus was preparing the disciples to be the future leaders of his kingdom on earth. Jesus himself was sent to do his Father's will (John 4:34), and these twelve men would emulate Jesus (John 8:31), and so would all the future leaders of God's kingdom and the church of Jesus Christ (John 14:23–24). Jesus, in person and human form, was the way, the truth, and the life back to God (John 14:6–7). When Jesus returned to be with his Father, he sent the Holy Spirit to inhabit the disciples (John 14:26; Acts 1:8), and they became teachers of the way, the truth, and the life back to God. The same Holy Spirit moved through every generation, including ours, and made the leaders into vessels of the way, the truth, and the life back to God (John 17:13–26). For those leaders, who make disciples, the Spirit of God the Father, and of the Son, and the Holy Spirit are with them while they serve here on earth (Matthew 28:16–20).

"Jesus, the author and finisher of man's faith" (Hebrew 12:2), as he promised (John 14:25–26), gave the disciples verbal instruction, for the Holy Spirit to verify, of what they had to become to be the bearers of the way, the truth, and the life (John 14:26).

ALL THE INGREDIENTS

|||||||||||||||||||||||||||||||||||||||

The Sermon on the Mount has all the ingredients the church leaders need to lead their people into the kingdom and into heaven. The Holy Spirit keeps transferring the grace and truth that the Son of God brought down to earth (John 1:17) into leaders, who faithfully live out and pass on the content of the Sermon on the Mount (Matthew 5:20). There is no doubt who the recipients and the executors of the Sermon on the Mount were. Jesus looked straight at the twelve and delivered the instructions to them. The Holy Spirit guided Jesus's witnesses to write the instructions down. These instructions have become an international and universal guide for the benefit of all men and women.

"You are the salt of the earth; but if the salt has lost its taste, how can its saltiness be restored? It is no longer good for anything except to be thrown out and trodden under foot by men. You are the light of the world. A city set on a hill cannot be hid. Nor do men light a lamp and put it under a bushel, but on a stand, and it gives light to all in the house. Let your light so shine before men, that they may see your good works and give glory to your father who is in heaven. Think not that I have come to abolish the law and the prophets; I have come not to abolish them but to fulfill them. For truly, I say to you, till heaven and earth pass away, not an iota, not a dot, will pass from the law until all is accomplished. Whoever then relaxes one of the least of these commandments and teaches men so, shall be called least in the kingdom of heaven; but he who does them and teaches them shall be called great in the kingdom of heaven. For I tell you, unless your righteousness exceeds that of the scribes and Pharisees, you will never enter the kingdom of heaven." (Matthew 5:13–20)

THE TEN COMMANDMENTS ARE NOT DEAD

‖‖‖‖‖‖‖‖‖‖‖‖‖‖‖‖‖‖‖‖‖‖‖‖‖‖‖‖‖‖‖

The statement of Paul in Romans 10:4—"For Christ is the end of the law"—is consistent with Paul's belief in Romans 7:12—"So the law is holy, and the commandment is holy and just and good." And it must have alarmed the Jewish Christian editors of the Gospel of Matthew to use Jesus's authority to prioritize the law. In my own mind, this was another human attempt to lessen the value of the law and give more credence to faith, which can save a person without works.

The Greek word *telos* means to reach a goal, a high point, and not fizzle out as a failed project. The idea that faith replaced the law did not fly with Jesus. Hence, Romans 10:4 should read, "Christ is the fulfillment of the law." Now, instead of lessening or softening the demands of the law, Jesus increased the demands of the law and showed how the law could serve his disciples and apostles. That was what the law did for me for my ninety years. The Sermon on the Mount is the best guide human beings can have in this life. Jesus laid out some helpful examples for his successors.

> "You have heard that it was said to the men of old, 'You shall not kill; and whoever kills shall be liable for judgment.' But I say to you that every one who is angry with his brother shall be liable to judgment; whoever insults his brother shall be liable to the council, and whoever says, 'You fool!' shall be liable to the hell of fire. So if you are offering your gift at the altar, and there remember that your brother has something against you, leave your gift there before the altar and go; first be reconciled to your brother, and then come and offer your gift. Make friends quickly with your accuser, while you are going with him to court, lest your accuser hand you over to the judge, and the judge to the guard, and you be put in prison; truly, I say to you, you will never get out till you have paid the last penny. You have heard that it was said, 'You shall not commit adultery.' But I say to you that everyone who looks at a woman lustfully has already committed adultery with her in his heart. If your right eye causes you to sin, pluck it out and throw it

away; it is better that you lose one of your members than that your whole body be thrown into hell. And if your right hand causes you to sin, cut it off and throw it away; it is better that you lose one of your members than that your whole body go into hell. It was also said, 'Whoever divorces his wife, let him give her a certificate of divorce. But I say to you that everyone who divorces his wife, except on the ground of unchastity, makes her an adulteress; and whoever marries a divorced woman commits adultery. Again you have heard that it was said to the men of old, 'You shall not swear falsely, but shall perform to the Lord what you have sworn.' But I say to you, Do not swear at all, either by heaven, for it is the throne of God, or by the earth, for it is in his footstool, or by Jerusalem, for it is the city of the great King. And do not swear by your head, for you cannot make one hair white or black. Let what you say be simply 'Yes' or 'No'; anything more than this come from evil. You have heard that it was said, 'An eye for an eye and a tooth for a tooth.' But I say to you, Do not resist one who is evil. But if anyone strikes you on the right cheek, turn to him the other also; and if any one would sue you and take your coat, let him have your cloak as well; and if any one forces you to go one mile, go with him two miles. Give to him who begs from you, and do not refuse him who would borrow from you.

You have heard it said, 'You shall love your neighbor and hate your enemy.' But I say to you, Love your enemies and pray for those who persecute you, so that you may be sons of your Father who is in heaven; for he makes his sun rise on the evil and on the good, and sends rain on the just and on the unjust. For if you love those who love you, what reward have you? Do not even the tax collectors do the same? And if you salute only your brethren, what more are you doing than others? Do not even the Gentiles do the same? You, therefore, must be perfect, as your heavenly Father is perfect." (Matthew 5:21–48)

LEADERS MUST LEAVE A FAVORABLE IMPRESSION
||||||||||||||||||||||||||||||||||||

Act and behave in such a manner that we, the disciples of Christ, do not embarrass ourselves and shame our Lord Jesus Christ. Being in the flesh, I am subject to the law that helps me live in grace. Grace does not act outside the law. It is up to you and me to live in grace and to keep our sinning under control (Romans 6:12–19). In Matthew 6, Jesus gave his disciples a taste of what it means to live in grace and stay out of trouble. The Holy Spirit endorses these things through humankind's conscience. At least, that is how I feel I am led to do what Jesus commanded and taught:

> "Beware of practicing your piety before men in order to be seen by them; for then you will have no reward from your Father who is in heaven. Thus, when you give alms, sound no trumpet before you, as the hypocrites do in the synagogues and in the streets, that they may be praised by men. Truly, I say to you, they have received their reward. But when you give alms, do not let your left hand know what your right hand is doing so that your alms may be in secret; and your Father who sees in secret will reward you. And when you pray, you must not be like the hypocrites; for they love to stand and pray in the synagogues and at the street corners, they may be seen by men. Truly, I say to you, they have received their reward. But when you pray go into your room and shut the door and pray to your Father who is in secret; and your Father who sees in secret will reward you. And in praying do not heap up empty phrases as the Gentiles do; for they think that they will be heard for their many words. Do not be like them, for your Father knows what you need before you ask him. Pray then like this: Our Father who art in heaven, Hallowed be thy name. Thy kingdom come, Thy will be done, On earth as it is in heaven. Give us his day our daily bread; And forgive us our debts, As we forgive our debtors; And lead us not into temptation, But deliver us from evil. For

if you forgive men their trespasses, your heavenly Father also will forgive you; but if you do not forgive men their trespasses, neither will your Father forgive your trespasses. And when you fast, do not look dismal like the hypocrites, for they disfigure their faces that their fasting may not be seen by men. Truly, I say to you, they have their reward. But when you fast, anoint your head and wash your face, that your fasting may not be seen by men but by your Father who is in secret; and your Father who sees in secret will reward you. Do not lay up for yourselves treasures on earth, where moth and rust consume and where thieves break in and steal, but lay up for yourselves treasures in heaven, where neither moth nor rust consumes and where thieves do not break in and steal. For where your treasure is, there will your heart be also. The eye is the lamp of the body. So, if your eye is sound, your whole body will be full of light; but if your eye is not sound, your whole body will be full of darkness, how great is the darkness! No one can serve two masters; for either he will hate the one and love the other, or he will be devoted to the one and despise the other. You cannot serve God and mammon." (Matthew 6:1–24)

When Jesus had washed his disciple's feet, and taken off his garments, and resumed his place, he said to them, "Do you know what I have done to you? You call me Teacher and Lord; and you are right, for so I am. If I then, your Lord and Teacher, have washed your feet, you also ought to wash one another's feet. For I have given you an example, that you also should do as I have done to you. Truly, truly, I say to you, a servant is not greater than his master; nor is he who is sent greater than he who sent him. If you know these things, blessed are you if you do them." (John 13:12–17)

SUMMARY

- Jesus prepared the disciples to be the future leaders of his kingdom on earth.
- Jesus himself was sent to do his Father's will (John 4:34).
- Jesus, in person and human form, was the way, the truth, and the life back to God (John 14:6–7).
- When Jesus returned to his Father, he sent the Holy Spirit to inhabit the disciples (John 14:26), and they provided the way back to God. The same Holy Spirit has moved through every generation, including ours.
- Christ is the fulfillment of the law.
- The Sermon on the Mount is the best guide that humankind has in this life.

~

CHAPTER 31

THE APOSTLES'
MANUAL, PART II

The kingdom of God is too demanding. How, then, shall its servants live? Jesus promised that his Father would provide. The ministers and the full-time workers in the kingdom of God had no time to build nest eggs or hoard earthly treasures, which would fill their eyes and keep them from spreading the good news of Jesus Christ. A servant of Jesus Christ has to make friends with those who dispense the means of mammon and work part-time to supplement their ministry. One of the first things Jesus did was try to address the anxiety that the disciples had when they had given up their jobs for Christ. How were they to live without the means to feed themselves and their families? During and after World War II, my family—and millions of our people—agonized over sustenance, while facing starvation for years. Jesus's answer to his disciples became our only choice and that was that we had to live one day at the time. Our little faith helped us daily to find sustenance (Matthew 7:7–8).

> "Therefore I tell you, do not be anxious about your life,
> what you shall eat or what you shall drink, nor about your
> body, what you shall put on. Is not life more than food,
> and the body more than clothing? Look at the birds of
> the air: they neither sow nor reap nor gather into barns,

and yet your heavenly Father feeds them. Are you not of more value than they? And which of you by being anxious can add one cubit to his span of life? And why are you anxious about clothing? Consider the lilies of the field, how they grow; they neither toil nor spin; ye I tell you, even Solomon in all his glory was not arrayed like one of these. But if God so clothes the grass of the field, which today is alive and tomorrow is thrown into the oven, will he not much more clothe you, O men of little faith? Therefore do not be anxious saying, 'What shall we eat? What shall we drink? Or 'What shall we wear?' For the Gentiles seek all these things; and your heavenly Father knows that you need them all. But seek first his kingdom and his righteousness, and all these things shall be yours as well. Therefore do not be anxious about tomorrow, for tomorrow will be anxious for itself. Let the day's own trouble be sufficient for the day." (Matthew 6:25–34)

WHAT DID JESUS DO BEFORE HE BEGAN HIS MINISTRY?

Jesus did not leave his family and his adopted family stranded, as far too many people do in the world. He provided them with friends of means who could and did take them in when he had to leave. They did not just live on faith but also on friends.

In 1945, while we were homeless and destitute, we, too, lived by faith in strangers who were friendly toward us and helped us (Luke 16:9). What did Jesus say that those people who hurt their little ones should do? They should have a millstone put around their necks and drown in the sea (Mark 9:42; Luke 17:2; Matthew 18:6).

The evangelist Dr. Luke left us some hints. Jesus had eighteen years to make friends with people of means to prepare for the care of his followers. And Jesus told his disciples to make friends with mammon, for such a time when he would be taken from them (Luke 2:41–52; 16:9). Jesus's parents took Jesus to Jerusalem for twelve years, and it is unlikely that he did not long annually to see his Father's house. Jesus was very familiar with Jerusalem and, in particular, with the place of the upper room, where he sent his disciples to prepare to eat his last Passover meal. The place was built like a fortress and provided safe housing for Jesus's family, the apostles, and the disciples during his ordeal and afterward. The present owner was a wealthy widow with her son, John Mark. The Romans did not destroy the building, and a visitor from Rome sketched it in AD 135, when Jerusalem was no longer inhabitable.

The disciples stayed with Jesus while he served as the Christ, and they were provided for. The other believers, like Nicodemus, Joseph of Arimathea, and John Mark's family, were wealthy and supported Jesus and his ministry. John Mark, in his account of Jesus, added some women who supported Jesus and his disciples with sustenance.

Take note of the wife of Chuza, Herod's steward, and Mark's own family who provided a place where they stayed in Jerusalem, known as the upper room, which could accommodate many people (Mark 1:12–16; Luke 22:7–13; Acts 1:12–14). Herod had a court member named Manaen, who was a leader in the church of Antioch in Herod's district (Acts 13:1). Jesus also made friends like Lazarus and his sisters (John 11), Simon the leper (Mark 14:3), Zacchaeus (Luke 19:1–10), Cleopas (Luke 24:18), and no doubt others who could take in Jesus's orphans, for whom he well provided.

> Soon afterward Jesus went on through cities and villages, preaching and bringing the good news of the kingdom of God. And the twelve were with him, and also some women who had been healed of evil spirits and infirmities: Mary, called Magdalene, from whom seven demons had gone out, and Joanna, the wife of Chuza, Herod's steward, and Susanna, and many others, who provided for them out of their means. (Luke 8:1–3)

When Jesus left the disciples, the following occurred:

> They returned to Jerusalem from the mount called Olivet, which is near Jerusalem, a sabbath day journey away; and when they had entered, they went up to the upper room, where they were staying, Peter and John and James and Andrew, Philip and Thomas, Bartholomew and Matthew, James the son of Alphaeus and Simon the Zealot and

Judas the son of James. All these with one accord devoted themselves to prayer, together with the women and Mary the mother of Jesus, and with his brothers. (Acts 1:12–14)

Before Jesus was taken up, he gave these instructions:

> "But you shall receive power when the Holy Spirit has come upon you; and you shall be my witnesses in Jerusalem and in all Judea and Samaria and to the end of the earth." And when Jesus had said this, as they were looking on, he was lifted up, and a cloud took him out of their sight. And while they were gazing into heaven as he went, behold, two men stood by them in white robes, and said, "Men of Galilee, why do you stand looking into heaven? This Jesus, who was taken from you into heaven, will come in the same way as you saw him going into heaven." (Acts 1:8–11)

The disciples remembered that Jesus had made promises to come back and take them with him to heaven. So the heaven-bound people disposed of earthly holdings and formed a commune, ready to depart from earth.

> Now the company of those who believed were of one heart and soul, and no one said that any of the things which he possessed was his own, but they had everything in common. And with great power the apostles gave their testimony to the resurrection of the Lord Jesus, and great grace was upon them all. There was not a needy person among them, for as many as were possessors of lands or houses sold them, and brought the proceeds of what was sold and laid it at the apostle's feet; and distribution was made to each as any had need. Thus Joseph who was surnamed by the apostles Barnabas (which means, Son of encouragement), a Levite, a native of Cyprus, sold a field which belonged to him, and brought the money and laid it at the apostles' feet. (Acts 4:32–37)

JESUS DID MORE THAN PROVIDE WHAT WE NEED ON EARTH—JESUS PROMISED TO BE WITH US IN SPIRIT ALL THE TIME

|||||||||||||||||||||||||||||||||||||||||

Where is Jesus now? Most answers have been that he is seated at the right hand of God in heaven (Mark 14:62; Luke 22:69; Matthew 26:64). But what about the promise of being with the disciples and living with them and protecting them in the world? Personally, I, too, have been in the care of heaven, for it is humanly impossible that I would have survived for over ninety years. I have been a very costly follower of the Lord.

"And lo, I am with you always, to the close of the (your) age." (Matthew 28:20b)

"If you love me, you will keep my commandments. And I will pray the Father, and he will give you another Counselor, to be with you forever, even the Spirit of truth, whom the world cannot receive, because it neither sees him nor knows him; you know him, for he dwells with you, and will be in you. I will not leave you desolate; I will come to you. Yet a little while, and the world will see me no more, but you will see me; because I live, you will live also. In that day you will know that I am in my Father, and you in me, and I in you." (John 14:15–20)

Jesus answered him (Judas not Iscariot), "If a man loves me, he will keep my word, and my Father will love him, and we will come to him and make our home with him. He who does not love me does not keep my words; and the word which you hear is not mine but the Father's who sent me. These things I have spoken to you, while I am still with you. But the Counselor, the Holy Spirit, whom the Father will send in my name, he will teach you all things, and bring to your remembrance all that I have said to you." (John 14:23–26)

"I am praying for them; I am not praying for the world but for those whom thou hast given me, for they are thine; all mine are thine, and I am glorified in them. And now I am no more in the world (body), but they are in the world, and I am coming to thee. Holy Father, keep them in the name which thou hast given me, that they may be one as we are one. While I was with them, I kept them in thy name which thou hast given me; I have guarded them, and none of them is lost but the son of perdition, that the scripture might be fulfilled." (John 17:9–12)

Now Judas (Iscariot), who betrayed Jesus, also knew the place; for Jesus often met there with his disciples. So Judas, procuring a band of soldiers and some officers from the chief priests and Pharisees, went there with lanterns and torches and weapons. Then Jesus, knowing all that was to befall him, came forward and said to them, "Whom do you seek?" They answered him, "Jesus of Nazareth." Jesus said to them, "I am he." Judas, who betrayed him, was standing with them. When Jesus said to them, "I am he," they drew back and fell to the ground. And again he (Jesus) asked them, "Whom do you seek?" And they said, "Jesus of Nazareth." Jesus answered, "I told you that I am he; so, if you seek me, let these go." This was to fulfill the word which Jesus had spoken, "Of those whom thou gavest me I lost not one." (John 18:2–9)

"My sheep hear my voice, and I know them, and they follow me; and I give them eternal life, and they shall never perish, and no one shall snatch them out of my hand. My Father, who has given them to me, is greater than all, and no one is able to snatch them out of the Father's hand. I and the Father are one." (John 10:27–30)

"See that you do not despise (or abort) one of these little ones; for I tell you that in heaven their angels always behold the face of my Father who is in heaven. What do you think? If a man had a hundred sheep, and one of them has gone astray, does he not leave the ninety-nine on the mountains and go in search of the one that went astray? And if he finds it, truly, I say to you, he rejoices over it more than over the ninety-nine that never went astray. So it is not the will of my Father who is in heaven that one of these little ones should perish (robbed of the right to live)." (Matthew 18:10–14)

And they were bringing children to Jesus, that he might touch them; and the disciples rebuked the parents. But when Jesus saw it he was indignant, and said to them (and others), "Let the children come to me, do not hinder them; for to such belongs the kingdom of God. Truly I say to you, whoever does not receive the kingdom of God like a child shall not enter it." And he took them in his arms and blessed them, laying his hands upon them. (Mark 10:13–16)

There is no safer place for me and you than being in the arms of Jesus. His arms are full of love, grace, and forgiveness. But in this world, you and I have become his arms.

SUMMARY

- Jesus provided his family with friends of means who could take them in when he had to leave.
- Jesus told his disciples to make friends with mammon, for such a time when he would be taken from them (Luke 2:41–52; 16:9).
- The upper room was built like a fortress and provided safe housing for Jesus's family, the apostles, and the disciples.
- Jesus promised to be with us and live in us (John 14:15–20; 10:27–30).
- There is no safer place for us than being in the arms of Jesus.

CHAPTER 32

THE APOSTLES' MANUAL, PART III

Jesus concluded his instructions to his apostles with commands that would keep the apostles in his kingdom. Their position in the kingdom was not yet secure. Their righteousness had not measured up. It was still very much like the righteousness of the scribes and Pharisees (Matthew 5:20). In that sense, we, too, suffer from the same lack of righteousness that will keep us out of the kingdom of heaven.

In this world, I skated on thin ice, and when I stayed too long in one spot, I began to sink, like Peter. Most of the time, with my own mistakes, I created my sinkholes. My tongue, particularly, has judged me too many times, which I regret deeply. Jesus issued this warning:

> "I tell you, on the day of judgment men will render account for every careless word they utter; for by your words you will be justified, and by your words you will be condemned." (Matthew 12:36–37)

FIRST AND FOREMOST, AVOID JUDGING, FOR IT WILL COST US DEARLY

"Judge not, that you be not judged. For with the judgment you pronounce you will be judged, and the measure you give will be the measure you get. Why do you (I) see the speck that is in your (my) brother's eye, but not notice the log that is in your (mine) own eye? Or how can you say to your brother, 'Let me take the speck out of your eye,' when there is the log in your (my) own eye? You hypocrite, first take the log out of your (my) own eye, and then you will see clearly to take the speck out of your brother's eye." (Matthew 7:1–5)

"Judge not, and you will not be judged; condemn not, and you will not be condemned; forgive, and you will be forgiven; give, and it will be given to you; good measure, pressed down, shaken together, running over, will be put in your lap. For the measure you (I) give will be the measure you (I) get back." (Luke 6:37–38)

Do not be deceived; God is not mocked, for whatever a man sows, that he shall also reap. For he who sows to his own flesh will from the flesh reap corruption; but he who sows to the Spirit will from the Spirit reap eternal life. And let us not grow weary in well-doing, for in due season we shall reap, if we do not lose heart. So then, as we have opportunity, let us do good to all men, and especially to those who are of the household of faith. (Galatians 6:7–10)

He (Jesus) also told this parable to some who trusted in themselves that they were righteous and despised others: "Two men went up into the temple to pray, one a Pharisee and the other a tax collector. The Pharisee stood and prayed thus with himself, 'God, I thank thee that I am not like other men, extortioners, unjust, adulterers, or even like this tax collector. I fast twice a week, I give tithes of all that I get.' But the tax collector, standing far off, would not even lift up his eyes to heaven, but beat his breast, saying, 'God, be merciful to me, a sinner!' I tell you, this man went down to his house justified rather than the other; for every one who exalts himself will be humbled, but he who humbles himself will be exalted." (Luke 18:9–14)

The Spirit of Jesus the Christ shows us clearly that we have our hands full with ourselves while we work out our salvation with fear and trembling (Philippians 2:12).

SECOND, STOP DEMEANING OURSELVES

There are 802 million uses of the word *holy* in the world, and humankind tops the list as God's primary creation in his image and likeness, and with his Spirit (breath). God entrusted the world to us to manage! God gave us the ability to choose between right and wrong and the power to become whatever they want. Who, then, caused human beings to demean themselves but human beings themselves?

I began to form an opinion of myself and compared myself to others. When I began to read the Bible, I came across this idea: "For as he (a man) thinketh in his heart, so he is" (Proverbs 23:7 KJV).

At times, I discovered that I was down and at other times up but never at a total loss. Then, when I began attending church, I was told that all human beings are totally depraved and have no chance of self-redemption. I, too, endorsed that view until I wrote my doctoral thesis, and one examiner was very disturbed by my attitude of using 150 scholars to defend my view on Christ. He had no objection to my view of Christ, but why had I allowed my mind to be saturated by the thinking of others, which robbed me of my ability to be saturated by Christ myself? He sent me back to the scriptures to find out what they say and not to rely on what proof I needed to agree with someone else's view.

The examiner was right. I personally had to meet and study Christ! My dear friend, so must you! And when you meet Jesus, your Lord, you must also do what he said and what he commands to qualify for his kingdom. I know I am repeating myself, but woe unto me if I do not warn my fellow human beings of wrongdoing (Ezekiel 3:16–21; 1 Corinthians 9:16; 26–27). Our salvations are at risk if we do not work them out with fear and trembling (Philippians 2:12). It is I who sin and gather guilt, and it is I who expose my life to be trampled on by evil. It is in me where good or evil can dwell (Matthew 12:33–37; 15:19; Luke 6:45). It is you and I who will appear before the highest tribunal in the universe, and we have to answer for our actions and not for our faith on Judgment Day (2 Corinthians 5:16; Revelation 20:11–15). To avoid eternal internment, let us do what Jesus and his Spirit tell us that we must do. Humankind is not a wimp; neither am I. We bear our Creator's image and his likeness, and we house his Spirit (Genesis 1:26; 2:7). Let us use the power, as children of God, to resist evil (John 1:12).

> "Do not give to dogs what is holy; and do not throw your pearls before swine, lest they trample them under foot and turn to attack you." (Matthew 7:6)

> Yet thou has made him little less than God, and dost crown him with glory and honor. Thou hast given him dominion over the works of thy hands; thou hast put all things under his feet. (Psalm 8:5–6; John 10:34)

> But you are a chosen race, a royal priesthood, a holy nation, God's own people, that you may declare the wonderful deeds of him who called you out of darkness into his marvelous light. (1 Peter 2:9; Exodus 19:6; Revelation 1:6)

> Do you not know that your body is the temple of the Holy Spirit within you, which you have from God? You are not your own; you were bought with a price. So glorify God in your body. (1 Corinthians 6:19–20)

> Do not be mismated with unbelievers. For what partnership have righteousness and iniquity? What accord has Christ with Belial? Or what has a believer in common with an unbeliever? What agreement has the temple of God with idols? For we are the temple of the living God; as God said, "I will live in them and move among them, and I will be their God, and they shall be my people. Therefore come out from them, and be separate from

them, says the Lord. and touch nothing unclean; then I will welcome you, and I will be a Father to you, and you shall be my sons and daughters, says the Lord Almighty." (2 Corinthians 6:14–18)

Let not sin therefore reign in your mortal bodies, to make you obey their passions. Do not yield your members to sin as instruments of wickedness, but yield yourselves to God as men who have been brought from death to life, and your members to God as instruments of righteousness. For sin will have no dominion over you, since you are not under the law but under grace. (Romans 6:12–14)

THE LORD EXPECTS TO HEAR FROM US IN OUR PRAYERS

Jesus said that "[we] ought always to pray and not lose heart" (Luke 18:1). Prayer is an endless pleading and seeking and doing what we can. We must not stop asking, seeking, and knocking! And we must not demand that God give us what is possible to human beings. Jesus did not turn stones into bread. Jesus did not jump off a steeple to impress people. And Jesus did not bow for fame that dishonors God (Matthew 4:1–11; Luke 4:1–13). God himself has limits! And God confined them for us to the perimeter of his kingdom on earth. He will not give us a stone when we need bread or a serpent when we need a fish.

Physically, I was born twice—as an infant and then at the age of twenty-one, when a fire returned me to an infant state. Thus, for over a year, I had to be cared for like a helpless baby. The Lord did not let me die because I had yet to work in his vineyard. He did not have his servants restore me to my former looks. The Lord did not give me back the full use of my hands, but the Lord allowed me to become sufficiently physically and mentally restored so I could serve in God's kingdom.

From the day I set my mind on becoming a minister of his gospel, the Lord answered all my prayers within the perimeter of his kingdom. My dream was to obtain the best education so that I could honor my Lord with preaching, teaching, authoring, and blogging. I also wished for a lovely young lady to share my life, and the Lord granted my wish, which now has lasted over sixty years. He has blessed us with three outstanding sons and their lovely and talented wives, who blessed us with eight wonderful grandchildren. We had hoped for nine, but the Lord took home one grandson in infancy. Yes, the Lord was good to us, and his mercy has endured for me for over ninety years, thus far.

"Ask, and it will be given you; seek, and you will find; knock and it will be opened to you. For every one who asks receives, and he who seeks finds, and him who knocks it will be opened. Or what man of you, if his son asks him for bread, will give him a stone? Or if he asks for a fish, will he give him a serpent? If you then, who are evil, know how to give good gifts to your children, how much more will your heavenly Father who is in heaven give good things to those who ask him? So whatever you wish that men would do to you, do so to them; for this is the law and the prophets." (Matthew 7:7–12)

WHAT ARE WE TO PRAY FOR?

Jesus was very concise: "Thy kingdom come, Thy will be done, On earth as it is in heaven" (Matthew 6:10).

To get in and build the kingdom or do what God wills, the manual tells us what we must do and whom we must follow.

"Enter by the narrow gate; for the gate is wide and the way is easy, that leads to destruction, and those who enter by it are many. For the gate is narrow and the way is hard, that leads to life, and those who find it are few. Beware of the prophets, who come to you in sheep's clothing but inwardly are ravenous wolves. You will know them by their fruits. Are grapes gathered from thorns, or figs from thistles? So, every sound tree bears good fruit, but the bad tree bears evil fruit. A sound tree cannot bear evil fruit, nor can a bad tree bear good fruit. Every tree that does not bear good fruit is cut down and thrown into the fire. Thus you will know them by their fruits. Not everyone who says to me, 'Lord, Lord,' shall enter the kingdom of heaven, but he who does the will of my Father who is in heaven. On that day many will say to me, 'Lord, Lord, did we not prophesy in your name, and cast out demons in your name, and do many mighty works in your name?' Then I will declare to them, 'I never knew you; depart from me, you evil-doers.'" (Matthew 7:13–23)

WHAT MUST WE DO TO QUALIFY FOR OUR TRIP INTO THE KINGDOM?

Everyone who does not follow the manual or the Sermon on the Mount will forfeit his or her place in the kingdom of heaven, here on earth. We begin to live for God here on earth, the God of those who are still alive and not dead (Luke 20:38; Mark 12:27; Acts 17:28). The dead cannot praise God (Psalm 115:17). Without a human body, no one can serve God or humankind. A sinful and wicked body is also mentally and spiritually unable to honor God and humankind. Such a person can be reborn by giving up his or her sinful life, living for Christ and starting a new life, and praising the Lord. Particularly those who were predestined to serve in God's kingdom, Christ will snatch from death and raise them up to live for the praise and honor of God (John 5:24). I consider myself as having been snatched from death several times and given an extended time to live in grace and share it with my fellow human beings. It is not God's will that anyone should perish (Matthew 18:14).

"Every one then who hears these words of mine and does them will be like a wise man who built his house upon the rock; and the rain fell, and the floods came, and the winds blew and beat upon that house, but it did not fall, because it had been founded on the rock. And every one who hears these words of mine and does not do them will be like a foolish man who built his house upon sand; and the rain fell, and the floods came; and the winds blew and beat against that house, and it fell; and great was the fall of it." (Matthew 7:24–27; Luke 6:46–49)

To conclude this reminder about the usefulness of the Apostles' Manual and the Sermon on the Mount, I am reminded of the Parable of the Rich Man and Lazarus. The rich man begged Abraham to send one from the dead to stop his brothers from following him. Abraham reminded him that they had Moses, and the prophets who could save them (Luke 16:19–31). But we have one who has returned from the dead and left us his direction in person. What will the judge tell those who do not heed Jesus's words?

Therefore we must pay closer attention to what we have heard (read), lest we drift away from it (salvation). For if the message declared by angels was valid and every transgression or disobedience received a just retribution, how shall we escape if we neglect such a great salvation? (Hebrews 2:1–3a; 10:26–31)

SUMMARY

- Avoid judging, for it will cost you dearly.
- Stop demeaning yourself.
- God entrusted humankind to manage the world.
- When we meet Jesus, we must also do what he says and commands to qualify for his kingdom.
- Humankind bears our Creator's image and his likeness, and we house his Spirit (Genesis 1:26; 2:7).
- Humankind needs to use the Holy Spirit to become children of God to resist evil.
- Jesus said, "Man must always pray and not lose heart" (Luke 18:1).
- If humankind does not follow the Sermon on the Mount, they will forfeit their place.

CHAPTER 33

WHAT IS A CHRISTIAN DOING IN THIS WORLD?

FEBRUARY 21, 2021

The Holy Spirit had come to keep the apostles and their followers in the world and not take them out of the world (John 17:15–19). They were to be kingdom builders and not space travelers. Their memories, however, of what Jesus had said that they were to do were suppressed by their endeavor to depart from this world in a hurry. It was after their commonality failed that they let the Holy Spirit help them recall Jesus's charge and Jesus's teachings. The Apostles' Manual or the Sermon on the Mount are the words of Jesus, the Son of God, and Son of God the Father (John 6:63; 14:24). They summarize everything we need in this world to represent Jesus, our Lord, and build the kingdom of heaven on earth. That is why spirit-filled people speak of the Sermon on the Mount as being kingdom ethics. Ethics of the world and not ethics of heaven, where we no longer need a manual to live by.

THE COMMONALITY WAS NOT LIKE THE KINGDOM OF GOD

The first Christians in Jerusalem were led by their faith and not by a manual, but their community was bound for heaven. God's intentions and schedule did not conform to humankind's hope and prayers (Mark

13:32–37; Acts 1:7; Deuteronomy 18:20–22). The two witnesses, regarding the return of Jesus, gave the apostles presumptuous hope, contradicting Jesus's request to keep the apostles and their disciples as witnesses in the world (John 17:15–21; Matthew 28:16–20; Acts 1:8). Obviously, their faith was unrealistic and misdirected, a tendency that we humans all have—hoping and praying for things that God, who is all knowing, cannot give to us. Much that we wish for and desire may cause more harm than we can possibly bear or endure (Matthew 6:8). The fact that we end up doing so much that does not end in good faith but in fate is evidence that God does not interfere in our choices. It is the Lord's wish and will that humankind will seek first his kingdom and his righteousness (Matthew 6:33). It is up to humankind, however, as to whether they will do the will of the Lord (Matthew 7:21; Luke 6:46). Even the apostles, who were to leave Jerusalem after the Holy Spirit arrived, did not leave when the first persecution scattered all the followers of Jesus except the apostles (Acts 8:1).

RUNNING INTO TROUBLE

The idea of having all things in common ran into trouble when there were no more owners who parted with their properties, and those who had misgivings about giving it all to the apostles were treated severely with death (Acts 5:1–11). That was presumed to be the work of the Holy Spirit. The action of Peter frightened the new believers, and therefore, it kept others from joining, and it also drained the supply of sustenance. With the shortage of food and other necessary things, the Gentile widows were not receiving equal treatment from the Jewish distributors. So, seven men were selected to alleviate the disparity (Acts 6).

Instead of appealing for help to a huge crowd of interested prospects in the Jesus's way movement, the hyper-zealous Stephen hammered the people with guilt, which turned the crowd against him and Jesus's followers. Stephen was stoned, and the converts of Christ were scattered over Judea and Samaria (Acts 7–8). The Holy Spirit led these scattered converts of Jesus to spread the good news. The apostles did not leave Jerusalem for a very astute reason (Acts 8:1).

COMMONALITY FAILED, MISSION IGNITED

The first attempt at a commonality of life failed, but the mission of Christ was ignited, and the calculated decision of the apostles to stay in Jerusalem paid off. A huge influx of people from all over the Roman Empire came to learn about the man who was dead and now was alive. The Jews tried to bury Jesus, but now they were facing the apostles and hundreds of witnesses who had seen the man—who was dead, yet not dead. The first violent persecution was triggered by Stephen, and it was carried out by a Jewish mob. The Jewish religious authority followed Gamaliel's advice to let God take care of their problem (Acts 5:33–39).

The leaders listened to Gamaliel, but a man from Tarsus by the name of Saul, who guarded the clothes of Stephen's stoners, persuaded them to give him the authority to continue persecuting the followers of Jesus. With the approval in writing from the highest Jewish council, Saul set out for Damascus to bring back men and women in chains to Jerusalem. And as Gamaliel had warned, they stepped on God's purpose, and Jesus stopped Saul and the persecution. To add insult to their helpless intentions to end Jesus's mission, their main persecutor ended up with the apostles in Jerusalem as a witness against the Jewish leaders.

Imagine the impact that the convert Saul-into-Paul had on the hostile council and on the followers of Jesus. There was peace, and the church grew larger and spread her wings over Judea, Galilee, and Samaria (Acts 9:1–31).

GAMALIEL'S PREDICTION HELPED
TO EXPAND THE CHURCH

The Holy Spirit used the persecution to strengthen the faith of the followers of Jesus and scatter them into the world with Christ's message of redemption. The apostles were left alone, but the seven deacons—three, in particular—emerged as leaders of the faith in Jesus as the Christ. These were Stephen, who was stoned for his faith (Acts 7); Philip, who led Samaria and an Ethiopian to Christ (Acts 8:4–13; 26–40); and Nicolaus, a proselyte of Antioch, where the followers of Jesus were first called Christians and where the world missions began (Acts 11–13).

During this time, Peter and John went to Samaria (Acts 8:14–25), to

Lydda-Joppa, and to Cornelius in Caesarea (Acts 9:32–10:48). Then, Peter, John Mark, Barnabas, Paul, Silas, and others met and settled in Antioch as the headquarters of Gentile Christianity (Acts 11–13). It was John Mark who joined Barnabas and Paul on their first missionary journey and not John Zebedee, who was a pillar in Jerusalem (Acts 13; Galatians 2:9). At this point, Herod, too, became a persecutor of the followers of Jesus. Antioch was in his jurisdiction, and it was overpopulated for its size.

What aroused and incited Herod the Tetrarch against the Christians? He was not concerned when his steward Chuza's wife, Joanna, followed and supported Jesus (Luke 8:3). He was happy when Pilate sent Jesus to him, but he did not take part in removing Jesus (Luke 23:6–12). He did nothing when his court member Manaen was a leader in the church of Antioch in his district (Acts 13:1). However, when Peter and his companion arrived in Samaria, Herod felt that the trouble Peter had caused in Jerusalem had come to his backyard (Acts 8:14–25).

Peter had not caused any trouble in Jerusalem. Aside from his mishaps with Ananias and Sapphira (Acts 5:1–11) and the misunderstanding regarding the imminent return of Christ, Peter made a name for himself and his fellow apostles (Acts 5:12–16). The authorities stopped jailing them (Acts 5:17–42), and the election of seven men to serve the neglected Hellenist widows was regarded as the right choice. Things went well with the arrangement, and the church grew immensely (Acts 6:1–7).

But one of the seven, called Stephen, was not the man he was chosen for. He ended up as the most outspoken witness for Jesus, and he dared to blame the Jews for Jesus's death. That hastened Stephen's own stoning and deprived the church of a very valuable teacher. Stephen's boldness triggered the first violent attack on the Christians and drove them out of Jerusalem, but the pillars of the church—Peter, James, and John—were left intact (Acts 8:1; Galatians 2:9).

HEROD THE TETRARCH WAS UNFAMILIAR WITH GAMALIEL'S WARNING

The leaders of the church were aggressive and not as diplomatic and tactful as Jesus had suggested in his Sermon on the Mount. In a sense, they challenged Herod, presuming that the Lord would protect them.

Well, the Lord, at times, lets the wolf have one sheep so the others can be saved. Just as God the Father left Jesus in the hands of the Jewish leaders, so God left James Zebedee to die at the hands of Herod's men. God did not, however, let Herod have Peter or John. The messenger of God freed Peter from prison, and he went to the home of Mary, the mother of John Mark. Herod, too, was struck by the destroyer with a sickness that was mortal. He could not stop the church from expanding, even with the removal of the three pillars (Acts 12).

The Tetrarch's persecution had a profound impact on the church's leadership and direction. To a student of Jesus's intention, the Lord used the Herods more than he used the apostles to carry the gospel into the world. The three pillars were replaced by Galileans and outsiders. Jesus's half-brothers, James and Jude, took over the leadership of the church in Jerusalem. They were backed by Joseph Barnabas, a Levite of Cyprus (Acts 4:36); Paul (Saul), a teacher and Pharisee of Tarsus (Acts 9:11; 11:25); Silas Silvanus, a proficient Aramaic and Greek scribe (Acts 15:22; 1 Peter 5:12); and John Mark, cousin of Barnabas and son of Mary, prominent and very wealthy and respected by Jewish leaders and Romans. These men were missionaries and were eager to reach the Gentiles. Paul, Barnabas, and Mark were the first team commissioned by the church in Antioch (Acts 13). On the second tour, Paul partnered with Silas, and Timothy joined during their trip (Acts 16:3). Barnabas partnered with Mark and sailed to Cyprus (Acts 15:39). Following the split between Paul and Barnabas over John Mark, Paul's health required constant attention, and Luke, physician and writer, joined the team in Macedonia and stayed with Paul to his very end. Luke had already traced and written down the life and ministry of Jesus and was keenly interested in recording Paul's mission work. We know that Luke was with Paul before he died in Rome (2 Timothy 4:6–11; Luke 1:1–4; Acts 1:1–11).

THE CHURCH GREW IN SPITE OF PERSONAL DIFFERENCES CAUSED BY MARK

God does not stop because men disagree over a certain way things had to be done in his kingdom. John Mark left immediately after Paul blinded the nasty magician Elymas (Acts 13:6–11), and Paul branded Mark as a quitter, and so did Luke (Acts 13:13; 15:36–41). This is surprising when Luke used all of Mark to write his account of Jesus and did not acknowledge it. Could it have been that Mark's brief Gospel became the heart of the other Gospels that propelled the church of Christ past Paul into the future? Paul had to tell his own followers in Corinth that it was about Jesus the Christ and not himself (1 Corinthians 3).

In my studies, I found no one with the credentials of John Mark—prominent in the Jewish community as an unidentified ruler (Luke 18:18), very rich (Mark 10:22), and educated in Aramaic, Greek, and Latin. Who else but Mark's mother could accommodate 120 people and take in the families of Jesus and his disciples and not be interfered with by the authorities? My mind cannot fit John Zebedee into such a huge task, when he disappeared after Herod killed James, his brother, and Peter escaped Herod's executioner.

There is more that made me think of John Mark as the man behind all these men who spread the message of Christ. He first appeared in the background of Jesus's last Passover meal with his disciples (Mark 14:12–16), then he was at Gethsemane while the three pillars slept (Mark 14:37–41, 51–52), and he ended up following Peter to Annas and helped him inside the court of the high priest (John 18:15–16). It also is the other disciple who went with Peter to the empty grave and believed that Jesus was alive (John 20:1–8).

Now, where were Jesus's mother and family, the disciples, and the women who had followed, staying in hiding at this time, and were being taken care of? It was in Mary's place, who was the mother of the disciple to whom Jesus committed his mother. John Zebedee or any other disciple was not in any position to take care of anyone. All of them had become homeless, and they were in fear of their lives. No one of the eleven disciples was present at Jesus's crucifixion. Who was this disciple who had earned the love of Jesus and was not afraid to appear with Jesus's mother during the humiliation and death of her son (John 19:25–27)? Could it be the young ruler whom Jesus loved, who walked away and then came back, and became the other disciple of Jesus? (Mark 10:17–22). Well, someone like him or John Mark did appear as Peter's spiritual son in Antioch and in Babylon (Rome) (1 Peter 5:13; Acts 12:12). Mark also traveled with Paul and Barnabas (Acts 13:5; 16:36–40) and went with Timothy to be with Paul in Rome (2 Timothy 4:11).

WHAT HAPPENED TO THE ZEBEDEE BROTHERS?

For a long time, I was led to believe that Jesus had twelve disciples, whom he promoted to be apostles, but I overlooked comments like, "And when it was day, he (Jesus) called his disciples, and chose from them twelve, whom he named apostles" (Luke 6:12–16). The author of Mark was even more specific on why Jesus needed apostles and what kind of men they were:

> And he (Jesus) went up into the hills, and called to him those whom he desired; and they came to him. And he appointed twelve to be with him, and to be sent out to preach and have authority to cast out demons: Simon whom he surnamed Peter; James the son of Zebedee and John the brother of James, whom he surnamed Boanerges, that is, sons of thunder; Andrew, and Philip, and Bartholomew, and Matthew, and Thomas, and James the son of Alphaeus, and Thaddaeus, and Simon the Cananaean, and Judas Iscariot, who betrayed him. (Mark 3:13–19a)

James and John were ambitious, selfish, and annoying. They stopped a man from doing what Jesus did (Mark 9:38–41), and they also were ready to burn down a Samaritan village that did not let them stay overnight (Luke 9:51–56). Then they demanded to sit on both sides with Jesus in his new kingdom. It was at this time that Jesus did not regard them as leaders in the future kingdom but that they too would die.

> And Jesus said to them, "The cup that I drink you will drink; and with the baptism with which I am baptized, you will be baptized; but to sit at my right hand or at my left is not mine to grant, but it is for those for whom it has been prepared." (Mark 10:39b–40)

Herod the Tetrarch killed James, drove Peter out of town, and made John Zebedee disappear (Acts 12). One hundred fifty years later, the Greek Latin Church had distanced itself from Christ. To restore that affinity, John Zebedee became a pastor of Ephesus, the author of the Gospel of John, and the recipient of the book of Revelation. Peter became the source for the Gospel of Mark, and Matthew Levi, the father of the Gospel of Matthew. Luke, who had brought honor to the Jews and Gentiles, was left to speak for himself. At the end, it is what the Holy Spirit has preserved for us, the way back to our origin: "Yet he (God) is not far from each one of us, for 'In him we live and move and have our being'" (Acts 17:27b–28a).

God did this so "that they should seek God, in the hope that they might feel after him and find him. Yet he is not far from each one of us, for 'In him we live and move and have our being;' as even some of your poets said, 'For we are indeed his offspring.'" (Acts 17:27–28)

SUMMARY

- The Holy Spirit had come to keep the apostles and their followers in the world (John 17:15–19).
- It is up to humankind to seek first the kingdom of God (Matthew 6:33).
- The first attempt for a commonality of life failed.
- Herod the Tetrarch could not stop the church from expanding (Acts 12).

CHAPTER 34

WHY DOES GOD NOT STOP EVIL?

FEBRUARY 28, 2021

It is true that in God we live, move, and have our being (Acts 17:28). God, however, decided to make an independent, self-sustaining human being, in whose life on earth God will not interfere. On my long journey of grace, I was left on my own to face good and evil in this world. It has been up to me to choose what was right and what was wrong. Most of my choices made or lessons learned were reached by trial and error. To assist me, I followed the large manual, the Bible. After seventy years of studying the Bible, I would like to share some things that helped me make it through this world. The first question is this:

WHY DID GOD LIMIT HIMSELF?

What is divine limitation? Humankind has always wondered and speculated how far-reaching God's power is. Many believers insist that God's power is limitless. Yet so many things happen in the world that seem to rule that out or disprove divine intervention. Many events are so evil that one cannot help but perceive that there is an evil power behind it.

The ancients believed that God made a perfect world and that Satan took it upon himself to ruin it (Isaiah 14:12–15). After all, the first couple,

Adam and Eve, allowed the snake, or the symbol of perversion, to divert their objective (Genesis 3).

Christians believe that there are principalities and powers in the air that disrupt God's affairs in the world (Ephesians 6:12). To counter those powers, Christ Jesus was sent. But what happens when evil is not restrained?

How do we explain the evil actions of humankind as the outright orders of God? Are atrocities judgments ordained by God, or are they the misguided acts of humankind? What about earthquakes, floods, hurricanes, tornadoes, and other disasters? We call them "acts of God." Where does God's power begin, and where does God's power end? Are there divine limitations?

DIVINE LIMITATIONS BY GOD'S OWN WORD

Contrary to popular belief, God has limited himself by his own Word and by his own laws. Not a dot can be altered or aborted (Matthew 5:18). God has determined to place the world in humankind's hands, and he will not interfere (Genesis 1:26). Even after the flood, the Lord God did not release humankind from managing the world. In fact, God strengthened the covenant with Noah by granting Noah more respect and more authority (Genesis 9).

Many believe that these happenings, regardless how devastating they may be, are God's punishments for humankind's transgressions. Of course, that is one answer that may satisfy those who see God as one who chooses to step in and out of human history. The people of the Old Testament believed that the Lord God stepped in and out to either bail them out or to punish them. Thus, when Israel liquidated the people of Canaan before they took possession of the land, their actions were interpreted as divine orders. But when Israel and, later, Judah sinned, both were carried into captivity. In fact, every nation that sinned, no matter how powerful it was, fell or even ceased to exist. Is there invisible handwriting on the wall of history? Has God chosen some power, like Babylon of old, to teach his people a lesson?

I FIND THIS TROUBLING
||||||||||||||||||||||||||||||||||||

I personally find all this very troubling. It is not at all characteristic of the God whom Jesus called his Father, that he was the only one in the universe who was God. It is far more likely that humankind, by disrupting what God has created, brings disaster upon themselves. God does not need to destroy the world. Humankind has found the knowledge of good and evil, and they are quite capable of changing the ecology and human behavior. They have designed tools for survival and weapons for self-destruction. All God has to do is let humankind find another planet like Earth, so that they can repopulate and mess it up again. This idea of another planet like the earth is not as far-fetched as we may think. The technology is already available to travel in space for centuries until such a place is found.

LET'S NOT SPECULATE JUST YET
||||||||||||||||||||||||||||||||||||

Before we get caught up in speculation, let us touch on the subject of our intent. Let us look at divine limitations. The Bible tells us that God created a good and self-sufficient world. In fact, it was a paradise called Eden. God then created humankind to manage it.

Humankind messed up, and they lost paradise. Humankind became the fallen angel, and they took the devil with them. In the new world, humankind was completely on their own. Again, humankind mismanaged by allowing evil to misguide them.

God interfered for the last time with a flood. God then made a covenant with Noah that he would never again destroy the world (Genesis 9). God would send his Spirit to touch some individuals, but that, too, has been abused by humankind. People who were not sent by God speak for him (Jeremiah 28). They might even use the Lord's name to do mighty works, but they will be evildoers (Matthew 7:21–23). They shall see themselves in the light of God's favor and mercy but deny his presence by their deeds (2 Timothy 3:5).

Even those who the Spirit of the Lord touched did not always interpret the Spirit of the Lord accurately. For example, Abraham became the father of Ishmael before he became the father of Isaac. To please the men of his day, Moses changed the law on divorce. Solomon turned wisdom into a diplomacy of sin. Peter was supposed to save souls, but he had Ananias and Sapphira killed. Paul made a man blind and stopped a girl from witnessing in his favor.

The point is this: humankind does misread and misinterpret God's intentions, and God may do nothing about it in this life. The only thing humankind cannot do is kill the soul and the breath of life itself.

Humankind is managing the world, not God. That is how God set things up. That is why Satan, whom man follows, could offer the world to the Son of the Creator (Matthew 4:8–9; Luke 4:5–7). We can sing all we want that, "This is my Father's world." The truth declared by Jesus was and still is, "My kingdom is not of this world" (John 18:36).

> Jesus answered, "My kingship is not of this world. If my kingship were of this world, my servants would fight, that I might not be handed over to the Jews; but my kingship is not from this world." (John 18:36)

GOD IS NOT RESPONSIBLE

God has absolutely nothing to do with humankind's destructive behavior!

First, God is good and perfect, and God is the Father of the light that comes from above. God does not change like the shifting shadows (James 1:16–17).

Second, God loves the world, and he has no intention of destroying the world. God sent Jesus, His Son, to save the world (John 3:16). The term *world* means the entire cosmos. That includes all of creation and not just humankind (Romans 8:19–22). We have been led to think that humankind alone needs redemption. In reality, it is creation that is in bondage to humankind and groans to be delivered from them (Romans 8:22). Humankind is the culprit that has devastated creation. Christ came to give humankind a new heart and a new perspective, but they have conveniently turned even that idea to their own benefit.

God No Longer Judges

Third, God no longer judges. God is the Father of all creatures. And for that reason, God has turned the problem of humankind over to Jesus, his Son. Jesus has been entrusted with judgment (John 5:22). Jesus became a man, and he set the example of how to live and how to manage human affairs. Therefore, humankind has no excuse (John 15:22).

Fourth, Jesus Christ arranged it so that humankind becomes their own judge by rejecting him, by the way they believe, by the way they behave, and by the way they bring forth good or evil (John 5:24–29). Even a careless word will haunt them on Judgment Day (Matthew 12:36).

Humankind Shapes Their Own Destiny

This is consistent with what God said when Adam and Eve disobeyed: "Man has become like one of us, he knows good and evil" (Genesis 3:22). Guilt and innocence rests entirely on their shoulders. Woe unto that person who wants to hold God accountable for his or her actions.

Humankind's argument has been, "The devil made me do it." Again, they have twisted the truth. They make the devil do it. They solicit the devil's help, use his techniques, give the devil permission, and then believe his lies.

Dear friend, the devil does not have to do anything. We take the drugs, which disable us mentally and pervert us sexually. We let doubt and fear into our hearts. Turn on any newscast. Do you see the devil preaching fear? It is the foolish reporters who scare us to death with a handful of bad news. It is bad enough to have one case, but why must an entire nation be held captive? In spite of the positive rhetoric of the leaders, we are on a train headed for doomsday.

It so happens that I lived through World War II, and I believe that the American free press unintentionally prolonged the war with its irresponsible reporting. The bad news helped the Nazis believe that America would soon quit and that they would succeed in the end. Now that we are at war with the terrorists, the news reporters are doing it again. Just listen to their questions and the stories you pass on. You do not need the devil to create fear. You are doing rather well without his help. Reporters have such power that they drive the politicians out of their minds. Politicians know that if they are not on good terms with reporters, they will be smeared in public, and that will cost them the election. What is even worse is that the public believes the yarn that reporters spin. Contemplate for a moment how many lives are put at risk. Stop being bearers of bad messages; they are sharper than a two-edged sword.

SATAN STRIPPED OF HIS POWER

Concerning Satan or the devil, too much is said about his influence. Satan is not as strong as he is made out to be. If he is a roaring lion, then Jesus has knocked out his teeth (1 Peter 5:8). He can no longer bite or hurt anybody. The good news is that Satan, the devil, has been stripped of his power. Jesus has cast him out and rendered him ineffective (John 12:31). Satan is already condemned (John 16:11). He cannot touch Jesus. In this world now, however, he is on the loose (John 14:30).

> "And now I have told you now before it takes place, so that when it does take place, you may believe. I will no longer talk much with you, for the ruler of this world is coming. He has no power over me; but I do as the Father has commanded me, so that the world may know that I love the Father. Rise, let us go hence." (John 14:29–31)

All one has to do is submit to God and resist the devil, and he will flee (James 4:7). The devil cannot stand against people who live godly and clean lives. Satan prefers people who render lip service, rather than live out godly acts of compassion and mercy. Satan believes in God—only fools do not—but Satan trembles (James 2:19). He is deceptive. He likes to appear as if he is an angel of light (2 Corinthians 11:14). That is, Satan can only appear; he cannot be real. He steals the truth and alters the Word of God by putting doubt into people's thoughts (Luke 8:12).

The work of Satan and that of his followers can be identified easily. He who commits sin is of the devil (1 John 3:8). Anyone who entertains murder is a child of the devil (John 8:44), and so is the one who betrays Christ (John 6:70; 13:2). The truth is simply this: without voluntary human consent, Satan, the devil, and his angels and demons cannot touch or use humankind. People must want to do Satan's bidding and also believe his teaching. Satan uses one argument only, and that is, "God could not really mean what he said."

DISCERNING WHETHER THEY ARE OF GOD

It is important that we discern whether the spirits are of God (1 John 4:1). How does one know whether the spirit is beneficial? Let us look at some examples.

A Samaritan village did not welcome Jesus because he was on his way to Jerusalem. Two of his disciples were ready to have fire fall from heaven and punish them. Jesus's reply was, "You do not know of what kind of a spirit you are" (Luke 9:55 KJV). The two in question were James and John. And John was the disciple whom Jesus loved.

Take Peter, for instance, the third of the three who went everywhere with Jesus. When Jesus informed his followers that he had to die to give credence to his mission, Peter tried to be helpful and told Jesus, his teacher, that he would not let this happen. Jesus told him, "Get behind me Satan! You are a hinderance to me; for you are not on the side of God, but of men" (Matthew 16:23).

The disciples were arguing over who among them was the greatest. Whatever Peter did, Jesus addressed him, "Simon, Simon, behold, Satan demanded to have you, that he might sift you like wheat, but I have prayed for you that your faith may not fail; and when you have turned again, strengthen your brethren" (Luke 22:31–32).

Peter did not get it. Peter kept on insisting that he would prove to Jesus how great he was. And what did Jesus tell this man who was supposed to be the rock of his church? He predicted that he would deny his Lord three times before the rooster crowed. Obviously, Peter had not taken inventory of his spirit. Jesus had sent out seventy-two to do his work.

They returned with glowing stories of success. How did Jesus receive them? "I saw Satan fall like lightning from heaven," he told them (Luke 10:18). Again, Jesus had to stop Satan from getting the better of the seventy-two. The spirit of pride and success almost kept them out of the kingdom.

SUMMARY

|||||||||||||||||||||||||||||||||||||||

- God decided to make an independent, self-sustaining human being.
- It is up to humankind to choose what is right and what is wrong.
- Contrary to popular belief, God has limited himself by his own Word and by his own laws (Matthew 5:18).
- God has determined to place the world in humankind's hands, and he will not interfere (Genesis 1:26).
- Humankind, by disrupting what God has created, is bringing disaster upon themselves.
- Humankind has mismanaged by allowing Satan/evil to misguide them.
- Humankind has found the knowledge of good and evil, and they are quite capable of changing the ecology and human behavior, tools for survival, and weapons for self-destruction.
- The only thing humankind cannot do is kill the soul and the breath of life.
- Humankind is managing the world, not God.
- That is why Satan could offer the world to Jesus, the Son of the Creator God (Matthew 4:8–9; Luke 4:5–7).
- The truth declared by Jesus was and still is, "My kingdom is not of this world" (John 18:36).

CHAPTER 35

How to Face Deception and Temptation

MARCH 7, 2021

Let us spend a little time on Jesus's temptation in the desert. It has always been a puzzle for me. Why did Jesus have to be tempted before he began his ministry?

According to one Christian writer, Jesus was tempted like any other man so that he could help his followers (Hebrews 2:18). If that is the case, then Jesus's encounter with Satan is a blueprint for us.

First of all, Satan did not tempt Jesus when he was physically strong but when he was exhausted and hungry. Second, Satan questioned Jesus's relationship with God—if Jesus was the Son of God, he should have no trouble turning stones into bread. The issue was not what Jesus could or could not do; rather, the question was, "What was Jesus's duty as a man?" Jesus was to abide by God's law built into creation, and he was not supposed to alter it, such as making a new creation through turning stones into bread just because he was hungry. It was a matter of obeying God's law and Word, rather than pleasing the temptation. In this case, hunger was on the tempter's side. In order to satisfy the needs of the human body, should we be allowed to break a law or two? "Not so," said Jesus.

We can live without bread, but we cannot live without God's Word, which sustains all of creation. No miracle was called for here, but complying with the Word of God is always called for. That, of course, opened the door for Satan to quote scriptures, and he was rather skillful at it. Beware of what purpose Satan uses the scripture.

Next, Satan took Jesus to the highest point on the roof of the temple and challenged Jesus to break another one of God's laws; namely, gravity. Being the Son of God, it would not at all hurt to put his Father in heaven to the test. After all, it was written that God would send his angels, who would carry his Son in their hands so that he would not strike his foot against a stone. The request was foolish, and the quote was out of context.

Psalm 91 was a prayer of a God-fearing man who trusted in the Lord. It was not a promise or command of God. Jesus's answer was a reference to Deuteronomy 6:16, when the people tested God at Massah. To please the quarreling people, Moses struck the rock to get water, and this cost Moses the promised land.

Satan had neglected to read that particular command from the man whose prayer he quoted. In both instances, Satan attacked God's limitations. God has limited himself by his Word and by his law. Only Satan can devise the idea that man should turn stones into bread and jump off high places. According to Jesus, God was not interested in such miracles. Instead, God is interested in abiding and living within his Word and his law.

YOU CAN HAVE THE ENTIRE WORLD

The third attempt of Satan to throw Jesus off course was to give Jesus all the kingdoms of the world in exchange for denying God only once. All it would take to become the greatest man in the history of humanity was to pay homage to Satan. Satan asked only for one single acknowledgement that he was worthy of reverence. It did not seem much, yet it was an act that would have been an insult to God.

For Jesus, it was a matter of having respect in this world and respect in heaven. Satan wanted to limit the power of God Almighty. On earth, Satan knew that man could do that, but what man does on earth determines whether he ends up in heaven or in hell.

If you break one law, you break all the laws. You can only serve one master or one God. Satan did not want all of Christ's allegiance, only one. All sins and transgressions begin as a single act. If the action is unchecked, sin multiplies until it becomes normal. God, however, will not share his Son with another extraterrestrial being; neither will God share his Son's followers with Satan. There are no exceptions. Satan is just not big enough to make that claim. Satan himself is only a fallen angel. Since his fall, God found it necessary to create a special place for him called hell (Matthew 25:41). Those who serve him will join him.

Satan is the accuser. Every mistake humankind makes, Satan quickly takes before God to embarrass the Almighty (Revelation 12:10). We need to refresh our thinking on Satan, the accuser, by reading the book of Job. And then, we should make certain that Christ is our defender (Romans 8:34). Satan is limited and does not spare a trick to pervert our feelings, needs, and ambitions, but Satan must gain our consent.

Let us turn to Jesus.

THE LORD RESPECTS THE WILL OF HUMANKIND

Prior to Jesus's Resurrection, he had authority over the Sabbath, the demons, and sin. Jesus could multiply bread and fish, stop trees from growing, and walk on the water. But when it came to humankind, Jesus had to have their consent.

Jesus could do no mighty work at home due to their lack of faith in him (Matthew 13:58). Jesus did not divide the inheritance between two brothers (Luke 12:13). Jesus did not grant permission for James and John to sit on his right and left in his kingdom (Mark 10:40). Jesus did not know when the end would come (Mark 13:32). Jesus could not alter his destiny (Mark 14:36). And Jesus could not avert the hour of darkness (Luke 22:53).

Jesus saved others, but he could not save himself (Mark 15:31). Jesus had to function within the limits that had been put in place before creation came into being (John 17:24). Jesus's disclosure was planned (Matthew 13:35), and Jesus's sacrifice was also in place (Revelation 13:8). We live lives within limits and in a world within limits. These limits are God's eternal law. And God's eternal law is fixed for our good. God's law gives us an opportunity to prove ourselves. It is up to us whether we are productive or destructive. It has been predetermined where we will spend eternity if we fail. That place has also been prepared beforehand (Matthew 25:41). We do not have to go there. If we do, then it is all our doing.

Joshua's challenge still rings down the corridor of history with the appeal to humankind's ability to choose. "Choose you this day whom you will serve." The options he presented were the man-made gods of the neighboring nations or the living God of his fathers (Joshua 24:15). The creature called humankind is fully capable of choosing and managing their and the world's affairs. The Creator has endowed them with the ability to do so.

Consider, for a moment, the statement, "Let us make man in our own image, in our likeness" (Genesis 1:26). This is not just a reference to the inner nature of humankind but also their ability to make choices. This is supported by the following statement that they have been placed in charge of all the affairs of the world (Genesis 1:26). In fact, humankind is in charge of life itself. Humankind can kill the body, and they will (Matthew 10:28). Humankind will even kill the Son of God in the flesh (Matthew 17:23). People will kill God's messengers and people that preach God's law (Matthew 23:37). The only things humankind cannot destroy are their souls (Job 19:26). Humankind has been given the ability to develop and invent awesome weapons to manage and govern. They are capable of altering the environment and disrupting nature. Humankind, not God, causes abnormalities and accidents, but God will hold people accountable for everything they have done (Revelation 22:12). In the final analysis, humankind are only stewards, whom God has put in charge of the world and everything in it. It is entirely up to us to manage in such a way that will earn us worthy recognition (Matthew 25:21–23).

IS THERE ANY LINK?

Is there any link with God? The truth is that God has never turned the world over to humankind without witnesses (Acts 14:17; Hebrews 1:1–2). Their encounters and their testimony with the Almighty have culminated in the Bible. Many, unfortunately, have not taken God's witnesses seriously.

To begin with, God's Spirit was in the world at the time of creation and in the lives of all the godly people in history, including in Jesus. And God's Spirit will come to every godly person who invites him, even today.

"If you then, though you are evil, know how to give good gifts to your children, how much more will your Father in heaven give the Holy Spirit to those who ask him!" (Luke 11:13)

But there are also many evil spirits in the world that can be identified only by those who are Christ-centered (1 John 4:1–6). The head of these false spirits had the audacity to tempt Jesus Christ himself (Matthew 4:1–11). Satan's angelic performance has swept the world off its feet (2 Corinthians 11:14; John.14:30). And Satan's children have already left an ugly path of blood (John 8:42–47).

Humankind disobeyed God and tasted the fruits of good and evil (Genesis 3:22). Instead of repenting and correcting their error, they went on and called evil good (Isaiah 5:20). On top of that, the highest authority in the land legalizes behaviors that are an abomination to God (Romans 1:32). For such people, there is no connection with God (Romans 1:18–31) and no redemption through Christ (Hebrews 10:26–31).

IF MAN DOES NOT USE HIS WILL, SATAN WILL

Satan no longer can bite or hurt anyone, unless we give Satan our permission. The good news is that Satan has been stripped of his power. Jesus has cast Satan out. Jesus has rendered Satan ineffective.

"Now is the judgment of this world, now shall the ruler of this world be cast out." (John 12:31)

Satan is already condemned.

"Of judgment, because the ruler of this world is judged." (John 16:11)

Satan cannot touch Jesus, but Satan is in the world, and he is on the loose.

"I will no longer talk much with you, for the ruler of this world is coming. He has no power over me." (John 14:30)

All one has to do is submit to God and resist the devil, and the devil will flee,

> Submit yourselves therefore to God. Resist the devil and
> he will flee from you. (James 4:7)

Satan cannot stand people who live godly and clean lives. Satan prefers that human beings render lip service, rather than godly acts of compassion and acts of mercy.

Satan believes in God, but Satan trembles. Only fools do not believe in God. John reminds us,

> You believe that God is one; you do well. Even the demons
> believe—and shudder. (James 2:19)

Satan is deceptive. Satan likes to appear as if he is an angel of light. Paul states, "And no wonder, for even Satan disguises himself as an angel of light" (2 Corinthians 11:14). That is, Satan can only appear. He steals the truth and alters the Word of God by putting doubt into people's thoughts. Regarding the different kinds of seed sown by the Word of God:

> "The ones along the path are those who have heard; then
> the devil comes and takes away the word from their hearts,
> that they may not believe and be saved." (Luke 8:12)

The work of Satan and his followers can easily be identified.

> He who commits sin is of the devil; for the devil has sinned
> from the beginning. The reason the Son of God appeared
> was to destroy the works of the devil. (1 John 3:8)

Anyone who entertains murder is a child of the devil.

> "You are of your father the devil, and your will is to do your
> father's desires. He was a murderer from the beginning,
> and has nothing to do with the truth, because there is no

truth in him. When he lies, he speaks according to his own nature, for he is a liar and the father of lies." (John 8:44)

The one who betrays Christ is also of the devil.

And during supper, when the devil had already put it into the heart of Judas Iscariot, Simon's son, to betray him. (John 13:2)

The truth is simply this: without the voluntary human being's consent, Satan, the devil, and his angels or demons cannot touch humankind or even use humankind. People must want to do the devil's bidding and believe in the devil's teaching. Satan only uses one doubt and only one argument, and that is, "God could not really mean what He said."

It is important that we discern the spirits—whether they are of God.

Beloved, do not believe every spirit, but test the spirits to see whether they are of God; for many false prophets have gone out into the world. (1 John 4:1)

How, then, does one know whether the spirit is beneficial? Let us look at some examples.

A Samaritan village did not welcome Jesus because Jesus was on his way to Jerusalem. Two of Jesus's disciples were ready to have fire fall from heaven and punish them. Jesus's reply was, "You do not know of what kind of a spirit you are" (Luke 9:55 KJV). The two disciples in question were James and John. And John was the disciple whom Jesus loved.

Peter, the third of the three disciples, went everywhere with Jesus. When Jesus informed his followers that he had to die to give credence to his mission, Peter tried to be helpful and told Jesus that he would not let this happen. Jesus told him, "Get behind me Satan! You are a hindrance to me; for you are not on the side of God, but of men" (Matthew 16:23).

The disciples were arguing over who among them was the greatest. Whatever Peter did, Jesus addressed him,

Simon, Simon, behold, Satan demanded to have you, that he might sift you like wheat, but I have prayed for you that your faith may not fail; and when you have turned again, strengthen your brethren. (Luke 22:31–32)

Peter did not get it. Peter kept insisting that he would prove to Jesus how great he was. And what did Jesus tell this man, who was supposed to be the rock of his church? Jesus predicted that Peter would deny his Lord three times before the rooster crowed. Obviously, Peter had not taken inventory of his spirit. Jesus had sent out seventy-two to do his work. They returned with glowing stories of success. How did Jesus receive them? Jesus told them, "I saw Satan fall like lightning from heaven" (Luke 10:18).

SUMMARY

- Satan did not tempt Jesus when he was physically strong but when he was exhausted and hungry.
- Satan questioned Jesus's relationship with God.
- Satan offered to give Jesus all the kingdoms of the world in exchange for denying God only once (pay homage).
- God does not share his Son with another extraterrestrial being (Satan); neither will God share his Son's followers with Satan.
- Satan is an accuser.
- To follow Satan and do his bidding, he must gain our consent.
- It is up to humankind, whether they are productive or destructive, to choose whom they will serve.
- Humankind, not God, causes abnormalities and accidents.
- Satan no longer can bite or hurt anyone unless we give Satan our permission.
- To resist Satan, the devil, all humankind has to do is submit themselves to God, and Satan has to flee (James 4:7).
- Humankind shapes their own destiny.

CHAPTER 36

WHO CAUSES DECEPTION AND TEMPTATION?

MARCH 13, 2021

During my ninety-plus years, everything I did has my mark on it and no one else's. There were many times when I had to put the brakes on my desire. James, the half-brother of Jesus, has been a profound guide in maintaining my journey of grace.

James wrote,

> Blessed is the man who endures trial, for when he has stood the test he will receive the crown of life which God has promised to those who love him. Let no one say when he is tempted, "I am tempted of God"; for God cannot be tempted with evil and he himself tempts no one; but each person is tempted when he is lured and enticed by his own desire. Then desire when it has conceived gives birth to sin; and sin when it is full-grown brings forth death. Do not be deceived, my beloved brethren. Every good endowment and every perfect gift is from above, coming down from the Father of lights with whom there is no variation or shadow due to change. Of his own will he brought us forth by the word of truth that we should be a kind of first fruits of his creatures. Know this, my beloved brethren. Let

every man be quick to hear, slow to speak, slow to anger, for the anger of man does not work the righteousness of God. Therefore put away all filthiness and rank growth of wickedness and receive with meekness the implanted word, which is able to save your souls. But be doers of the word, and not hearers only, deceiving yourselves. For if any one is a hearer of the word and not a doer, he is like a man who observes his natural face in a mirror; for he observes himself and goes away and at once forgets what he was like. But he who looks into the perfect law, the law of liberty, and preserves, being no hearer that forgets but a doer that acts, he shall be blessed in his doing. (James 1:12–25)

I—AND NO ONE ELSE—HAVE TO KEEP MY DESIRE IN CHECK

I am human, and my eyes have traveled, but my will has not followed. I am not on a leash to anyone, especially not God, who has made me in such a marvelous way that I can function on my own, even when I became handicapped at the age of twenty-one.

I have never quite understood why translators say that the Greek verb *eisenegkes* (from *eisphero*) refers to being led by someone, instead of using "yielding" by myself, without anyone dragging me into temptation (Luke 11:4; Matthew 6:13).

God does not lead, nor does God mislead anyone. Therefore, God has provided humankind with the law and the prophets and with words of his Son and with the witness of the apostles. These laws and witnesses have kept me on the straight and narrow for over ninety years. If I had not anchored myself in the scripture, I would have fallen many times, as Jesus had predicted. It always was up to me to stop gratifying the desire of the flesh. I am no one's slave but my own! The Lord has helped me not to yield to temptation, and he never has led me into one temptation.

"Every one then who hears these words of mine and does them will be like a wise man who built his house upon the rock; and the rain fell, and the floods came, and the

255

winds blew and beat upon that house, but it did not fall, because it had been founded on the rock. And every one who hears these words of mine and does not do them will be like a foolish man who built his house upon sand; and the rain fell, and the floods came; and the winds blew and beat against that house, and it fell; and great was the fall of it." (Matthew 7:24–27; Luke 6:46–49)

Let not sin therefore reign in your mortal bodies, to make you obey their passions. Do not yield your members to sin as instruments of wickedness, but yield yourselves to God as men who have been brought from death to life, and your members to God as instruments of righteousness. (Romans 6:12–13)

But I (Paul) say, walk by the Spirit, and do not gratify the desires of the flesh. For the desires of the flesh are against the Spirit, and the desires of the Spirit are against the flesh; for these are opposed to each other, to prevent you from doing what you would. But if you are led by the Spirit you are not under the law. Now the works of the flesh are plain: fornication, impurity, licentiousness, idolatry, sorcery, enmity, strife, jealousy, anger, selfishness, dissension, party spirit, envy, drunkenness, carousing, and the like. I warn you, as I warned you before, that those who do such things shall not inherit the kingdom of God. But the fruit of the Spirit is love, joy, peace, patience, kindness, goodness, faithfulness, gentleness, self-control; against such there is no law. And those who belong to Christ Jesus have crucified the flesh with its passion and desires. If we live by the Spirit, let us also walk by the Spirit. Let us have no self-conceit, no provoking of one another, no envy of one another. (Galatians 5:16–26)

Put on then, as God's chosen ones, holy and beloved, compassion, kindness, lowliness, meekness, and patience, forbearing one another and, if one has a complaint against another, forgiving each other: as the Lord has forgiven you, so you also must forgive. And above all these put on love, which binds everything together in perfect harmony. And let the peace of Christ rule in your hearts, to which indeed you were called in the one body. And be thankful. Let the word of Christ dwell in you richly, as you teach and admonish one another in all wisdom, and as you sing psalms and hymns and spiritual songs with thankfulness in your hearts to God. And whatever you do, in word or deed, do everything in the name of the Lord Jesus, giving thanks to God the Father through him. (Colossians 3:12–17)

WATCH OUT FOR DECEPTION

Our Lord gave us a glimpse of what our world will be like. Jesus warned us to watch out for deceivers, false Christs, false signs, and false miracles (Mark 13; Matthew 24; 7:15–23). If we are ashamed of him and his Word, he will reciprocate (Mark 8:38; Luke 9:26). If we confess Christ before humankind, Christ will also confess us before the angels and God (Matthew 10:32–33; Luke 12:8–9).

ANOTHER SPIRIT WILL BE AT WORK

A spirit will be at work that is not the Spirit of God or the Spirit of Christ (Ephesians 2:2).

And you he made alive, when you were dead through the trespasses and sins in which you once walked, following the course of this world, following the prince of the power of the air, the spirit that is now at work in the sons of disobedience. Among these we all once lived in the passions of our flesh, following the desires of body and mind, and so we were by nature children of wrath, like the rest of mankind. But God, who is rich in mercy, out of the great love with which he loved us, even when we were dead through our trespasses, made us alive together with Christ (by grace you have been saved). (Ephesians 2:1–5)

This spirit will form alliances but not with the Spirit of God (Isaiah 30:1). They will proclaim a "false message and a false hope" (Ezekiel 13:3–7). A "spirit of prostitution" will detain them from returning to God or repenting from their sin (Hosea 5:4).

THEIR MESSAGE WILL SOUND GOOD

There will be false prophets (Matthew 7:15; 24:11; Revelation 16:13; 19:20). Their message will sound good. There will come false apostles and false teachers (2 Corinthians 11:13; 2 Peter 2:1–3). There will also be a false Christ (Matthew 24:24; Mark 13:22). There will even be a false trinity— the beast, the prophet, and the dragon (Revelation 16:12–14).

Do not believe every spirit. Test them (1 John 4:1–13). This is what Jesus said the Spirit of God will do: (John 14:15–26; 16:5–15). The scary part is that all sins can be forgiven, even speaking against the Son of man, but not the sin against the Holy Spirit (Matthew 12:31–32; Luke 12:10).

BY LIMITING GOD TO SPECIFICS

A special effort will be made to bypass the law of God by limiting it to specifics. We see this everywhere in our world today. They will say, "That's not what God meant in the scripture."

For example, adultery (*moicheuw*) is not just about stepping outside a marriage, but it is violating God's creative act of wanting more than one partner. God sanctioned only one male and one female to be together. "You shall not commit adultery" (Leviticus 20:13) also means you shall not engage in sex with anyone else—any other woman, any other man, or any beast—because this is an abomination to God. The body is the temple of God's Spirit, and therefore, the body is not to be an object of any perversion. Perversion is not just a sin against humankind; it is a perversion against God, and all perversion, including sex perversion, infringes on many, if not all, of the other laws of God. In addition to dishonoring and disobeying God, adulterers covet, steal, lie, and even end up killing for sex (Matthew 5:17–20; 5:27–30; 19:3–6; 1 Corinthians 6:12–20; Psalm 51; James 2:8–11).

Disobedience to God is also called adultery (Isaiah 57:3–5; Jeremiah 7:9–15; 23:9–12; Ezekiel 23:42–44; Revelation 2:20–24), and adultery is called "the great harlot, and the mother of prostitution and confusion" (Revelation 17).

A WORLD OF CONFUSION

It shall be a world of confusion, where good will become bad, and bad will become good (Romans 1). It will be like in the days of Noah and Lot (Matthew 24:37–38; Luke 17:26–28). It will be Babylon on earth and worldwide confusion; namely, the home of every foul spirit and demon (Revelation 18). Even the church of Jesus Christ will be driven into the desert and from her primary mission in the world (Revelation 2–3; 12).

The dragon will strip her of her influence and turn her into another social organization. Satan will do everything to destroy "faith in Jesus the Christ" (Luke 18:8). Christians will abandon the scriptures and follow deceiving spirits (1 Timothy 4:1). Sound biblical teaching will not be tolerated (2 Timothy 3:12–17; 4:1–5). A Christlike language will be used to enhance deception (Romans 3:13; 16:18). Therefore, mostly human interests shall be served at the expense of good morals (1 Corinthians 3:18; 6:9–20). Bad company will corrupt good character (1 Corinthians 15:33). Leaders will be deceitful, and Satan will masquerade as an "angel of light" (2 Corinthians 11:13).

Therefore, people will reap what they sow (Galatians 6:7). Too many opinions will keep people from adopting the attributes of Christ (Ephesians 4:14). The falling away from the church has begun, and the lawless Antichrist is actively leading the rebellion (2 Thessalonians 2:3–11). God has allowed this delusion and has taken away his Spirit from among us (2 Thessalonians 2:10–11). Those who no longer confess Jesus, who keep sinning and allow themselves to be led astray, are following the devil (1 John 1–5). Be not hardened by deceitfulness (Hebrews 3:13) and a spirit of stupor (Revelation 11:8). Due to the similarities with Christ, people will not even realize that they are worshipping the beast (Revelation 19:20).

WHAT KIND OF AN ATTITUDE DO WE
NEED TO OVERCOME THE WORLD?

Our prayer ought to be, "Grieve not the Holy Spirit" (Ephesians 4:30), and please, Lord, "Do not take Your Holy Spirit from us" (Psalm 51:11). Our desire must remain to be close to God's laws and Christ's life, God's work, and God's Word.

It is our solemn task to abide in Christ and do what he commanded so that the Godhead can continue to live in us (John 14:23). It is when we remain faithful to Jesus to our very end that we shall be saved (Mark 13:13). We need a mind like Jesus had (Philippians 2:5–11).

Our Lord has a major concern—that humankind's faith in the Son of man will decline. Humankind will stop being persistent. Jesus put it this way:

When the Son of man returns, will he find faith on earth? (Luke 18:8)

What exactly will happen to Jesus's concern? First of all, for Jesus, faith, along with justice and mercy, were part of the law (Matthew 23:23). It was the Son of man who brought mercy and grace to the law (John 1:17). Second, to remove faith in the Son of man also removes faith from the law. That makes the law weak and ineffective. Third, to remove faith from the law ceases the connection with God. And when you remove faith, then there is no longer any fear of God. Without the fear of God, then God only becomes love. The argument is then that God is incapable of holding guilty human beings responsible for their criminal activities.

NO MORE FEAR OF GOD

That is precisely where we are. There is no more fear of God because we again argue, "Love has cast out fear." Therefore, our excuse becomes simply, "Human beings are what they are because they were born that way. How can they be held accountable for being what they are?"

Interpreters of professing Christians propound this stunning logic. The interpreters today and the critics both try to disown Jesus of Jesus's sayings; therefore, they are inclined to turn Jesus himself into a myth.

These interpreters and critics prefer to assign most of Jesus's words and deeds to secondary sources; namely, as the fabrication of Jesus's followers. This, of course, is nothing new. Three days after Jesus's death, the chief priests and leaders of the people paid the Roman guards to lie about Jesus's Resurrection (Matthew 28:12–15). That lie has been perpetrated, tarnished, and even cleverly concealed to our own day.

BE OF GOOD CHEER

Jesus said, "Be of good cheer, I have overcome the world" (John 16:33). How do we overcome the world? The key is, "Repent and believe the good news" (Mark 1:15). A change in us has to take effect before we can live in a world in which we no longer feel a part (John 17:14). Proving that our Lord is real becomes more difficult when the eyes of the world are upon us. How do we do that?

John took great pains to write a Gospel based on "believing by seeing." All the things Jesus did and said were signs to prove that Jesus was who Jesus claimed to be. When Jesus turned water into wine, his disciples believed in him (John 2:1–11). The Samaritans believed in Jesus (John 4). The blind man believed in Jesus (John 9:35) and so did Mary, Martha, and Lazarus (John 11). The other disciple saw the empty grave, and he believed (John 20:8). Mary of Magdala found believing more difficult, and she required seeing, hearing, and touching Jesus (John 20:10–16).

Thomas was not satisfied with the testimony of his fellow disciples. Thomas demanded personal proof, and Jesus obliged (John 20:10–16). In a way, Thomas spoke for all of us who were yet to be born into the world and into God's kingdom. In like manner, Jesus answered for all of us when he said, "Blessed are those that have not seen, and yet have believed" (John 20:29). For it is they who believe in the Son of God and magnifies him with their lives who have eternal life (John 3:36; Matthew 10:32; Luke 12:8).

BELIEVE AND KEEP HIS COMMANDMENTS

Everyone who believes that Jesus is the Christ is a child of God, and every one who loves the parent (Godfather) loves the child. By this we know that we love the children (one another) of God, when we love God and obey his commandments. For this is the love of God, that we keep his commandments. And his commandments are not burdensome. For whatever is born of God overcomes the world; and this is the victory that overcomes the world, our faith. Who is it that overcomes the world, but he who believes that Jesus is the Son of God?

This is he who comes by water and blood, Jesus the Christ. Not with the water only, but with the water, and the blood. And the Spirit is the witness, because the Spirit is the truth. There are three witnesses, the Spirit, the water, and the blood; and these three agree. If we receive the testimony of men, the testimony of God is greater; for this is the testimony of God that he has born to his Son. He who believes in the Son of God has the testimony, in himself. He who does not believe God, has made him a liar, because he has not believed in the testimony that God has borne to his Son. And this is the testimony that God gave us eternal life; and this life is in his Son. He who has the Son, has life; he who has not the Son, does not have life. (1 John 5:1–12)

SUMMARY

- God does not lead, nor does God mislead anyone (Luke 11:4; Matthew 6:13).
- Jesus warned us to watch out for deceivers, false Christs, false signs, and false miracles (Mark 13; Matthew 24; 7:15–23).
- Perversion is not just a sin against humankind; it is a perversion against God, and it infringes on the other laws of God.
- We live in a world of confusion, where good will become bad, and bad will become good (Romans 1; Revelation 18).
- Satan will try everything to destroy faith in Jesus Christ (Luke 18:8).
- Humankind reaps what it sows (Galatians 6:7).

- The lawless Antichrist is actively leading the rebellion (2 Thessalonians 2:3–11; 2:10–11).
- To overcome the world, humankind must abide in Christ and do what he commanded (John 14:23).
- Jesus's concern was, "When the Son of man returns, will he find faith on earth?" (Luke 18:8).
- To overcome the world, humankind must repent, believe the good news, and do what Jesus commanded (Mark 1:15; 1 John 5:1–12).

CHAPTER 37

CHOSEN IN CHRIST BEFORE THE WORLD BEGAN

MARCH 20, 2021

Long before the incarnation of Christ and his death on the cross, God's Son already had been chosen as the way through whom the world could be saved. As a human being, Jesus proved that one can live by God's conditions and attain God's promises. God, in his infinite wisdom and foreknowledge of humankind's fall before the world was created, designed predestination as a way of salvation through the promises and the conditions humankind can follow. This election is God's greatest promise of grace bestowed on humankind in Christ Jesus.

Paul, the apostle to the Gentiles, summed it up as follows:

> Blessed be the God and Father of our Lord Jesus Christ, who has blessed us in Christ with every spiritual blessing in the heavenly places, even as he chose us in him before the foundation of the world, that we should be holy and blameless before him. He destined us in love to be his sons through Jesus Christ, according to the purpose of his will, to the praise of his glorious grace which he freely bestowed on us in the Beloved. In him we have redemption through his blood, the forgiveness of our trespasses, according to the riches of his grace which he lavished upon us. For

he had made known to us in all wisdom and insight the mystery of his will, according to his purpose which he set forth in Christ as a plan for the fullness of time, to unite all things in him, things in heaven and things on earth. (Ephesians 1:3–10)

PREDESTINATION

Predestination is generally defined as a predetermined, preordained, and preplanned act of God. It was all decided before humans were created. Everything that has happened was determined to take place. No matter what man may want to do, he will only do what he has been reprogrammed to do. If this is what *predestination* means, then humankind has a reason to be scared out of their wits. They have to live in uncertainty, not knowing where they will spend eternity, whether it is in heaven or in hell. Then, humankind absolutely has no choice regarding their condemnation or their salvation. If humankind has no choice, then why would they be held responsible for everything that they do in this life? Why, then, did Christ suffer? Why, then, did Christ die if his redemptive role has no bearing on humankind's future? These are some of the questions interpreters who hold to the idea of predestination must ponder. Our task is to search the scriptures and try to understand what is meant by *predetermination* or *predestination*.

PREDETERMINATION OR PREDESTINATION

First and foremost, before we dive into the Bible, let us remember that we all are human beings, and we may not always see things the way God wants us to see. After all, God's thoughts are not our thoughts, and neither are God's ways our ways (Isaiah 55:8).

By God's choice, we human beings are free agents. God expects us to choose wisely. Unlike God, we have not been given foresight. In our history, we have Adam and Eve, who brought sin and death into the world. We have an impatient Abraham fathering Ishmael. We have King Saul acting as a priest, when he ought to have been the king. Saul lost his kingdom to David. David, too, made many bad choices. Judas betrayed his Master, Jesus. Peter denied his Lord. Paul persecuted Jesus's followers. Yet, these men were still used to shape Heilsgeschichte, or salvation history.

NOT PERFECT BUT WILLING TO CHANGE

First, God was not using perfect men but men willing to yield to change. God knew what they would do, and that is why God chose them before they were born (Jeremiah 1:5). Jesus declared, "You did not choose me, but I chose you" (John 15:16, 19). One of the twelve was a devil, not by predestination but by choice (John 6:70). Jesus told Judas, "What you are going to do, do quickly" (John 13:27). The Lord God has foreknowledge, but the Lord God does not predestine free agents to do what they do not want to do. It is humankind's choice to choose either good or bad (Genesis 3:22).

Second, God is dealing with human beings, not with "perfect" human beings. God, as the only Supreme Being, does not change, but God had to make possible that which was impossible for human beings. This is what Jesus announced (Luke 18:27). Being God, he knew that he would need a plan of redemption for humankind.

God had to stop the first couple, Adam and Eve, from "forever living in sin and death." This *forever living in sin and death* meant the destruction of the soul and the spirit. Therefore, God chose Noah to preserve the human race. God chose Abraham to represent the ways of the Lord in the world (Genesis 18:19). The Lord called Moses to deliver Israel and provide the people with laws and regulations to live by. The Lord God wanted to be Israel's king, but the people wanted a human monarch, and God yielded to their wishes (1 Samuel 10:17–19; 12:6–19). When Saul failed, Israel still demanded a human king, and again, with hesitation, God chose David (1 Samuel 16:1–13). The people did not realize that they had separated religion from their politics. From then on, two powers would compete for governing a nation. God allowed this to happen and still does in our time.

THE COVENANT

A third thing occurred, and it is the most significant change that God allowed. When the Lord was King, God had two arms to govern his people: Moses and Aaron. After Joshua, the priests governed the people.

The priests were set apart for God (Deuteronomy 18:5). Unfortunately, under Eli, the priests became corrupt. Then Samuel was chosen to govern until Israel demanded a human king (1 Samuel 2:27–36). Henceforth, God would accept only those who honored him. In other words, it appeared as if God had to change what humankind thought was unchangeable. In reality, God merely followed up on his covenant with the patriarchs, Moses, Aaron, and the kings.

The covenant was a promise of the almighty God for a people who would obey and for a people who would keep the Almighty's conditions and God's laws. Abraham was told, "I am God Almighty; walk before me, and be blameless" (Genesis 17:1b). Moses was reminded that God remembered his covenant (Exodus 2:24) and that not even the mighty pharaoh of Egypt could stand in the way (Exodus 3:14). These were the words of the Lord that Moses had to pass on to the people:

"You have seen what I did to the Egyptians, and how I bore you on eagles' wings and brought you to myself. Now therefore, if you will obey my voice and keep my covenant, you shall be my own possession among all peoples; for all the earth is mine, and you shall be to me a kingdom of priests and a holy nation." (Exodus 19:4–6a)

To make it easier for people to recognize what the covenant was, God gave them the Ten Commandments and pages of explanations on how to live and behave (Exodus 20; Leviticus 1:27). And what did the people say?

"All that the LORD has spoken we will do, and we will be obedient." (Exodus 24:7b)

Moses was told to seal the covenant with the sprinkling of blood on the people (Exodus 24:8). This agreement between God and the people bears great similarity to Jesus's covenant with Jesus's followers:

"This is my blood of the covenant, which is poured out for many." (Mark 14:24b)

HOW DID ISRAEL RESPOND TO GOD'S
COVENANT AND GOD'S CONDITIONS?

Humankind has a short memory. At least, they take things for granted. When things go well, humankind assumes that they are being blessed. In reality, they may be drifting too far offshore. Even leaders have a tendency to drift along. Moses relaxed the law on marriage, and so did David. People took liberties, which destroyed the covenant. Moses was given a glimpse of the entire history of the people that were to be "the apple of God's eye" (Deuteronomy 32:10b). In spite of the warnings that there would be blessings for those who abided by the covenant, and there would be curses for those who disobeyed, Israel failed, and they discontinued as a nation (Deuteronomy 28).

God let Israel have a king on the condition that they live within the covenant (Deuteronomy 17:15). God gave Israel prophets and spokesmen, with a final leader like Moses (Deuteronomy 18:14–22). At the end, disobedience won the day.

Israel ceased to exist, and then Judah ceased to exist. Why did this happen? Again, it was Moses, who was allowed to see the demise of the covenant people.

"It is because they forsook the covenant of the Lord, the God of their fathers, which he made with them when he brought them out of the land of Egypt." (Deuteronomy 29:25) .

And when that last and final prophet came—namely, Jesus—he had this to say:

"O Jerusalem, Jerusalem, killing the prophets and stoning those who are sent to you! How often would I have gathered your children together as a hen gathers her brood under her wings, and you would not! Behold, your house is forsaken and desolate. For I tell you, you will not see me again, until you say, 'Blessed be he who comes in the name of the Lord.'" (Matthew 23:37–39)

WHAT THE PROPHET MOSES SPOKE ABOUT WAS THE SON OF GOD IN PERSON

"Do not think that I shall accuse you to the Father; it is Moses, who accuses you, on whom you set your hope. If you believed Moses, you would believe me, for he wrote of me. But if you do not believe his writings, how will you believe my words?" (John 5:45–47)

Jesus did not come to abort the original covenant; Jesus came to finalize the original covenant. Not even a tiny dot will be deleted.

Do not think that I have come to abolish the law and the prophets; I have not come to abolish them but to fulfill them. For truly, I say to you, till heaven and earth pass away, not an iota, not a dot, will pass from the law until all is accomplished. (Matthew 5:17–18)

This is not something that came out of the mind of God after human beings got themselves into an impossible dilemma. This was already in place before the world was created. Jesus told those who believed that they were covenant children of Abraham. "Before Abraham was, I am" (John 8:58b). Christ was chosen to be the Redeemer before the creation of the world (1 Peter 1:20).

Paul told the Ephesians, "Even as he chose us in him before the foundation of the world, that we should be holy and blameless before him" (Ephesians 1:4). It was in this connection that Paul saw himself; therefore, Paul also saw others as predestined to be adopted as children in and through Christ.

He destined us in love to be his sons through Jesus Christ, according to the purpose of his will, to the praise of his glorious grace which he freely bestowed on us in the Beloved. (Ephesians 1:5–6)

Christ is the new covenant, established by the shedding of Jesus's blood as a ransom for many (Luke 22:20; Hebrew 9:22; Matthew 20:28).

Paul believed that the ransom was for all (1 Timothy 2:6). According to Jesus, no one can come to the Father or the kingdom or into heaven but by him (John 14:6). In Christ, we are predestined for heaven, but outside of Christ, we are not. It is entirely up to us whether we want to conform to the covenant or live without the covenant. God will not change a single line of his promises, nor has he ever.

In order to inherit a small piece of heaven, we must change. We, not God, must confirm his calling and his election (2 Peter 1:10). We must choose life or death (Deuteronomy 30:11–20). In the old covenant, God is life. In the new covenant, Christ is life. There is nothing in between the two, for God and Christ are one and the same (John 14:6–11).

THE ROAD TO HEAVEN IS NOT PAVED WITH GRACE

To me, grace is God's commodity, available to all humans so that they can pave their own ways into eternity. That commodity has been made available through Jesus Christ, Son of God (John 1:17). And Jesus Christ passed it on to his disciples (John 20:21–23). Every believer and every follower is a "vessel of grace and truth" in the world. And it is by our deeds that we glorify our heavenly origin (Matthew 5:16).

The road to heaven is not automatic. The road to heaven is not mechanical, nor is the road to heaven robotic. The road to heaven is a cooperation between the one who has set the redemptive system—the conditions—in order and those who are willing to accept the redemption and then pass it on to those who are yet to be chosen.

Predestination means that the system is in operation. The puzzle begins when those who were called, chosen, elected, and invited did not choose to accept predestination. Jesus explained this in the Parable of the Wedding Banquet in Matthew 22:1–14. Those who were initially called did not regard the invitation as a priority. The second invitation went out to the people who were not expected at the wedding. Yet they came dressed for the occasion. One guest, however, did not bother to dress for the wedding, and therefore, he was ejected. Then Jesus concluded, "For many are called, but few are chosen."

Do Not Presume

If the parable teaches us anything, it is that we must not presume that we are already elected and predestined for eternal life. The Lord does single out people from the world (John 15:19) because the Lord has the foreknowledge that they will do God's will (John 7:17) and that they will produce eternal fruit (John 15:16). The uplifted Son of man draws all people, but not all people will respond (John 3:14) or abide in him (John 6:14). And while one lives in Christ, one must submit to the pruning and the trimming of the Gardner, who happens to be the Father in heaven, and the Father in heaven does the drawing.

> "No one can come to me unless the Father who sent me draws him, and I will raise him up at the last day." (John 6:44)

Belief Must Precede the Election

The other puzzling reference has been credited to Luke in Acts 13:48. Most English versions reproduce the verse as follows: "And all who were appointed for eternal life believed" (RSV). The Living Bible has, "As many as wanted eternal life believed." What does the Greek text say? The Greek text has no problem because it is a language that does not reverse words to say what they mean. The Greek renders it in this order: "And all who believed were ordained for life eternal." *There is absolutely no doubt, in the Greek text, that belief must precede the election.* The Lord will be convincing at times, as he was with Moses or Paul, but the Lord never crams salvation down our throats. God wants us to respond in love and out of gratitude for what God prepared before time began.

The Biggest Puzzle

Paul has presented Christians with the biggest puzzle. Paul used the word *proorizen* (Romans 8:29–30). Proorizen means "to mark out beforehand or to establish a system or to decide ahead." Proorizen can be very confusing if the meaning of the word is taken out of context. In this context, proorizen is not at all a puzzle. Of course, it was heartbreaking for Paul to see that his own race, except for a remnant, had placed itself outside the election (Romans 11:5). All Paul could do was to wish that all of Israel would turn when the Deliverer comes to restore the covenant (Romans 11:26–27). But what will happen when the Deliverer has already come and Israel has refused to accept her own Messiah? According to Jesus, the Deliverer has already come. Yes, Jesus, the Deliverer, has come, but his own people have rejected the Deliverer.

WHAT, THEN, SHALL WE MAKE OF ROMANS 8:29–30?

Paul has been misunderstood, with an overemphasis on grace and an underemphasis on works. In like manner, Paul has been misunderstood on predestination. Paul knew rather well that his people had not chosen to do what was expected of them and that God did not accept people who broke his covenant. In the text in question, God extended his prearranged plan of salvation to those who love him and to those who are willing to carry out God's purpose (Romans 8:28). God foreknew and foresaw that the Gentiles were willing to conform to the image of his Son (Romans 8:29). Once they are in Christ, they too are predestined, called, justified, and glorified (Romans 8:30).

Of all people, Paul insisted that Christ was the only one through whom humankind could be adopted into the family of God (Ephesians 1:5). In Paul's context, Romans 8:29–30 is not concerned with predestination but with the fact that when the believer is in Christ, nothing in heaven or on earth can separate him or her from the love of God that has been revealed in Christ Jesus, our Lord (Romans 8:31–39).

NO ONE BUT OURSELVES

No one can tear us out of the hands of God and Jesus, his Son (John 10:28–29), except ourselves. That is why we should work out our salvation with fear and trembling (Philippians 2:12). This advice comes from the man, Paul, who supposedly believed that he was predestined by grace alone. Paul forced himself to serve Christ, in fear of not being able to reach his goal (1 Corinthians 9:26–27) so that he would be rewarded with a crown in heaven.

> For I am already on the point of being sacrificed; the time of my departure has come. I have fought the good fight, I have finished the race, I have kept the faith. Henceforth there is laid up for me the crown of righteousness, which the Lord, the righteous judge, will award to me on that Day, and not only to me but also to all who have loved his appearing. (2 Timothy 4:6–8)

SUMMARY

- Before the world was created, Jesus, God's Son, already had been chosen as the way through whom humankind could be saved.
- Jesus, as a human being, proved that humankind can live by God's conditions and attain God's promises.
- By God's choice, humankind is a free agent. The Lord God does not predestine free agents to do what they do not want to do (Genesis 3:22).
- Christ is the new covenant, established by the shedding of Jesus's blood as a ransom for all humankind. (Luke 22:20; Matthew 20:28).
- Humankind must choose either life or death (Deuteronomy 30:11–20).
- God and Christ are one and the same (John 14:6–11).
- No one can tear us out of the hands of God and Jesus, his Son, except we ourselves (John 10:28–29).

CHAPTER 38

WALKING IN THE
SHOES OF GRACE

APRIL 15, 2021

The recipient in the book of Revelation picked up this message and passed it on to the inhabitants of the world:

> Here is a call for the endurance of the saints, those who keep the commandments of God and the faith of Jesus. And I heard a voice from heaven saying, "Write this: Blessed are the dead who die in the Lord henceforth." "Blessed indeed," says the Spirit, "that they may rest from their labors, for their deeds follow them!" (Revelation 14:12–13)

FAITH AND DEEDS GO HAND IN HAND
TO REACH THE PROMISED LAND

Grace has two shoes—faith and deeds—which have helped me believe and serve Christ for over ninety-one years. I have learned that grace is a human characteristic, and when practiced, it will result in gracious reciprocation. Human beings are not heartless; even those who do not believe, even sinners, tend to be gracious to those in need. The grace in man is the evidence that God the Spirit is still present and active in the world.

Deeds of grace practiced in this life earn rewards in this life and beyond. Jesus gave us some profound examples of how grace will be rewarded.

> John said to him (Jesus), "Teacher, we saw a man casting out demons in your name, and we forbade him, because he was not following us." But Jesus said, "Do not forbid him; for no one who does a mighty work in my name will be able soon after to speak evil of me. For he that is not against us is for us. For truly, I say to you, whoever gives you a cup of water to drink because you bear the name of Christ, will by no means lose his reward." (Mark 9:38–41)

> "Then the King will say to those at his right hand, 'Come, O blessed of my Father, inherit the kingdom prepared for you from the foundation of the world; for I was hungry and you gave me food, I was thirsty and you gave me drink, I was a stranger and you welcomed me, I was naked and you clothed me, I was sick and you visited me, I was in prison and you came to me.' Then the righteous will answer him, 'Lord, when did we see thee hungry and feed thee, or thirsty and give thee drink? And when did we see thee a stranger and welcome thee, or naked and clothe thee? And when did we see thee sick or in prison and visit thee?' And the King will answer them, 'Truly, I say to you, as you did it to one of the least of these my brethren, you did it to me.'" (Matthew 25:34–40)

The nobleman recognized and rewarded the productive the servants with higher tasks and turned his attention to the one who did nothing with his pound. He, too, came to the nobleman and said,

> 'Lord, here is your pound, which I kept laid away in a napkin; for I was afraid of you. Because you are a severe man; you take up what you did not lay down, and reap what you did not sow.' He said to him, 'I will condemn you of your own mouth, you wicked servant! You knew

that I was a severe man, taken up what I did not lay down and reaping what I did not sow? Why then did you not put my money into the bank, and at my coming should have collected it with interest? And he said to those who stood by, 'Take the pound from him, and give it to him who has the ten pounds.' (And they said to him, 'Lord, he has ten pounds!') 'I tell you, that to every one who has will more be given; but from him who has not, even what he has will be taken away. But as for these enemies of mine, who did not want me to reign over them, bring them here and slay them before me.'" (Luke 19:20–27)

LIVING IN GRACE IS LIVING IN THE CARE OF CHRIST

Grace is best seen in the fruits of the Spirit that we need to live in this world (Galatians 5:23–24). To me, that means that I live constantly under the tutelage and pruning of the Spirit of Christ. I have been a lifelong disciple and student of Jesus, my Lord and my teacher. Yet I still feel that I am only a beginner. The field of grace in which we live, move, and have our beings is far too enormous to finish the smallest task in a lifetime of one person. I am immeasurably grateful for having had a chance to serve my Savior, who has repeatedly added years to my life and kept me in his vineyard. There is no greater privilege than being a dispenser of grace.

"I am the true vine, and my Father is the vinedresser. Every branch of mine that bears no fruit, he takes away, and every branch that does bears fruit he prunes, that it may bear more fruit. You are already made clean by the word which I have spoken to you. Abide in me, and I in you. As the branch cannot bear fruit by itself, unless it abides in the vine, neither can you, unless you abide in me. I am the vine, you are the branches. He who abides in me, and I in him, he it is that bears much fruit, for apart from me you can do nothing. If a man does not abide in me, he is cast forth as a branch and withers; and the branches are gathered, thrown into the fire and burned. If you abide in me, and my words abide in you, ask whatever you will, and it shall be done for you. By this my Father is glorified, that you bear much fruit, and so prove to be my disciples. As the Father has loved me, so have I loved you; abide in my love. If you keep my commandments, you will abide in my love, just as I have kept my Father's commandments and abide in his love. These things I have spoken to you, that my joy be in you, and that your joy may be full. This is my commandment, that you love one another as I have loved you. Greater love has no man than this, that a man lay down his life for his friends. You are my friends if you do what I command you. No longer do I call you servants, for the servant does not know what the master is doing; but I have called you friends, for all that I have heard from my Father I have made known to you. You did not choose me, but I chose you and appointed you that you should go and bear fruit and that your fruit should abide; so that whatever you ask the Father in my name, he may give it to you. This I command you, to love one another." (John 15:1–17)

To Keep Up with Christ Requires Much Pruning

We had a row of grapes that looked great but not in the eyes of pruners. Friends, who know how to treat these vine plants, came and cut off everything that was in the way of bearing grapes and left bare skeletons standing. A year later, the grape vines were beautiful, healthy, and productive. In a way, my spiritual life has been like that. I, too, tried to look impressive in the eyes of men. To do so, I let unnecessary foliage and dead wood cover me up and cut off the good branches, which I needed to carry my own cross and not be an extra burden to our Lord (Matthew 10:38; 16:24; Luke 9:23; 14:27).

While Jesus was a human being, he required help from Simon of Cyrene to carry his cross (Mark 15:21). I, too, had many people assist me in carrying my cross, and so must I be on hand for them. We are cross-burden bearers and administrators of God's redemptive grace to our fellow human beings. The apostle Paul offered these words to guide us:

> Brethren, if a man is overtaken in any trespass, you who are spiritual should restore him in a spirit of gentleness. Look to yourself, lest you too be tempted. Bear one another's burdens, and so fulfill the law of Christ. For if any one thinks he is something, when he is nothing, he deceives himself. But let each one test his own work, and then his reason to boast will be in himself alone and not in his neighbor. For each man will have to bear his own load. Let him who is taught the word share all good things with him who teaches.
>
> Do not be deceived; God is not mocked, for whatever a man sows, that he will also reap. For he who sows to his own flesh will from his flesh reap corruption; but he who sows to the Spirit will from the Spirit reap eternal life. And let us not grow weary in well-doing, for in due season we shall reap, if we do not lose heart. So then, as we have opportunity, let us do good to all men, and especially to those who are of the household of faith. (Galatians 6:1–10)

GRACE AS BURDEN-BEARER WAS NOT APPEALING

Most of my fellow ministers are sold on being saved by grace without human effort, but in their sermons, they turn their people into burden-bearers and do-gooders. I felt that I was not understanding Jesus and his followers correctly; they were told that they would face harsh and violent opposition in the world (John 15:18–27). To build a treasury fit for heaven here on earth is extremely difficult (Matthew 6:19–21; Luke 12:32–34).

Luke and Mark understood what Jesus expected his servant would do to earn merits in heaven. The parables remind me of my life and my family's life. We lost everything earthly during World War II, and then, when we had built a nest egg for our old age, when our children were in trouble, we gave up everything without being paid to help them. Their lives and needs were more important to us than our own.

And he (Jesus) told them a parable, saying, "The land of a rich man brought forth plentifully; and he thought to himself, 'What shall I do, for I have nowhere to store my crops?' And he said, 'I will do this: I will pull down my barns, and build larger ones; and there I will store all my grain and my goods. And I will say to my soul, Soul, you have ample goods laid up for many years; take ease, eat, drink, be merry.' But God said to him, 'Fool! This night your soul is required of you; and the things you have prepared, whose will they be?' So he who lays up treasure for himself, and is not rich toward God" (Luke 12:16–21).

And as he (Jesus) was setting out on his journey, a man ran up and knelt before him, and asked him, "Good Teacher, what must I do to inherit eternal life?" And Jesus said to him, "Why do you call me good? No one is good but God alone. You know the commandments: 'Do not kill, Do not commit adultery, Do not steal, Do not bear false witness, Do not defraud, Honor your father and mother.'" And he said to him (Jesus), "Teacher, all these I have observed from my youth." And Jesus looking upon him loved him, and said to him, "You lack one thing; go, sell all that you have, and give it to the poor, and you will have treasure in heaven; and come, follow me." At that saying his countenance fell, and he went away sorrowful; for he had great possessions. (Mark 10:17–22)

WHAT WAS JESUS LOOKING FOR IN PETER AND IN ALL HIS SERVANTS?

When they had finished breakfast, Jesus said to Simon Peter, "Simon, son of John, do you love me more than these?" (John 21:15). Did Peter understand what Jesus wanted? I do not think he did, and it took me a lifetime to realize it.

The lectures and sermons I listened to and preached myself were about loving God, not about putting the disciples first. Would Peter have understood if Jesus had said, "Peter, do you love these [ten disciples] more than me?" I think that Peter would still have answered, "Lord, you know that I love you," and Jesus still would have said, "Feed my lambs. Tend my sheep. Feed my sheep" (John 21:16–19).

Like Peter, we, too, try to love God and Christ more than our fellow human beings and even ourselves. It sounds noble and religious, but it deters us from helping other human beings in need. The apostles James and John had that problem.

> But be doers of the word, and not hearers only, deceiving yourselves. For if any one is a hearer of the word and not a doer, he is like a man who observes his natural face in a mirror; for he observes himself and goes away and at once forgets what he was like. But he who looks into the perfect law, the law of liberty, and preserves, being no hearer that forgets but a doer that acts, he shall be blessed in his doing. If any one thinks he is religious, and does not bridle his tongue but deceives his heart, this man's religion is vain. Religion that is pure and undefiled before God and the Father is this: to visit orphans and widows in their affliction, and to keep oneself unstained from the world. (James 1:22–27)

> By this we know love, that he (Christ) laid down his life for us; and we ought to lay down our lives for our brethren. But if any one has the world's goods and sees his brother in need, yet closes his heart against him, how does God's love abide in him? Little children, let us not love in word or speech but in deed and in truth. (1 John 3:16–18)

> We love, because he (Christ) first loved us. If any one says, "I love God," and hates his brother, he is a liar; for he who does not love his brother whom he has seen, cannot love God whom he has not seen. And this commandment we have from him (Jesus), that he who loves God should love his brother also (first). (1 John 4:19–21)

Luke gave us a glimpse of what Peter was like when Jesus was about to hand over his disciple to him. It was at Jesus's last meal when he told his followers that one of them would hand him over to be killed. The disciples quarreled over who would run the new kingdom, and Jesus had to warn Peter.

> "Simon, Simon, behold, Satan demanded to have you, that he might sift you like wheat, but I have prayed for you that your faith may not fail; and when you have turned again, strengthen my brethren." And he (Peter) said to him, "Lord, I am ready to go with you to prison and to death." He (Jesus) said, "I tell you, Peter, the cock will not crow this day, until you three times deny that you know me." (Luke 22:31–34)

Peter did deny three times that he knew Jesus; he repented and briefly led the believers in Jerusalem (Luke 22:54–62; Acts 1–6). James, half-brother of Jesus, took over the leadership, and Peter was sent out to places where the "new way" was gaining converts. The Lord had a serious bout with Peter over admitting Nicodemus and people into the kingdom of heaven and forced him to walk in the "shoes of grace" to open the doors of the kingdom to the Gentiles (Acts 10, 15). When Peter stepped into the shoes of grace, he lost his narrow eyesight and saw other nationalities and races as God's children. That has happened to many of Jesus's followers, and I have been graced with all these years to become one of them. I remember the words of Paul:

> Every athlete exercises self-control in all things. They do it to receive a perishable wreath, but we are imperishable. Well, I do not run aimlessly, I do not box as one beating the air; but I pommel my body and subdue it, lest after preaching to others I myself should be disqualified. (1 Corinthians 9:25–27)

SUMMARY

- Faith and deeds go hand in hand to reach the promised land (Matthew 25:34–40).
- Living in grace is living in the care of Christ (Galatians 5:23–24).
- To keep up with Christ requires much pruning.
- While Jesus was a human being, he, too, required help from other people (Mark 15:21).
- We love because Christ first loved us (1 John 4:19–21).

Editor's note: This was Daniel's final blog post.

CHAPTER 39

EACH OF US HAS OUR TURN

LIVING AS AN ACT OF GRACE

You may disagree with many things in this book, or perhaps you may agree with all of them. Nevertheless, that is not what you should focus on. The point of these writings is to get you to think—to stop and think about the life you are living and the choices you are making. What matters most now is how you choose to live your life from this moment going forward. What will you do today? Will you accept God's grace? Will you show grace toward others?

> Let your speech always be gracious, seasoned with salt, so
> that you may know how you ought to answer ever one.
> (Colossians 4:6)

Hopefully, by reviewing a few things we've discussed in this book, we can give you some confidence to act with grace, each and every day, from this moment on.

YOUR VERY LIFE IS A GIFT OF GRACE

The very miracle of creation, the sheer number of things that have happened throughout history—each has made it possible for you to be alive right now. Our flesh is not immortal. You are supposed to be here. Your life is a gift of God's grace.

WE ARE NOT ALONE

The Holy Spirit is alive and well and at work in our world, and it is up to you to call upon, accept, believe, and protect your belief. If you believe this to be true, it is true. You do not have to feel alone or live alone anymore. Believe in God's grace, and you will have it.

JESUS WAS TEMPTED, AND WE ALSO ARE TEMPTED

It is foolish to think that we will never be tempted when Jesus himself was tempted. We can call upon our Lord, however, to help us, protect us, and keep us saved in his grace. We can overcome these temptations and stay in God's grace.

There are those who serve an evil purpose. They seek to separate us from the truth of God's grace by encouraging us to doubt. But doubting is by our own choice, and we can choose to have doubt taken from us. Jesus has defeated the evil one and sent the Holy Spirit to be with us each and every day. We can live in victory over these doubts and chase them away when they arise. Sure, they will come again, but we can chase them away again.

SAVED BY GRACE, BUT WE HAVE WORK TO DO

Just like the Parable of the Talents, we have been given God's grace, and we are commissioned to do good works. We are not saved by grace so we can live in sin; that is absurd. We are not to go about life each day as though God isn't real except on Sundays. That is also absurd. God created us, as his workmanship, to care for each other so we can experience the love and grace of Jesus Christ, of God himself, in our lives. We are to help others, serve others, love each other, and show each other grace.

AFRAID

This does not mean we won't be afraid. This doesn't mean we won't fail. Quite the contrary. Even the apostles failed, as we noticed when we looked at the story of Peter. But taking a lesson from our failures, just like

Peter, we carry on. We pray, ask for forgiveness, and move forward. We must continue to strive to be more than we are, to show grace. It's what we are called to do.

Perhaps You Have a New Understanding

You know that you have responsibilities. What happens when you have responsibilities to take care of and you do not do it? Well, if no one else takes care of it either, trouble usually ensues. Whether it's dirty dishes, dirty laundry, or maintenance on the house, on the car, or some eyesore, if no one takes care of it, it will worsen. The same is true of grace. If you do not show grace, and that cycle continues, no one will show grace. The trend must begin somewhere.

It's Now Up to You

Dan's time on this earth has passed, and it is now your turn. Each of us has our own turn, and it is up to each one of us to make graceful things happen in our world. It is now your turn. You are not dependent on anyone but yourself. God made you with the abilities to sustain yourself, to care for others, and to both receive and extend the grace he gives you to others. Go now and show God's grace to others.

Thank You

Thank you for reading my father's book.
It's now up to you to live your own journey of grace.

—Danny Kolke Jr.

CHAPTER 40

Remembering Rev. Daniel A. Kolke

by Selma Kolke

Daniel A. Kolke 3/13/1930–6/24/2021

Daniel Arthur Kolke was born March 13, 1930, in Kurgany, Poland, to Arthur and Mathilde (Oelke) Kolke. Daniel was named after his mother's brother, and as a child, he was called Danush, Danja, and Danl. Later, he became known as Dan. Growing up, he had little time to play, as he was employed at age six, doing chores, attending cows, and helping his father with blacksmithing. Dan's family was poor, so they made balls out of cow hair and toys out of discarded materials.

Dan began school in Antonufka, Poland, where his parents had purchased a home, and his father started his blacksmith business, working mostly on farm equipment. After Dan's father served two years in the Polish army, he remained on standby reserve. At the onset of World War II, when Dan was nine years old, his father had to rejoin his old army regiment to fight the Germans. This was a scary time for the family because they were a German family living in Poland. One night, they were chased from their home by a mob of Polish locals. Dan's mom took the children and hid in the woods for three weeks until the fighting was over.

The family lost everything, including their home and business. The German army then relocated the Kolke family on a farm in Biala, Poland, to produce needed crops for the war effort. They stayed in Biala until

286

January 1945, when they fled from the advancing Russian forces. They spent nine months traveling by horse and covered wagon, moving farther west to ensure that they did not settle inside the Russian sector. For two years, they lived in Wrexen, and then they moved to a farm in Laubach, Germany. The war was over, and the family was once again safe inside the American sector. Dan fell in love with life on the farm.

In 1951, Dan turned twenty-one, and his parents encouraged him to immigrate to Canada. His parents and friends called Canada "the land of milk and honey." They finally convinced him to give it a try. In July 1951, Dan traveled across the Atlantic on *Miss Nelly*. He found a variety of jobs. Dan was discouraged, feeling this was not the life in Canada he had hoped for. He began planning to return to Germany, but it was at Larder Lake Lumber Camp where Dan would experience the most transformational event of his life.

Dan was holding a lamp when a coworker accidentally pushed Dan. Dan slipped and fell with the lamp on two cans of kerosene. Dan became a living torch. All Dan remembers was throwing himself on a bed while covering his eyes with his hands and screaming, *"Ich bin verloren!"* (I am lost). Eternity flashed before Dan's eyes. Two men quickly covered him in a blanket and rolled him on the ground. It was a miracle he survived the initial accident. Dan was wrapped, put on a train, and eventually transferred to Toronto General Hospital, where he would undergo numerous surgeries and procedures, with a long and painful recovery ahead. Being at death's door, swaying between life and death, was an indescribable experience. It would be eighteen months and twenty surgeries before Dan was finally discharged.

In the hospital, Dan was severely depressed. On top of his debilitating condition, he did not understand or speak English. Dan's hands were severely burned; therefore, they fused his fingers so that he was able to grasp things and help himself. Dan called his fingers "my hooks." The hospital staff reached out to a local German church, and they sent a group of young adults to visit Dan. One of these men was Desmond Eagle, who faithfully visited and taught Dan English. Des and Dan remained lifelong friends. Reverend Alfred Price, who encouraged Dan that his life was not over, suggested that Dan should become a minister. Dan was amazed because he had no education, and he was only beginning to learn English.

Nevertheless, Dan's decision to accept the challenge brought peace to his troubled soul. Dan began pursuing his education, starting with his high school diploma while still recovering from his injuries.

Hardworking and driven to share the gospel, Dan would spend the next seventeen years furthering his education. He attended the Christian Institute at Edmonton, Alberta, and earned a bachelor of arts degree from the University of Manitoba in 1958. In the summer months, he served at a youth camp in Moosehorn, Manitoba. The summer of 1959 was a special highlight for Dan. While studying Hebrew at Princeton, Dan visited his uncle on weekends in Union City, New Jersey. This is where Dan met Selma Fahl. They fell in love and set their wedding date for May 28, 1960.

In 1961, Dan received his bachelor of divinity degree from the North American Baptist Seminary in Sioux Falls, South Dakota. He was ordained and served as lead pastor at Ebenezer Baptist Church in Shattuck, Oklahoma. In December 1961, their first son, Desmond, was born.

Dan wanted to further his education, so he accepted a call in 1962 to the Second German Baptist Church in Hell's Kitchen, New York City. And in July 1963, their second son, Raymond, was born. In 1964, Dan earned his master's degree in sacred theology from Biblical Seminary in New York City. Dan also studied the Islam faith for one year under a Palestinian visiting professor at the University of New York City. While doing his residential work at Toronto, Dan briefly served the Immanuel Church in St. Catharines, Ontario. In April 1965, Dan returned to the Second German Baptist Church in New York, sold the church, and relocated to Little Neck to build a new church. The secretary of the American Baptist, however, invited Dan to a church that needed help. With the help of Frank Pastore, the Second German Baptist merged with the Alden Terrace Baptist to become the Valley Stream Baptist Church. In 1967, Dan returned to Toronto to do more studying for his doctorate.

In 1968, Dan pastored Central Park Baptist Church in Buffalo, New York. While there, he taught at the University of Buffalo, "With Jesus through the Ages," "The Origin of Christianity," and "Introduction to the New Testament"—for which Dan wrote his own texts. In December 1970, their third son, Daniel Jr., was born. In 1971, Dan earned his doctorate in theology and was knighted at Victoria University, the University of Toronto.

In 1973, he published his first book, *The Church and Her Walls.* From 1973 to 1978, Dan served the First Baptist Church in Ilion, New York. In 1975, guest speaker Dr. O. Dean Nelson united Protestants and Catholics by encouraging them to "Get Closer to God and Each Other" in a week of spiritual renewal. In 1976, all Ilion churches joined in celebrating the bicentennial of the USA. Due to Dan's many civic activities, Dan became a US citizen in 1976. From 1978 to 1980, Dan served the First Baptist Church in Fulton, New York. There, he continued his writing by publishing a weekly column for the *Oswego Valley News* titled "Stop and Think."

In 1980, Dan's family moved to Washington State to be closer to his parents, who lived in Vancouver, British Columbia. Dan served the Gorst First Baptist Church for two years, and then Edmonds First Baptist, where he stayed until he retired in 1993. After retirement, Dan served part-time as an interim pastor in Hansville, Port Townsend, and Kittitas, Washington. In all, Dan served thirteen churches in his career and taught at two colleges and three seminaries: Central Baptist Seminary in Toronto; New York State University in Buffalo; Linfield College in Oregon; Far West Seminary in Oakland, California; and Fuller Seminary in Pasadena, California. He also led many ministers' and teachers' training sessions.

One of Dan's joys was writing poems to Selma, "Expression of Appreciation, Love, Care, and Life Together," throughout their sixty-one years of marriage. Dan was a prolific writer, authoring numerous articles and publishing one book. He completed forty additional manuscripts and 130 studies or articles, and he published over 1,373 articles on his weekly blog, "Stop and Think." Dan's writings represent religion and ideologies through the eyes of different cultures and languages, using the original texts, which he fervently studied to present Jesus's words as the ultimate authority of our faith.

Dan's favorite Bible verse was John 14:6—"I am the way and the truth and the life; no one comes to the Father, but to me." His favorite hymn was "The Love of God Is Greater Far." He also liked "Peace I Leave with You," "I Believe," "It Is Well with My Soul," "Traumerei," and "Danny Boy." His favorite hobby was taking care of his country place, and his loves were his wife, Selma, and being with his children and grandchildren.

Dan touched hundreds of lives with his kind and caring ways. He was compassionate and genuine, always willing to give a hug and talk about what was important to you first or give encouragement and gentle direction when he saw something amiss. Dan said that he lived his life by these simple rules: "I kept out of trouble, kept busy with my work, and kept up with what I had." If you asked Dan how he was, he usually would just say, "I'm behaving."

On June 24, 2021, at the age of ninety-one, Daniel Arthur Kolke's wish was granted: "I am finally going home to be with Jesus, my Lord and Savior."

He is survived by his wife, Selma Kolke; sister Margaret MacDonald and brother Reinhart Kolke; his sons Desmond D. Kolke and wife Kristin (Enumclaw), Raymond D. Kolke and wife Crystal (Renton), and Daniel J. A. Kolke and wife Robyn (North Bend); and grandchildren Kaitlin, Josef, Russell, Spencer, Sheila Rae, Leslie, James, and Daniel III; as well as many relatives, friends, and acquaintances.

Dan was preceded in death by his parents, Arthur and Mathilde Kolke; his siblings Helga, Blumgart, Eric, and Ingrid; and his grandson Benjamin Kolke.

Printed in the United States
by Baker & Taylor Publisher Services